Florida Circumnavigational Saltwater Paddling Trail Guide (Text Only)

Seventh Edition

Florida Office of Greenways and Trails

Copyright 2009, 2011, 2012, 2014, 2016, 2018, 2019 by Florida Office of Greenways and Trails

All rights reserved

www.FloridaGreenwaysAndTrails.com

ISBN-13: 9781077655157

Text by Doug Alderson and Liz Sparks in cooperation with numerous trail volunteers, paddlers, clubs, outfitters, land managers, and local, state and federal officials. This guidebook would not have been possible without input from these many sources.

Photos by Doug Alderson.

Florida Office of Greenways and Trails
FL Department of Environmental Protection
3900 Commonwealth Blvd.
MS 795
Tallahassee, FL 32399-3000

Table of Contents

Introduction	1
Segment 1	4
Segment 2	10
Segment 3	16
Segment 4	25
Segment 5	33
Segment 6	44
Segment 7	56
Segment 8	65
Segment 9	73
Segment 10	81
Segment 11	85
Segment 12	91
Segment 13	97
Segment 14	106
Segment 15	115
Segment 16	129
Segment 17	138
Segment 18	143
Segment 19	147
Segment 20	152
Segment 21	157
Segment 22	163
Segment 23	172

Segment 24	178
Segment 25	183
Segment 26	188
Alternate Panhandle Route, Segs. 2-4	196
Alternate Keys Route, Segs. 15-16	207
Data Book Summary	215
Data Book	222
Panhandle Alternate Route, Segs. 2-4 Data Book	297
Keys Alternate Route, Segs. 15-16 Data Book	302
Trip Planning	306
Trip Tips and Safety	311
Recommended Gear	314
Trail Glossary	317

Introduction

A dream has become reality.

First conceived in the 1980s by paddling enthusiast David Gluckman, sea kayakers can now paddle around the entire state of Florida on the 1,515-mile Florida Circumnavigational Saltwater Paddling Trail, commonly referred to as the CT. This is the fifth edition of the printed guide for the trail. It has been created as a service to alleviate the need to download and print 26 different segment guides and other information from https://floridadep.gov/parks/ogt. However, as with all printed guides, certain information can become outdated. Periodically check the website for changes in the "What's New on the Trail" link, and check for new follow-up editions of this guide.

This guide only covers the trail guide text and data book. We kept costs down by printing this text guide in black and white and in a smaller format. Color maps should be downloaded and printed from our website. **All proceeds from the sale of this guide go directly to the non-profit Florida Paddling Trails Association (FPTA).** The FPTA serves as a volunteer steward of the trail as well as other paddling trails statewide (http://www.floridapaddlingtrails.com/).

Beginning at Big Lagoon State Park near Pensacola, extending around the Florida peninsula and Keys, and ending at Fort Clinch State Park near the Georgia border, the CT is a sea kayaking paradise. The trail includes every Florida coastal habitat type, from barrier island dune systems to salt marsh to mangroves. Several historical sites and points of interest are accessible by kayak along with colorful fishing communities and urban centers.

The CT is divided into 26 segments. Each segment is unique, ranging from the remote Big Bend Coast and Everglades/Florida Bay wilderness, to the more urbanized coastlines of Pinellas County and Fort Lauderdale. The trail is utilized by thousands of Florida residents and visitors alike who paddle the trail for a few hours, days, weeks or months. Some hardy souls have paddled the entire trail, and others seek to complete the trail in segments over several years, similar to how hikers often tackle the Florida or Appalachian Trail.

The CT is a strategic long-term priority of the Florida Department of Environmental Protection, being coordinated by the Office of Greenways and Trails, but it relies heavily on the involvement and cooperation of numerous other government agencies at the federal, state, regional and local levels, along with private outfitters, businesses, paddling clubs and individual volunteers.

The CT utilizes several existing local and regional trails such as the Big Bend Saltwater Paddling Trail, the Nature Coast Trail, the Gulf and Wilderness waterways in Everglades National Park, and several county blueway trails. Also, the National Park Service and the states of Virginia, North Carolina, South Carolina and Georgia worked together to create a Southeast Coast Saltwater Paddling Trail, so you can extend a CT journey by more than 800 miles!

Highlighting and educating paddlers about Florida's rich history and fragile coastal environment, the CT traverses 20 national parks, seashores, wildlife refuges and marine sanctuaries, 37 Florida aquatic preserves and 47 Florida state parks, along with numerous local parks and preserves. Sea kayaking is one of the country's fastest growing outdoor sports and requires less infrastructure and fossil fuels than most other coastal boating activities. It is especially suited for Florida's growing population of retirees and senior citizens because new materials and manufacturing designs are helping to make kayaks lighter and easier to maneuver.

So, enjoy the guide, but more importantly, enjoy the trail!

Doug Alderson
Florida Paddling Trails Coordinator
Florida Office of Greenways and Trails
FL Department of Environmental Protection'
Doug.alderson@floridadep.gov

Segment 1
Pensacola/Fort Pickens

Emergency contact information:

911

Escambia County Sheriff's Office: 850-436-9630
Santa Rosa County Sheriff's Office: 850-983-1100

Florida Fish and Wildlife Conservation Commission 24-hour wildlife emergency/boating under the influence hotline: 1-888-404-3922

Begin: Big Lagoon State Park

End: Navarre Beach Bridge

Distance: 35 miles

Duration: 3 days

Special Considerations: This guide will cover the route inside the barrier islands since it is more sheltered and opportunities for camping and/or motel stays are spaced at reasonable distances apart.

Advance reservations are recommended for motels and campgrounds, especially during holidays and spring break season.

Introduction

People of the Pensacola area can best be described as resilient. During the hurricane season of 2004-2005, they suffered through four named storms, the main one being Hurricane Ivan. Houses, buildings, roads and bridges were damaged or destroyed. The rolling dunes and tree-covered hamlets of the Gulf Islands National Seashore barrier islands were flattened, leaving a barren looking landscape of snow-white sand.

It is not the first time strong storms have battered the area. The first recorded hurricane occurred in 1559 when a killer storm struck only days after 2,000 Spanish soldiers and settlers sailed into Pensacola Bay to establish a permanent colony. All but two of the colonists' eleven ships were spared, crippling hopes for further exploration and resupply. The town was soon abandoned. St. Augustine, settled six years later, became the oldest European city on American soil.

On November 3, 1752, a hurricane and tidal wave hit Santa Rosa Island and destroyed all buildings of a Spanish settlement except for a storehouse and hospital. From 1877 through 2005, more than 45 hurricanes have struck within 60 miles of the area, and yet Pensacola has persevered and continues to prosper.

The circumnavigation trail begins at Big Lagoon State Park. Almost 700 acres, the park offers hiking trails and a top-notch campground. You can also view outstanding examples of upland coastal forests. For camping reservations, log on to Reserve America or call (800) 326-3521. There is also a paddler's only primitive campsite near the kayak launch site that can be reserved for one-night only through the park: (850) 492-1595.

The trail traverses the Fort Pickens Aquatic Preserve, 34,000 acres of seagrass beds, salt marshes and the undeveloped portions of eastern Perdido Key and western Santa Rosa Island. The preserve provides valuable habitat for wildlife, birds and marine life, including several threatened and endangered species.

The kayaking trail in this segment touches upon the Gulf Islands National Seashore in several places, mostly on the barrier islands. Some units, such as around Fort Pickens, have been closed in the past due to hurricane damage. Check here for latest information, or call (850) 934-2600.

1: Big Lagoon State Park to East End, Perdido Key, 6 miles

The scenic Big Lagoon State Park is an appropriate beginning for the Florida Circumnavigation Saltwater Paddling Trail. Make sure to climb the wildlife viewing tower to get a bird's eye view of the expansive marshes, forests, tidal creeks and waterways in the area. You can launch at the park's kayak launch near the viewing tower. There is also a primitive campsite near the launch for trail users, along with a log book. To reserve the site (one night only), call the park at (850) 492-1595. There is a nominal fee. Please sign the logbook as this is destined to become an historical account of the trail.

Paddling east from the launch, the lagoon is wide enough to hug the shallow shoreline and will allow you to largely avoid the Intracoastal Waterway, where boat traffic can be heavy.

Primitive camping is allowed on the eastern end of Perdido Key in the Gulf Islands National Seashore, beginning a half mile east of the end of Johnson Beach Road facing Big Lagoon (see map). You are asked to avoid the dunes and vegetated areas, and you must pack out what you pack in. Fires are allowed on the beach below the extreme high tide. If you are a long-distance paddler, this short day can be a great way to break in to the rigors of the trip.

After dark, from your camp on Perdido Key, you should be able to spot the Pensacola Lighthouse on the mainland.

Established in 1859, it is one of the oldest lighthouses along the Gulf Coast still in operation.

2. Eastern End of Perdido Key to Big Sabine Point, 17 miles

Take care in entering Pensacola Bay as this is an open water body and winds can create difficult paddling conditions. Also, be wary of currents and large ships as you cross the channel between Perdido Key and Santa Rosa Island. It is at this juncture that you will pass between Fort Barrancas on the mainland and Fort Pickens on Santa Rosa Island. Both forts underwent several stages during the 1800s and early 1900s before being deactivated when aircraft and missile defense systems made the need to protect vital ports with coastal fortifications obsolete.

If you like to explore history, you can land near Fort Pickens and walk around, although the actual fort may be closed due to hurricane damage. Check the Gulf Islands National Seashore website before embarking, or ask the rangers at Perdido Key. You cannot land at Fort Barrancas as this is part of a military security zone operated by the Navy.

Fort Pickens was the center of fighting early in the Civil War because it remained in Union hands. A Confederate takeover attempt in October of 1861 failed. What followed was a two-day bombardment in which both sides cumulatively fired several thousand shells. The noise and reverberations were so great that thousands of dead fish floated to the surface in Pensacola Bay and windows shattered in Pensacola, seven miles away. Fort McRee, which once stood across the inlet, was severely damaged. In 1862, Confederates abandoned the bay and Union forces took control of Pensacola harbor for the remainder of the war.

Leaving Fort Pickens, hug the shore along Santa Rosa Island as you paddle east. For several miles, you can land and take rest breaks on these undeveloped shores that are part of the national seashore.

Two motels are available near the Bob Sikes Bridge on Santa Rosa Island after about 11 miles. A Days Inn is on the west side (see map). It has a small beach for landing. Make reservations on the motel website, or call (850) 939-1761.

The Paradise Inn is about a quarter mile east of the bridge. There is a small seawall that you will have to hoist your boat over. Call (800) 301-5925 for reservations. By staying at either of these motels, you can easily stroll to Gulf beaches for a swim. Several restaurants and shops are in the area.

The scenic and easily accessible Big Sabine Point primitive campsite has benches, but no facilities. If desired, you can walk a half mile south across soft sand to a rest room and outdoor showers along the beach. No fires are allowed at the campsite.

The kayak campsite was an Eagle Scout project of Patrick Sheldon that had support from Escambia County, the Sea Scouts and Friends of Ship 411 of the Pensacola Yacht Club. It shows how a community can come together to support the trail.

3. Big Sabine Point to Navarre Beach Bridge, 12 miles

You have the option of paddling along Santa Rosa Island or the mainland as you head east through the Santa Rosa Sound. Much of the land along the island is undeveloped and part of the Gulf Islands National Seashore. Along the mainland, you can land at two small boat landings for rest breaks, but these offer no facilities. A wayside park and visitor's center with facilities is on the northwest side of the Navarre Beach Bridge. Just past the bridge on the mainland is the Best Western Navarre. You can land in the sand just before the large rocks and pull up your kayak for a short walk to grocery store and restaurants. Call (850) 939-9400 for reservations or click here.

For camping, you can set up a tent or rent a cabin at the Navarre Beach Camping Resort, (850) 312-7240, almost two miles past the bridge on the mainland. You will need to carry your kayaks over a small sea wall. The campground has full facilities, including a laundromat, heated pool, computer room and game room.

Segment 2
Santa Rosa Sound/Emerald Coast

Emergency contact information:

911

Okaloosa County Sheriff's Office: 850-651-7400

Walton County Sheriff's Office: 850-267-2000

Florida Fish and Wildlife Conservation Commission 24-hour wildlife emergency/boating under the influence hotline: 1-888-404-3922

Begin: Navarre Beach Bridge

End: Grayton Beach State Park

Distance: 46 miles

Duration: 3-4 days

Special Considerations: The second half of this segment covers the open waters of the Gulf where paddlers will first encounter the Emerald Coast's famous white sand beaches. While this means that paddlers can land virtually anywhere to stretch and take a rest break, it also means they will be more vulnerable to high winds and waves. Special care should be taken during stormy, windy or foggy periods. Advance reservations are recommended for motels and campgrounds, especially during holidays. There is an alternate 'inland' route across the north side of Choctawhatchee Bay and through the ICW to Apalachicola if weather conditions are hazardous (see page 196). If conditions improve there are several locations where the 'outside' route along the Gulf Coast can be rejoined.

Introduction

Part of the attraction of the Emerald Coast can be attributed to its stark white sand and emerald waters. The sand originated in the southern Appalachian Mountains, primarily from quartz rocks, and was carried down the Apalachicola River system eons ago. Many of the Gulf beaches in this area are currently isolated from sediment-laden rivers, so the water is often clear. Sunlight reflecting off harmless micro-algae suspended in the shallows gives off the emerald green hues.

The makeup of the shoreline has changed over time. All of Destin, for example, was once an offshore island. Storms, wind-driven sand and sea level changes prompted a gradual transformation into a peninsula.

Human history began with Native Americans about 12,000 years ago. Early paleo Indians were largely nomadic hunters who fished and followed game herds. Eventually, when agriculture was introduced, native people established large villages and ceremonial complexes. Remnants still exist. Modern-day visitors can tour a large Indian Temple Mound Museum in downtown Fort Walton Beach. The 17-foot tall mound, one of the largest along the Gulf Coast, was created by an estimated half-a-million basket-loads of earth.

During the Civil War, Confederate soldiers used the mound area as an encampment in order to guard part of the Santa Rosa Sound known as "The Narrows." Soldiers set up a tent to display artifacts found in the mound, but Union troops set it ablaze. Once known as Brooks Landing and Camp Walton, the town was named Fort Walton in 1932 when a Civil War cannonball was unearthed from the temple mound. Tourism became popular and the town's population grew by 700 percent between 1950 and 1970.

The town of Destin, named after an early fishing captain, eventually followed with a huge growth spurt. Once a quiet fishing village, the first condominiums framed the skyline in the 1980s, and the cranes are still at work. While about 14,000 people call Destin their year-round home, the population swells to two or three times that number during the summer tourist season and holidays.

In this segment, paddlers will continue through Santa Rosa Sound and eventually emerge into Choctawhatchee Bay and the Gulf of Mexico. Terrain varies from undeveloped military lands along Santa Rosa Island to Destin's condominium-lined shores.

Three Florida state parks are featured: Henderson Beach, Topsail Hill Preserve and Grayton Beach. All three contain unspoiled tracts of wind-sculpted dunes and coastal forest, with Topsail Hill and Grayton Beach being larger and more remote, featuring miles of nature trails and rare coastal dune lakes. The endangered Choctawhatchee beach mouse, which feeds on sea oats and other dune vegetation, can be found at Topsail.

Henderson Beach and Grayton Beach offer tent camping in shaded campgrounds. For reservations, visit Reserve America or call (800) 326-3521.

For primitive camping described in this guide, please utilize Leave No Trace principles.

1. Navarre Beach Bridge to Fort Walton Beach, 12-13 miles

You'll be paddling through the Santa Rosa Sound as it gradually narrows near Fort Walton Beach. There are few if any suitable places to stop along the mainland, and a large chunk of land is part of Hurlburt Field, home of the 16th Special Operations Wing and off limits to non-military personnel. Much of Santa Rosa Island in this segment, however, is undeveloped military land and is okay for rest stops.

Several spoil islands in the Santa Rosa Sound, beginning just before Fort Walton Beach, are available for primitive camping. We have provided a GPS point for one of them (see map).

If a motel stay is desired, the Roya Hotel & Suites (850-275-0300) is located just after a city park along the mainland, adjacent to a restaurant. You can land on a narrow beach and pull up your kayak near the motel. Several restaurants and a grocery store are within walking distance.

2. Fort Walton Beach to Henderson Beach State Park, 13-14 miles

After passing through a narrow stretch of the Santa Rosa Sound known as the Narrows, you'll enter the wide Choctawhatchee Bay. This is where the Alternate Inland Route for Segments 2,3, and 4 begins if weather conditions make it a better choice to travel to Apalachicola on the ICW. A short distance beyond the US 98 bridge is Ross Marler Park with bathrooms, several pavilions, an outdoor shower, and restaurants within walking distance. Keep skirting along Santa Rosa Island toward the Destin Bridge and be cautious of heavy boat traffic and strong currents and waves crossing the pass. There are a number of places to eat in Destin near the waterfront. A great place for a lunch break is the Clement R. Taylor Park about a half mile east of the bridge near Destin (see map). Mature live oaks and magnolias shade a covered picnic area. There are also restrooms and water.

Once you pass through East Pass, you'll be paddling along the Gulf of Mexico along white sand beaches. Henderson Beach State Park offers a natural alternative to Destin's row of condominiums. You may want to first land at the park's picnic area as it is only a quarter mile to the entrance station where you can register for a campsite. About a half mile or so farther down the beach is the end of the boardwalk leading to the campground. Since the campground is about 1400 feet away, you'll likely need to pull up your kayak away from the water and possibly lock it up on the boardwalk pilings, carrying your camping gear to your campsite. Make sure to take your paddle with you.

The Henderson Beach Campground is nestled in a pristine coastal forest of oaks and pines, many of which are twisted and bonsai-like due to coastal winds and storm surges. In this scrub habitat, look for wild rosemary, sand pine, wax myrtle oak, Chapman's oak, stunted southern magnolia, saw palmetto and ground lichens. The wild rosemary, which mostly grows in coastal and deep sand habitats, is the only member of the crowberry family found in Florida.

If you need to stock up on supplies, a supermarket is across the road from the state park. Several restaurants are in the area and a huge outdoor sports store is less than a mile east along U.S. 98.

3. Henderson Beach State Park to Topsail Hill Preserve State Park (first access point), 9.5 miles

Topsail Hill Preserve State Park is a must stop for exploration, with two large coastal dune lakes and a wide stretch of unspoiled coastal dunes and forest. At the first access point, you can utilize a composting toilet and find the trailhead of two nature trails. The second access point (about 1.3 miles past the first) is for the boardwalk and tram that leads to a tent campground. Like at Henderson Beach, you'll need to pull up your kayak near the dunes, with the option of locking it onto a boardwalk or post. The campground is about a mile from the beach, but you can utilize a park shuttle at the end of the boardwalk that leads to the ranger station. It runs every two hours in winter (9, 11, 1, 3 and 4:30 CST), and every hour in summer, beginning at 9AM and ending around 7:30 PM. The schedule shift is marked by daylight savings time. For reservations, visit Reserve America or (800) 326-3521.

A private campground about two miles before the state park is the Camp Gulf RV Park (see map). This is an RV campground, but tent camping is allowed near the office, not by the water. No reservations are allowed for tent camping. For more information, call (877) 226-7485.

4. Topsail Hill Preserve State Park to Grayton Beach State Park, 9.5 miles

In this scenic section, you will glide along more high dunes and white sand beaches. There are several small public beach access facilities that have restrooms, picnic pavilions and showers (see map). These spots are usually marked by flags that tell swimmers the level of safety for swimming. Red is for extreme caution (strong wind, strong surf, or strong currents and riptides), yellow is for normal conditions, and blue is for potential problems with jellyfish, stingrays or other marine life.

Near [Grayton Beach State Park](), you'll need to take an inlet leading into the park and to the campground (see map). Hurricanes or other strong storms may close this inlet to Western Lake, so you may need to make a short portage over sand. If staying in the campground, you should try to reserve even-numbered sites from 10 through 20 as these are on the water and accessible by kayak. There are also several trails that lead from the water to interior sites if waterfront sites are booked. Odd numbered sites from 9 through 23 might work for this option, but you'll need to use trails that do not cut through another camper's site. There are also cabins available for overnight stays. Take time to enjoy this 2,227-acre park that offers three coastal dune lakes, 13 distinct natural communities, and four miles of hiking trails.

If the campground is full, contact the park headquarters about tent camping at a nearby overflow site, (850) 267-8300. You can still land at the park's campground.

Segment 3
Panama City/St. Andrews

Emergency Contact Numbers:
911
Walton County Sheriff's Office: 850-267-2000
Bay County Sheriff's Office: 850-747-4700
Gulf County Sheriff's Office: 850-227-1115
Florida Fish and Wildlife Conservation Commission 24-hour wildlife emergency/boating   under the influence hotline: 1-888-404-3922

Begin: Grayton Beach State Park
End: St. Joseph Peninsula State Park
Distance: 63 miles, depending on side trips
Duration: 4-5 days
Special Considerations: Large storms and hurricanes may close several inlets, requiring some portaging to campsites and points of interest. No camping is allowed on Tyndall Air Force Base, so a 24-plus mile paddle is required from St. Andrews State Park to Mexico Beach, where motel accommodations can be made. To avoid this long distance an Alternate Inland Route for Segments 2-4 utilizing the ICW can be accessed if weather conditions are inclement (see page 196). There are several options for returning to the Gulf route if weather improves.

A GPS unit is critical in this segment as breakers along the beach may make it necessary to paddle farther offshore, and fog can shroud landmarks. Also, it is sometimes difficult to distinguish beachside motels from condominiums, and most motels are not marked on the Gulf side.

Introduction

Emerald waters, sugar-sand beaches and high dunes mark the first two-thirds of this section, followed by a remote stretch of wild barrier islands and peninsulas. There are several points of interest and a couple of nights where motel stays are necessary. Most motels are not marked from the Gulf side, so GPS points are given on the map for motels located at key intervals. Paddling is a straight west-east route parallel to the coast until barrier islands and peninsulas are seen after St. Andrews State Park.

For state park camping recommended in this guide, advanced reservations are essential. Access Reserve America or call 1-800-326-3521. Phone numbers are given in specific sections to reserve primitive campsites outlined in this guide. There is an 8-person and/or four 2-person tent maximum allowed at primitive campsites. Please keep sites clean and follow all regulations in order for these sites to remain open for paddlers. These sites are "pack-it-in, pack-it-out" only, with campers following Leave No Trace principles.

Large tracts of conservation lands and waters in the Panhandle are carefully managed for ecological, historical or recreational purposes and remain pristine and largely undeveloped. There are two state aquatic preserves, St. Andrews Aquatic Preserve and St. Joseph Bay Aquatic Preserve.

1: Grayton Beach State Park Campground to Beachside Resort, 14 miles

Comprising more than 2,227 acres, Grayton Beach State Park offers 37 campsites, 30 cabins, five picnic shelters, three coastal dune lakes, four miles of trails and 13 distinct natural communities, from beach dune to scrubby flatwoods. There are also 19 listed species of protected animals and plants occurring within the park boundaries. The park's beach and dunes, like most along the Panhandle coast, consist of quartz sand that floated down rivers and streams from the Appalachian Mountains.

The park has a boat ramp, but what makes this park so inviting to paddlers is that several campsites (even-numbered sites from 10 through 20) are directly along Western Lake, so paddlers can launch or land at their camping area. Western Lake is open to the Gulf via a narrow inlet except when big storms close it with sand. Some portaging may be necessary. Check with the ranger's office for local conditions (850) 231-4210.

From the campground along Western Lake, paddle west approximately a half mile to the Gulf inlet and proceed east along the shore. In about six miles, you'll see an unmarred area of dunes nestled between coastal developments. This is the 1,920-acre Deer Lake State Park. Growing atop the high dunes is a rare plant: the Cruise's golden aster. Numerous other flowering plants can be found in the park's 11 distinct natural communities, including white top and yellow pitcher plants, rosebud orchids and pine lilies.

The long boardwalk from the primary dune to the upland habitats is worthy a stroll as it traverses an unspoiled vista of rolling dunes with a scenic view of Deer Lake to the west. The parking lot area has water and a composting toilet.

Regular public camping is not allowed at Deer Lake. It is also not recommended as a launching spot as the Gulf is 200 yards or more from the parking lot down the long boardwalk unless you use a kayak cart to roll your boat.

About five miles from Deer Lake lies a spot you don't want to miss: Camp Helen State Park. It is marked along the Gulf by a decrepit pier jutting into the water. From the pier, you can reach a trail to the upland areas of the park by heading across the sand in a northerly direction.

Camp Helen, with its 1930s-era lodge and cottages, will give you a glimpse of how Florida tourists spent their vacations several decades ago. If you want to go back farther in history, you can envision the four thousand or more years Native Americans utilized this site. When standing atop the high hill, with striking views on three sides and a cooling breeze in your face, you can fully understand the desirability of this unique geologic landform. Make sure to stroll along the park's short loop hike through a scenic live oak hammock.

There is no camping allowed at the park, but water and bathrooms are available to visitors during daylight hours.

About two miles past Camp Helen along the Gulf is the first of many motels available to paddlers, the Beachside Resort. Advance reservations are recommended (call 1-850-234-5722). A GPS point is provided for you on the map. A small market is across the street; a supermarket is located about a mile west along the highway.

There are other motels as you proceed east, the next one being about a mile away, the Sugar Sands Beach Resort. You can scope out the various motels ahead at Panama City Beach Online. Advanced reservations are recommended, especially on weekends and during college spring break periods in March and April. Your choice of a motel will determine the length of your paddle to St. Andrews State Park.

2. Beachside Resort to St. Andrews State Park Campground, 17.5 miles

Paddle past the gleaming white beaches and numerous motels, condominiums and attractions of Panama City Beach to St. Andrews State Park. A handy reference point is the Dan Russell City Pier, about five miles from the Grand Cayman. A supermarket is about a mile west of the Dan Russell pier, along the beach road. The M. B. Miller County Pier is about three miles past the first pier. These public piers provide public restrooms, drinking water and outdoor showers. Numerous restaurants are in the vicinity. You can shorten your day by staying in another motel along the beach.

About three miles before St. Andrews is the Richard Seltzer Park, which also has restrooms, water and outdoor showers.

To reach the St. Andrews State Park Campground, make a sharp left at the pass between the jetties and Shell Island, and make another sharp left into Grand Lagoon and proceed just past the boat ramp. There are numerous campsites on the water where you can land your kayak (even numbers from 16-38, 96-114, and 101, 132, 134 and 143). There may be rip-rap (large rocks) and marsh grass in front of others. The park offers fresh water, showers and bathrooms.

Human history at St. Andrews State Park began with early Native Americans, who feasted on fish and abundant shellfish and left behind numerous middens (trash heaps of discarded shells, bones and other refuse). In the early 1900s, bathers frequently used the area, generally arriving by boat. The first known full-time resident during this period was a Norwegian-born sailor who wrecked his boat on the south bank of Grand Lagoon during a 1929 hurricane. "Teddy the Hermit" decided to homestead and remained until his death in 1954 at age 74. His makeshift shack once stood between campsites 101 and 102.

The purchase of land for a state park began in 1947 when 302 acres were acquired from the federal government for the bargain price of $2.50 an acre. Today, after the addition of several adjacent parcels, at a considerably higher cost, the popular park consists of more than 1,200 acres.

The inlets and bays around the park are part of the St. Andrews Aquatic Preserve. Considered one of the most diverse bays in North America, with over 2,100 recorded marine dependent species, St. Andrews Bay has the largest expanse of ecologically valuable seagrass beds in the Florida panhandle. These beds, along with expansive salt marshes, provide spawning and nursery habitats for a wide variety of fish and shellfish. The beaches and uplands along the preserve provide habitat and nesting areas for several protected species such as loggerhead and green sea turtles, the Choctawhatchee beach mouse, and snowy and piping plovers.

3: St. Andrews State Park Campground to Mexico Beach, 25 miles

This is a long stretch without camping, but one of the most pristine, with little or no coastal development visible. The shoreline appearance is reminiscent of a time before arrival of Europeans. Only occasional fighter jets and motorboats will jolt you back to this century.

From the campground, paddle across the channel and continue your journey west along Shell Island through St. Andrew Bay. This island was formerly known as Lands End Peninsula and was connected to the mainland, but the Army Corps of Engineers dredged the current pass as an easier and safer channel into St. Andrews Bay. Interestingly, in 2004, Hurricane Ivan closed the natural pass at the other end of Shell Island, known as East Pass. It is one more reminder that storms, winds and currents are constantly reshaping the coastal landscape. After you cross the channel take the Gulf side of Shell Island. Be careful of breakers along this pass and others. Take a wide turn around them.

The east end of Shell Island and the adjacent Crooked Island is controlled by Tyndall Air Force Base. You can land on these inviting, sandy shores for rest breaks, but no overnight camping is permitted. You'll need to stay on the Gulf side for the rest of this section. Otherwise, some portaging will be necessary (Crooked Island is not a true island).

Mexico Beach is a small coastal community that was severely impacted by Hurricane Michael in 2018. The town is slowly rebuilding and open establishments include a hardware store, restaurants, and a post office. While the Buena Vista Motel was destroyed, the El Governor Motel is rebuilding and may open in late 2020. Check website or call 850 648-5757 to check status. For more information, visit Mexico Beach.

If you want to use Mexico Beach for a mail drop, address letters or packages to: (your name) c/o general delivery, U.S. Post Office, Mexico Beach, FL 32456. The post office is located one mile inland on 15th Street.

4: Mexico Beach to St. Joseph Peninsula State Park, 6.5 miles.

Note: Due to damage from Hurricane Michael, the western part of the park, including the campgrounds and all primitive campsites, is closed until further notice. Check the "What's New on the Trail" web link for any updates.

St. Joseph Peninsula State Park is a fitting end to this section, offering a true coastal wilderness experience. The St. Joseph State Park's Wilderness Preserve, one of only six in the state park system, encompasses the northern 7.5 miles of the peninsula (over 1,750 acres). This is an unspoiled landscape of large dunes and coastal scrub and grasslands. The Preserve is accessible by foot or by boat, and circumnavigational paddlers can primitive camp in the preserve at a designated campsite with advance reservations. Call **850-227-1327 to reserve a site.** Calling ahead avoids conflict with other users. The site capacity is set to protect the wilderness quality of the area. Payment is due on the day of arrival and is normally paid at the ranger station, although a long-distance paddler can pay by phone with a credit card the day of arrival ($5.00 per person per night). No fires are allowed and campers must follow "Leave No Trace" principles. Paddlers need to check in at least two hours before sunset and check out with park personnel.

There are paddler campsites that can be accessed from the bay or from the Gulf. Campsites 2 & 7 can be accessed on the bay side. Campsite 3 can be accessed from the Gulf where you must hike in from the beach following marked trails and camp in the designated camping site. There is a limit of five campers per site and most sites can accommodate 2-3 small tents.

From the Wilderness Preserve, paddle through the clear waters of the St. Joseph Bay Aquatic Preserve. The shallow bay waters are homes and nurseries for numerous fish and sea animals such as sea urchins, scallops and snails. Seagrass beds are lush and abundant. Fishing and summer scalloping are popular recreational activities. Nearing the halfway point, water and restrooms are available at the southern end of the state park at the picnic area and boat ramp (see map). Outdoor cold showers are at the beach restrooms, across the road from the park's boat ramp along the bay. The park also offers canoe and kayak rentals. A small grocery store can be found about five miles outside the park boundary along 30E.

This stop is an excellent place to take an extra day off to paddle along St. Joseph Bay or to hike along the park's many trails. The peninsula is a birdwatcher's paradise; 247 species have been observed at the park. Following the passage of fall cold fronts, you can spot hundreds and sometimes thousands of migrating hawks and falcons passing over and resting at the park on their way to Mexico and South America. In winter, look for gannets, loons, cormorants and ducks. Spring migrants include snowy and piping plovers and black-throated and chestnut-sided warblers.

Summertime brings green and loggerhead sea turtles to the beaches for egg laying.

Horseshoe crabs along St. Joe Bay

Segment 4
Forgotten Coast

Emergency contact info:

911
Gulf County Sheriff's Department: 850-227-1115
Franklin County Sheriff's Department: 850-670-8500
Florida Fish and Wildlife Conservation Commission 24-hour wildlife emergency/boating under the influence hotline: 1-888-404-3922

Begin: St. Joseph Peninsula State Park wilderness area

End: Gap Point Campsite, Dr. Julian G. Bruce St. George Island State Park

Distance: 57 miles

Duration: 5 days

Special Considerations: Be wary of strong winds in open water sections (which is most of the route). Currents moving through all three passes can be strong, depending upon tidal fluctuations. After Stump's Hole, you'll need to paddle along the Gulf for several miles, where the surf can pose a challenge. A portable portage carrier is advised for the Stump's Hole land crossing.

Introduction

Vast segments of unspoiled public lands and islands are featured in this segment, from the high dunes of St. Joseph Peninsula State Park to the wild palm-lined shores of St. Vincent Island to the old-growth coastal slash pine forests of Cape St. George State Reserve. Paddlers will also enjoy the St. Joseph and Apalachicola bays, among the most productive waters in the state in terms of marine life. In addition, Apalachicola Bay provides the majority of the state's oyster harvest, and paddlers will likely see flotillas of characteristically shaped oyster boats with their small cabins. Oystermen pull up the rock-hard oysters by hand using long tongs, a practice that has changed little in more than a century.

These two bays are encompassed by the St. Joseph Bay Aquatic Preserve and the Apalachicola National Estuarine Research Reserve, respectively. The Apalachicola reserve is one of only 25 sites designated as a research reserve by the National Oceanic and Atmospheric Administration, designed to coordinate efforts to manage and protect the nation's most productive waters.

State Parks in Segment 4 include St. Joseph Peninsula State Park, Dr. Julian G. Bruce St George Island State Park, Cape St. George State Reserve and St. Joseph Bay State Buffer Preserve. These undeveloped lands help to protect either St. Joe or Apalachicola Bay while providing valuable wildlife habitat and outdoor recreation opportunities.

In addition, the trail traverses the massive 12,495-acre St. Vincent Island National Wildlife Refuge. Named St. Vincent by Franciscan friars in the 1600s, the island is one of the few sites where endangered red wolves are propagated and trained to live in the wild. Most of these wolves are eventually captured and released at either the Alligator River National Wildlife Refuge in North Carolina or the Great Smoky

Mountains National Park. Also, given the island's history as a private hunting retreat stocked with exotic animals, large sambar deer, native to southeast Asia, still roam the island and can occasionally be spotted. They may weigh several hundred pounds each.

Many of the primitive campsites in this segment are part of the Apalachicola Bay Aquatic and Buffer Preserve Kayak and Canoe Trail, developed by staff with the Apalachicola National Estuarine Research Reserve in coordination with other government entities. These sites are "pack-it-in, pack-it-out" only, with campers following Leave No Trace. All sites are on a first-come, first-serve policy with the exception of sites within state parks, whereupon reservations must be made through the individual parks.

For kayak rentals, shuttle support and other services, check the Franklin County website or Happy Ours Kayak and Canoe Outpost, Journeys of St. George Island, and St. Marks Outfitters who also offers on-the-water boat support.

Note: Due to damage from Hurricane Michael, the western part of the park, including the campgrounds and all primitive campsites, is closed until further notice. Check the "What's New on the Trail" web link for any updates.

1. St Joseph Park primitive campsite #7 to Deal Tract primitive campsite, 12.5 miles

The St. Joseph State Park's wilderness preserve, one of only six in the state park system, encompasses the northern 7.5 miles of the peninsula (over 1,750 acres). This is an unspoiled landscape of large dunes and coastal scrub and grasslands. The preserve is accessible by foot or by boat, and circumnavigational paddlers can primitive camp in the preserve at a designated campsite with advance reservations. Call 850-227-1327 to reserve a site. Calling ahead avoids conflict with other users. The site capacity is set to protect the wilderness quality of the area. Payment is due on the day of arrival and is normally paid at the ranger station, although a long-distance paddler can pay by phone with a credit card the day of arrival ($5.00 per person per night). No fires are allowed and campers must follow "Leave No Trace" principles. Paddlers need to check in at least two hours before sunset and check out with park personnel.

There are paddler campsites that can be accessed from the bay or from the Gulf. Campsites 2 & 7 can be accessed on the bay side. Campsites 3 can be accessed from the Gulf where you must hike in from the beach following marked trails and camp in the designated camping site. There is a limit of five campers per site and most sites can accommodate 2-3 small tents. The two full-service family campgrounds are accessible from the Gulf and must be reserved through Reserve America, 1-800-326-3521.

From the wilderness preserve, paddle through the clear waters on the St. Joseph Bay Aquatic Preserve. The shallow bay waters are homes and nurseries for numerous fish and sea animals, such as sea urchins, scallops and snails. Seagrass beds are lush and abundant. Fishing and summer scalloping are popular recreational activities.

Nearing the halfway point, water and restrooms are available at the southern end of the state park, at the picnic area and boat ramp (see map). Outdoor cold showers are at the beach restrooms, across the road from the parks boat ramp along the bay. The park also offers kayak rentals. A small grocery store can be found about 5 miles outside the park boundary along 30E.

The St. Joseph Bay State Buffer Preserve's Deal Tract primitive campsite is near a concrete dock and located on top of a concrete pad where a fire tower used to stand. No fires are allowed and campers must follow "Leave No Trace" principles. Muddy conditions along the bay may inhibit landing at low tide.

2. St. Joseph Bay State Buffer Preserve's Deal Tract primitive campsite to Indian Pass Campground, 11 miles

From the campsite, paddle south a short distance to the St. Joseph Bay Aquatic Preserve's canoe and kayak launch. Here, you'll have a challenging portage to the Gulf side. Portage wheels will make this much easier. The safest route is to travel the bike trail North on 30E for half a mile, turn West and cross 30E at the boardwalk that will lead you to the Gulf. From here, you'll paddle along the shore to Indian Pass. A welcome rest stop is the county-owned Salinas Park, where water, restrooms and picnic tables are available (see map).

The Indian Pass Campground is privately owned and has water, showers, restrooms, cabins, a swimming pool, and a small store. Fortunately, the tent camping area is easily accessible by water, enabling you to beach your kayak within easy view of your campsite. Land at the Indian Pass boat ramp and walk a short distance to the circular campground office to register before landing at the campground. [Reservations](#) are recommended, especially on weekends. Call 850-227-7203

The Indian Pass Trading Post (a.k.a The Raw Bar) is a couple of miles up the road, where you can sample area oysters and other seafood (closed on Mondays).

3. Indian Pass Campground to Government Dock Campsite, 15 miles

Paddling along [St. Vincent Island National Wildlife Refuge](#) on the bay side, you'll have many opportunities to land on a wild shoreline lined with cabbage palms, live oaks and slash pine. Indian pottery and oyster shells litter the shore as Native Americans utilized the island for thousands of years. Paddling along or standing on the shore, it is easy to envision the lifestyles and foods of these early inhabitants. Bear in mind that it is unlawful to remove artifacts.

A highlight of the island shoreline is the northwestern corner known as St. Vincent Point, a scenic area where a thick grove of cabbage palm trees line the water. Evidence of sea level rise and heavy erosion is evident as many trees are being inundated. From here, you can make a beeline across open water to the Government Dock primitive campsite on Cape St. George Island. The campsite is located just inland from the second dock.

As an alternative, you can paddle south along St. Vincent Island to the West Pass primitive campsite on Cape St. George. Along this route, you can explore some of St. Vincent's large lakes accessible from the bay side, although some lakes may be closed if bald eagles are actively nesting. If taking this route, it is 13.5 miles from Indian Pass to the West Pass campsite. Or, if you paddle the Gulf route along St. Vincent Island to West Pass, it is a little over 9 miles, although this route is less interesting. If you visit the West Pass or Sike's Cut on the east end of the island, please be aware of the closed areas for nesting shorebirds from about March-August. The threatened snowy plovers, Wilson's plovers, American oystercatchers, and terns are nesting on Little St George Island.

Alternate route: If you wish to explore more of the area's fishing culture, and to avoid unfavorable north winds, you can hug the northern shore after leaving Indian Pass and paddle to Battery Park in the town of Apalachicola, about 15.5 miles. From there, you can enjoy a Historic Apalachicola Walking Tour and select all types of quaint bed and breakfast inns, motels, restaurants and gift shops. Apalachicola is an historic fishing village where many residents still actively make their living from the sea, especially with regards to harvesting shrimp and oysters.

From Apalachicola, you can paddle across the bay six or seven miles to a number of campsites on either Cape St. George or St.

George Island. If you remain on the north side of the bay, the primitive campsite near Carrabelle is about 20 miles from Apalachicola (see segment 5). You can take a rest break at Eastpoint and purchase smoked mullet near the public boat ramp (see map).

4. Government Dock Primitive Campsite to Boy Scout Camp, 8.0 miles

The first half of this day is very scenic with slash pines that stand right up against the bay. Look for the angular cuts or "cat-faced" scars on older trees made by early workers to collect sap for making turpentine. The industry died out in the 1940s. Also, scan the skies and treetops for bald eagles that frequent the area in cooler months and sometimes nest along the bay in large pines. Give nesting trees a wide berth.

Government Cut or Sike's Cut marks the halfway point. This is an artificial pass dredged between the bay and Gulf in 1954 that separates Cape St. George from St. George Island. There is a campsite on the bay-side of the island about 400 yards west of the cut. The site is located back from the bay shore about 100 yards and is nestled behind a clump of palmetto bushes. There is a large stone fire ring marking the spot. As with any pass, be wary of strong currents. Just past the cut, you will pass an exclusive subdivision where docking or landing is prohibited. Proceed along the island to Nick's Hole, a wild cove, where a lone dock and sailboats mark the Boy Scout camp. Land on the small beach just past the dock. This campsite has porta-potties, picnic tables, sink, and fire rings. The water may or may not be turned on. Please be respectful and keep the site clean so it remains open for trail users.

5. Boy Scout Camp to Gap Point Campsite, 10.5 miles

A welcome rest stop is a sand landing on the east side of the St. George Island Bridge. Here, you can easily access stores and restaurants. A small grocery store is just east of the main road.

One option for camping is the Unit 4 campsite just east of the bridge along the bay. Primitive camping here is free and on a first-come, first-serve basis since it is outside the state park.

There are two primitive campsites in [Dr. Julian G. Bruce, St George Island State Park](#) at scenic Gap Point (see map). Gap Point is located across the bay from the state park's youth camp area and boat ramp (rental sit-on-top kayaks can be obtained here after making arrangements at entrance station). The Gap Point sites have no water or facilities and are located almost a half mile apart from each other. There is a 2.5 mile nature trail that traverses a terrain of old-growth slash pine and large bell-shaped rosemary plants. On the trail, look for "cat faces" on the trees from early turpentine operations. The island was also used for cattle grazing and as a practice bombing range during WWII. Like most barrier islands and shorelines in the region, you may see evidence of Native American occupation which predates European contact by thousands of years. Restrooms and hot showers are available in the family campground which is located at the end of the 2.5 mile trail from Gap Point. The youth camp, across the bay from the campsite, is also available to paddlers if not reserved by groups. There is a restroom and cold showers available at the youth camp area; check with the park about availability.

The third primitive campsite on the bay side is known as Sugar Hill and is not as enticing as the two sites at Gap Point. It is an exposed site next to a well-used trail, located 3 miles northeast of Gap Point. Cold water / outdoor showers, drinking water and restrooms are available 200 yards southeast from the Sugar Hill campsite on the ocean side at the end of a sand trail. Camp in the designated area. Please avoid walking on the fragile dunes. Call the park office between 8am and sunset at 850 927-2111 if you plan to utilize any of the three primitive campsites in the park or the youth camp. A small fee is required. Length of stay is limited.

Segment 5
Crooked River/St. Marks Refuge

Emergency contact information:
911
Franklin County Sheriff's Office: 850-670-8500
Wakulla County Sheriff's Office: 850-745-7100
Florida Fish and Wildlife Conservation Commission 24-hour wildlife emergency/boating under the influence hotline: 1-888-404-3922

Begin: St. George Island State Park
End: Aucilla River launch
Distance: 100-103 miles
Duration: 8-9 days
Special Considerations: Extreme caution is advised in paddling open water areas from St. George Island to Carrabelle and in paddling across Ochlockonee Bay.

Introduction
From traditional fishing communities to wild stretches of shoreline, tidal creeks and rivers, this segment is one where paddlers can steep themselves in "Old Florida." This is also the only segment where paddlers can follow two scenic rivers for a significant distance: the Crooked and Ochlockonee rivers. The Crooked River is the only area along the trail where paddlers have a good chance of spotting a Florida black bear. Several hundred black bears roam the Tate's Hell/Apalachicola

National Forest area, one of six major black bear havens in the state. Florida black bears are protected under Florida law. Keep food and garbage tightly packed and hanging in a bag from a tree branch at least ten feet off the ground.

In paddling the Crooked River paddlers will enjoy a slice of the untrammeled 200,000-plus-acre [Tate's Hell State Forest](). This scenic route also features [Ochlockonee River State Park]() where there is a full-service campground a short distance from the water. For camping reservations, visit [Reserve America]() or call (800) 326-3521.

Along the coast, paddlers can observe a major geologic change. St. George and Dog islands mark the end of a chain of barrier islands that have been formed by sediments deposited by the Apalachicola and Ochlockonee rivers. The numerous wild islands east of Ochlockonee Bay are chunks of land that have been isolated by a millennia of rising sea levels, thus the reason why their shapes are not as elongated.

[Dr. Julian Bruce, St. George Island State Park]() and [Bald Point State Park]() are natural highlights along the coast. Paddlers can enjoy camping in both of these premier parks and explore wild coves and shoreline. In the case of Bald Point, miles of winding tidal creeks lead to unspoiled lakes and ponds which must be accessed on a rising tide. Both parks also offer excellent fishing, wildlife viewing and hiking opportunities. Other public lands include a scenic county park at Mashes Sands along the east side of Ochlockonee Bay, and state lands along Dickerson Bay near Panacea that have been purchased under the Florida Forever program.

The last stretch of the trail, including three campsites, is part of the [St. Marks National Wildlife Refuge](). Permits must be obtained for camping and these may only be used by long distance paddlers traversing the entire refuge portion of this segment. A nominal one dollar per person per day fee is charged, the same fee charged for long distance Florida Trail hikers. Bear in mind that no camping is allowed other than at the designated sites. Click here for permit information or call (850) 925-6121. Obtain your permit at least two weeks prior to your arrival; you can change your date of arrival by phone later than that if you are unexpectedly delayed. The refuge needs to know the location of anyone camping on the refuge so they can safely plan management activities such as prescribed burning. The almost 70,000-acre refuge was established in 1931 to provide wintering habitat for migratory birds. Numerous small streams that wind through unspoiled expanses of marsh and coastal forests in the refuge offer countless hours of paddling enjoyment.

A good day trip off the main route of this segment is the Alligator Harbor Aquatic Preserve, which is enclosed by the Alligator Point sand spit. This area is a pristine coastal water body and its seagrass beds and salt marshes serve as important nursery grounds and refuges for a variety of sea life. There are also several clam leases in the preserve marked by PVC poles.

This segment complements the Apalachee Bay Maritime Heritage Paddling Trails, a network of ten coastal paddling trails through the St. Marks National Wildlife Refuge and Bald Point State Park.

For kayak rentals, shuttle support and other services, check Journeys of St. George Island, The Wilderness Way and St. Marks Outfitters who also offers on-the-water boat support.

Leave No Trace principles should be followed in camping at designated primitive sites in order to keep them open for paddlers.

1. Gap Point Campsite to Oxbow Campsite, 16.5 miles.

From the Gap Point Campsite, you can proceed northeast to the end of St. George Island before paddling diagonally across the bay towards Carrabelle. Along the mainland, you can take a rest break at the Carrabelle Beach Park, where there is fresh water, restrooms and picnic shelters (see map). Continue on the Crooked River about 3 miles past the US 98 Bridge to the shady Oxbow campsite on a small bluff overlooking a bend in the river. Make a reservation early as this is a popular site.

If a motel is desired, there are several places to stay in Carrabelle. Visit the Chamber of Commerce website here.

Carrabelle is a good supply stop where you can easily access a medium-sized supermarket, post office and a library from the city ramp along the Carrabelle River.

Campsites along the Crooked River in Tate's Hell State Forest are $10 per night and can be reserved online or by phone--877-879-3859.

The Crooked River is aptly named, with numerous twists and turns. After Carrabelle, most of the river is completely undeveloped. Note that during high water it may be difficult to go under the CR 67 Bridge, so portaging may be necessary.

2. Oxbow Campsite to Crooked River #1, 12.5 miles

Bear in mind that campsites at Warren Bluff, Sunday Rollaway and Loop Road are also hunt campsites that are occupied from mid-November through early February. Campsites at Rock Landing, Crooked River #1, Crooked River #2 and Womack Creek are mixed-use campsites that are available during the hunting season, so you should have better luck at reserving them at any time. Rock Landing has three sites in a row, good for groups, and Womack Creek Campsite has 13 sites, good for very large groups. Additionally, Womack Creek is the only camping area in Tate's Hell State Forest with restrooms that include hot showers. Showers can also be used by non-campers if paddlers pay the day use fee.

3. Crooked River Campsite #1 to Ochlockonee River State Park, 17 miles

From Crooked River Campsite #1, you have the option of a shorter day by camping at Rock Landing Campsite, about 7.5 miles, or paddling another 2 miles to Loop Road Campsite. If paddling to the Ochlockonee River State Park, leave the

Crooked River and head down the Ochlockonee River past the exposed pilings of an old railroad bridge. The state park is on the northern shore. You can land near the park boat ramp and access the main campground by walking about a quarter of a mile.

As an option to staying at the state park, you can proceed north about two miles from the Crooked River junction to Tate's Hell State Forest Womack Creek campsite. This is a more developed first-come, first-serve campground featuring hot showers.

If you are in a group, another option is to utilize the isolated youth camp on the shore of the Dead River just off the Ochlockonee River. It is available to adult groups of six or more on a first-come, first-serve basis, or you can make advanced reservations for organized youth groups. Call the park at 850-962-2771 for more information and to check on availability. Be sure to hike the park's scenic nature trail through open pine flatwoods. Scan the mature pines for cavities of the endangered red-cockaded woodpecker, the only native woodpecker that nests in living trees. You might also glimpse some of the park's unusual white squirrels.

4. Ochlockonee River State Park to Chaires Creek Campsite at Bald Point State Park, 11 miles

Head south on the ever-widening Ochlockonee River to the bay. One option for camping is the Holiday Campground just before the bay bridge on the left. The campground offers a bathhouse, laundromat, pool and recreation room. To make reservations, call (850) 984-5757 or book online. On the east side of the bridge is a small convenience store and several restaurants.

From the bridge area, cross the bay and hug the southern shore a little less than 2 miles to Chaires Creek in Bald Point State Park. Proceed up the creek about a mile to the primitive campsite on your left. Call the park headquarters at 850-349-9146 or 850-962-2771 if you plan to use this site.

For side trips, you can follow Chaires Creek all the way to Tucker Lake if the tide is high, or take more narrow creeks to small ponds. Part of the beauty of this marshy wilderness is the lack of human-made noises. Jet and highway noises are generally absent. Only occasional boats can be heard.

From the campsite, you can link up with the park's many miles of scenic hiking trails and unpaved roads. More than 500 different plant species and over 230 different animal species have been documented in the park. More species will likely flourish here as restoration of former slash pine timber plantations continues. With luck, you may glimpse one of the area's Florida black bears. In autumn, monarch butterflies often pause here before their bold migration across the Gulf of Mexico.

For birdwatchers, Bald Point is an exciting place to explore. According to the Great Florida Birding Trail guide, raptors such as peregrine falcons and harriers migrate along the shore in October. Black-bellied plovers and dunlins are seen in winter, and springtime often heralds colorful indigo buntings and other songbirds. Year-round residents include brown-headed nuthatches in the piney woods and clapper rails in the extensive marshlands.

5. Bald Point State Park to Spring Creek, 12-15 miles.

From Chaires Creek, be watchful of high winds as you cross the wide Ochlockonee Bay. Mashes Sands County Park, at the head of the bay on the east side, offers a good rest stop with picnic tables and restrooms. You can then wind around the islands of scenic Dickerson Bay with the option of stopping on a small beach in order to visit Gulf Specimen Marine Lab and Aquarium (small entrance fee required) just across the road. The aquarium features marine exhibits and touch tanks, focusing more on smaller marine life such as seahorses, rays, starfish, urchins, crabs, anemones, octopuses, jellyfish, spiny boxfish, sea turtles, small sharks, eels and a variety of fish. No leaping dolphin acts. You can picnic here or stop at a city park just to the east, where you can land along a tiny creek near a fishing pier. A blue crab festival occurs here during the first weekend in May. Both of these Panacea access points are marked on the map. Numerous restaurants and small stores are within easy walking distance.

Another access point and kayak launch marked on the map is the Wakulla County Visitor's Center, where you can use restrooms and learn more about the area. Across the road is the Panacea Mineral Springs Park, site of an old motel that once housed visitors seeking the healing qualities of this natural sulfur springs. A seafood retailer aptly named Mineral Springs Seafood on US 98 at east end of town offers excellent fresh and smoked fare, an excellent opportunity to sample a local favorite, smoked mullet.

Paddling into Dickerson Bay and stopping at Panacea will add two to three miles to your day. From Panacea, you can cruise on the inside of Piney Island and traverse Oyster Bay. You can take a short cut to Spring Creek via a small creek, or you can round the point near Shell Point and take Spring Creek north. At the town of Spring Creek, tent camping for a small fee is at a small RV camp at a boat landing. Be prepared to pay in cash. An abandoned white building that once served as a crab processing house borders one side of the camp. Restrooms are available, but no showers. A nearby restaurant is open for dinner.

Spring Creek is a traditional fishing community that is under tremendous development pressure as coastal land prices soar and historic fishing activities fade due to changes in net regulations. For now, you can enjoy a taste of Old Florida by viewing historic tin-roofed buildings, old docks, and derelict fishing vessels. More importantly, several residents are fifth-generation commercial fishermen who often regale visitors with tales of fishing on the open water and in the areas tidal creeks and bays.

Take time to explore around Spring Creek by kayak as several high magnitude springs can be seen in and around the camp and along small inlets. Researchers believe that these springs connect with Wakulla Springs to the north, although water discharge has mysteriously diminished, beginning in 2006.

As a side trip, you can paddle up palm-lined Spring Creek from the town about two miles until it narrows and becomes impassable with fallen trees. In spring, look for blooming purple flag irises, clusters of yellow senecio flowers, and the white blooms of duck potato. Bald eagles are commonly seen in cool months, and on warm sunny days, alligators often sun themselves along the shore and on fallen logs. As you travel inland, look for freshwater-loving cypress, live oak and bay trees. The brown tint of the water is generally due to harmless tannins released by fallen leaves and other decomposing vegetation from swamps that feed the stream. Most of this stretch falls under the protected auspices of the St. Marks National Wildlife Refuge.

6. Spring Creek to Apalachee Point campsite, 10 miles

As you journey down Spring Creek toward the Gulf, you can deviate from the marked serpentine channel if the tide has covered the numerous oyster bars, one advantage of a shallow-water kayak. You can take a break at the Shell Point Beach, a public park, where there are picnic tables and restrooms.

From Shell Point and Live Oak Island, paddle towards the St. Marks Lighthouse, visible along the eastern horizon in good weather conditions. In choppy conditions, you may want to hug the shoreline, although this will add more miles. A primitive campsite is on a spoil island near the mouth of the St. Marks River about two miles from the lighthouse. In the 1700s, the Spanish called this the Apalachee River after the local Native American tribe. The campsite has a small rise that provides for an excellent view of the area and it's a good spot to catch a breeze. Other names for this island are Fog Island and Rock Island.

A good access point for this area is Wakulla Beach, a small sand landing and beach that is an ideal access point for kayaks, although it is not advisable to leave vehicles parked overnight and low tide can make access challenging. It is the terminus of Wakulla Beach Road off Highway 98. Tidal creeks in the area make for great side trips through more wild lands of the St. Marks National Wildlife Refuge.

Note: There is no available fresh water until Econfina River State Park. Plan on leaving Spring Creek with one gallon per person per day for 4 days.

7. Apalachee Point Campsite to Ring Dike Campsite, 9.5 miles

A good rest stop is the St Marks Lighthouse, a national historic site. First built in 1829, but rebuilt more solidly two years later and then again in 1842 and 1866, the lighthouse has withstood many severe hurricanes and storms. One 1843 storm washed away every building except for the tower, killing several people in the area except for the lighthouse keeper's family, who clung to the garret floor near the top of the tower. Various lighthouse keepers lived at the site with their families until the light became fully automated in 1960. The lighthouse is only open to the public on rare occasions. There is no museum.

East of the lighthouse, you'll paddle an open stretch of water along an untrammeled shoreline of trees and marsh. The Ring Dike Campsite is a mile up Deep Creek from the Gulf. The campsite is distinguishable from the open marsh habitat by a ring of large live oaks. With open views in all directions, this campsite is one of the most scenic on the trail. Florida Trail hikers who are traversing the refuge also use this campsite. Click here for permit information or call (850) 925-6121. Obtain your permit at least two weeks prior to your arrival; you can change your date of arrival by phone later than that if you are unexpectedly delayed.

8. Ring Dike Campsite to Pinhook River Campsite, 8.5 miles

After cruising along a true Gulf Coast wilderness, you'll paddle approximately three miles up the Pinhook River. Keep to your left at both forks in the river. At the wooden bridge, there is a small beach on the northeast side where you can land. The campsite is approximately a hundred yards on the northwest side of the bridge along an unpaved road, then follow the blue blazes a short distance. This is also a Florida Trail campsite. You should be able to paddle the ditch alongside the road during high tide for closer access by boat.

9. Pinhook River Campsite to lower Aucilla River launch, 7 miles

After returning to the Gulf, you'll have more seemingly endless vistas of marsh and palm hammocks as you paddle to the mouth of the Aucilla River. Paddle upstream to the landing on the east bank if you are ending your trip here.

If you are on an extended trip, you may skip the Aucilla River launch and paddle directly to the Econfina River campsite, about 11.5 miles. See segment 6 for maps, text description and permit information.

Segment 6
Big Bend

Emergency contact information:

911

Jefferson County Sheriff's Office: (850) 342-0211

Taylor County Sheriff's Office: (850) 584-7288

Dixie County Sheriff's Office: 352-498-1220

Levy County Sheriff's Office: 352-486-5111

Florida Fish and Wildlife Conservation Commission 24-hour wildlife emergency/boating under the influence hotline: 1-888-404-3922

Begin: Lower Aucilla River launch

End: Cross Florida Greenway spoil island campsite near Yankeetown

Distance: 153.5 miles

Duration: 14-15 days

Special Considerations: This is a remote area where cell phone coverage can be non-existent. Being properly equipped and prepared and leaving a float plan is very important. Also, you may travel two to four days at a time without being able to replenish fresh water supplies, and opportunities for replenishing food supplies are also scarce, so plan accordingly.

The coast here can be very shallow and low tides can present a problem for navigation and when seeking to land or launch at campsites. Keep a tide chart to help plan your trip and count on tides making access a challenge. You may have to paddle a mile or two off the coast during extreme low tides.

Introduction

With the exception of the Ten Thousand Islands/Everglades segment, this is the remotest segment of the trail, featuring long stretches of unspoiled shoreline, marsh expanses, and sea islands. The Big Bend also has the most stable population of bay scallops in the state and the most intact seagrass beds. These seagrass beds serve as vitally important nurseries for fish, shrimp, crabs and a host of other marine species, one reason the Big Bend Seagrasses Aquatic Preserve covers much of this segment. Spanning more than 945,000 acres, the aquatic preserve is the largest and possibly the most pristine in the state.

Fortunately, much of the Big Bend coastline is in public ownership. The first 105-mile stretch of the trail, including six primitive campsites, is managed by the Florida Fish and Wildlife Conservation Commission (FWC) as part of the Big Bend Saltwater Paddling Trail. Free permits must be obtained before using any of the campsites and an online calendar makes checking availability and reservations simple. Campsites are marked by white poles and signs and limited to 8 persons and 4 backpacking size tents to better protect the fragile coastal environment, a general rule to follow along the entire segment. The six campsites are closed during the busy July and August scallop season. These are not the best months for overnight camping anyway with almost daily storms, biting insects and intense heat. The FWC trail guide is recommended for paddlers in this section as it provides more detailed information and waterproof maps. To purchase the trail guide, click here .

Near the Suwannee River, you'll pass through lands managed by the Lower Suwannee National Wildlife Refuge. The refuge covers numerous islands and more than twenty miles of the famed river of song. A number of excellent paddling trails maps are available.

Near Cedar Key, the Cedar Keys National Wildlife Refuge encompasses 13 historic and wildlife-rich islands ranging in size from 1 to 120 acres, totaling 762 acres,

It is unlawful to camp on either the Lower Suwannee or Cedar Keys National Wildlife Refuges.

Two state parks are part of this segment—Econfina River State Park and Waccasassa Bay Preserve State Park . Econfina River encompasses more than 3,000 acres of pine flatwoods, oak/palm hammocks, and broad expanses of marsh and tree islands. The 34,000-acre Waccasassa Bay Preserve State Park offers sweeping marsh vistas and tree islands between Cedar Key and Yankeetown.

There are many friendly trail towns in this segment that offer restaurants, small grocery stores, and some have motels. Advice and fishing yarns are generally free of charge. For kayak rentals, shuttle support and other services, check Suwannee Guides and Outfitters and St. Marks Outfitters who also offers on-the-water boat support.

Leave No Trace principles should be followed in camping at designated primitive sites in order to keep them open for paddlers.

1. Lower Aucilla River Launch to Econfina River State Park, 10-11 miles

From the Aucilla River mouth, it is about four miles to the mouth of the Econfina, and another 2.5 miles to the Econfina River State Park boat ramp.

The primitive paddler's campsite is about a mile upriver from the boat ramp and is on high ground in the river forest along the west bank. Shoals just above a small bridge before the campsite may inhibit passage at low tide or during low water conditions. If this is the case, you may want to wait an hour or so at the boat landing before attempting again with a rising tide or elect to stay at the private campground. The primitive campsite is free and requires no permit. However, the park would like for campers to notify them if using the site so they can gauge use, 850-922-6007. There is a two-night maximum stay.

If the primitive site is occupied or cannot be reached, then arrange for camping through the park concessionaire Econfina River Resort at 850-584-2135, or visit their store. The campground and store, along with showers and bathrooms, are a quarter mile north of the park boat ramp along a paved road. There is a fee. The store is closed on Mondays. You can also access the store from the primitive campsite by hiking a red blazed trail to the park road and turning left for a total of about a mile. The trail, like other hiking trails in the park, are best utilized in cool weather when venomous snakes and ticks are dormant. The area is known for having an abundance of pygmy rattlesnakes.

The river above the campsite is remote, uninhabited and full of wildlife. Large live oaks and other hardwoods arch over the waterway, and numerous wildflowers often bloom along shore.

2. Econfina River State Park to Rock Island Campsite, 10.5 miles

Big Bend - Saltwater Paddling Trail Permit Required

Leave Econfina River State Park with a 2-day supply of water.

An optional rest stop about halfway to Rock Island is the Hickory Mound Impoundment, where there is a picnic area and an observation tower. The tower will likely be visible from the water. You'll need the FWC trail guide for the best route up a tidal creek to the picnic area.

Rock Island is the larger of two offshore islands, where you can land in a narrow rocky cove on the north side. The island, about 20 acres in size, is interesting to explore, with its many tidal pools and exposed limestone. It can be buggy in warm weather, however. Be sure to stow away food to keep out vermin.

3. Rock Island Campsite to Spring Warrior Creek Campsite, 11 miles

Big Bend - Saltwater Paddling Trail Permit Required

Leaving Rock Island, it is a little over two miles to the mouth of the Fenholloway River, which may have an unpleasant smell due to effluent from a paper mill. A good rest stop is Big Spring Creek, about three miles past the Fenholloway, where you can access a picnic area and a spring run (3 miles roundtrip).

About 3 miles from the mouth of Big Spring Creek is the Spring Warrior channel marker. It is 1.6 miles to the campsite. Paddling up Spring Warrior can be challenging in a falling tide. Before the campsite, you can obtain fresh water from the Spring Warrior Fish Camp which also offers lodging option. If unattended, you can use a hose on the side of the building, but this water may not be potable. The campsite is along a bend on the right side about a half-mile upstream from the fish camp. The campsite was once a Thanksgiving gathering place for a local family. You can explore the scenic river for about another half mile upstream until logjams may restrict passage.

4. Spring Warrior Creek Campsite to Sponge Point Campsite, 12.5 miles

Big Bend - Saltwater Paddling Trail Permit Required

As you cruise along the marsh, you may notice small outcroppings where cedar trees are growing. These are often the brick and stone remnants of Confederate saltworks where furnaces and iron kettles were set up during the Civil War to boil seawater to obtain salt. Salt was vitally needed to cure meat for the Confederate Army. Many of the salt works were destroyed by Union raids near the end of the war.

A must stop is the county park at Keaton Beach where you can have a picnic, take an outdoor shower, replenish water supplies, and eat in a nearby restaurant. There are a couple of small convenience stores along the town's main road. Inexpensive beach house rentals are available through several local realty offices. Leave Keaton Beach with enough water for two days.

Sponge Point, marked by majestic coastal live oak trees, appears to be an island as it is separated from the mainland by an expanse of marsh. Its name was derived from spongers that once frequented the Big Bend Coast. A massive 1940s outbreak of red tide, coupled with the advent of synthetic sponges, severely curtailed the native sponge industry. Be watchful of prickly pear cacti when hiking the island.

For restrooms and a covered picnic shelter, you can paddle to Hagen's Cove a half mile to the east, although no camping is allowed.

5. Sponge Point Campsite to Dallus Creek Campsite, 8 miles

Big Bend - Saltwater Paddling Trail Permit Required

This is a short day along more shallow tidal creeks, but there are several options to further explore the area. From your campsite, you can paddle up Dallus Creek another 1.3 miles to a boat ramp and picnic area where you can hike a 1-mile loop trail. During high tide, you can paddle Dallus Creek past the boat ramp to its swampy origin or take a 3.5-mile loop around Clay Creek (see FWC guide).

The remote campsite is in a grove of coastal live oaks at the end of a cleared trail through needlerush. Be watchful of rattlesnakes during warm weather. The campsite may be difficult to reach during low tide or possibly inundated during a very high tide.

6. Dallus Creek Campsite to Steinhatchee, 8 miles

<u>Big Bend - Saltwater Paddling Trail Permit Required</u>

Steinhatchee is the largest town in this segment until you reach Cedar Key. Here, you can rent a motel room or campsite, sample restaurant fare, and stock up on supplies. One easily accessible overnight stop in Steinhatchee, and clearly marked from the water, is the <u>Sea Hag Marina</u> (352-498-3008). Another paddler-friendly option with an innovative kayak-friendly dock is the <u>Good Times Motel and Marina</u> (352-498-8088) on the south side of the river. There are two public boat ramps on both sides of the river (see map).

7. Steinhatchee to Sink Creek Campsite, 10 miles

<u>Big Bend - Saltwater Paddling Trail Permit Required</u>

Sink Creek, one of the more remote spots along the trail, is an island-like spot surrounded by tidal creeks, marsh and sand flats. It is about a half mile in from the mouth of the creek on the south bank. A high tide will make accessibility easier.

Behind the campsite at low tide, you can hike the salt flats--an open sandy ribbon between marsh and tree hammocks. Look for evidence of rising sea levels as many cedars and other trees have died, leaving behind their naturally sculpted trunks.

A brackish spring is a quarter mile upstream near a remote boat ramp. Here, you can take a swim, explore numerous small sinkholes, and hike the back roads for great vistas. The spring area is where mullet fisherman camped and traded salted fish for farm produce and other goods in the early 1900s. A fish house once stood on the shore, but like many of the Big Bend's shoreline areas, storms and rising sea levels have erased most obvious signs of human existence.

8. Sink Creek Campsite to Butler Island Campsite, 14 miles

Big Bend - Saltwater Paddling Trail Permit Required

From the campsite, Bowlegs Point is a good rest stop, about 2.5 miles away. Past the point, you can only cruise between Pepperfish Keys and the mainland at high tide. Otherwise, stay on the Gulf side. Northern Pepperfish Key is a bird rookery, so keep at least 300 feet (a football field length) from the island so as not to disturb nesting birds.

A good rest stop near the end of the day is a county park at the town of Horseshoe Beach. You can replenish water supplies—enough for two days--and walk a short distance to a convenience store and a restaurant. An overnight option is to rent a room at the El-Seas Fish Camp, accessible by floating dock along the main canal through town on right (just less than a quarter mile in from the Gulf). Call (352) 498-8036 for reservations and directions (see map).

The Butler Island Campsite is 1.7 miles from Horseshoe Point, on the south side of the island. Camping is beneath a canopy of live oaks, palms and a rare stand of mature cedars, but beware of poison ivy. As with other sites, the low-lying coontie palm grows here, a protected species. The starchy tubers—poisonous if not prepared properly--were once an important food source for Native Americans and early settlers.

9. Butler Island Campsite to Anderson Landing River Camp in Suwannee, 11.5 miles

From Butler Island, you'll pass through a maze of oyster bars across Horseshoe Cove. As you enter the Lower Suwannee National Wildlife Refuge, several tidal creeks offer scenic paddling opportunities, and Fishbone Creek has an observation tower about 1.5 miles from the mouth. If you want to explore the area further, one option is to stay at the county campground at Shired Island (pronounced Sheered), about 5 miles from Butler Island (fee required). The water is not potable and has a strong sulfur smell. Nearby, a large Indian shell midden about

12 feet high, with sides exposed due to erosion, is worth viewing.

Several islands in the refuge, such as Big Pine Island, offer inviting white sand beaches and palm-lined shores, great for rest stops. Bear in mind that Cat Island, near the mouth of Salt Creek, is privately owned but camping is allowed on an emergency basis and it is an enjoyable rest stop. From Cat Island, follow the gps point on the map to the canal along the east side of Suwannee and Highway 349. Paddle along the canal about a mile to Anderson Landing. There is a small fee for primitive camping and a motel is next door at Bills Fish Camp and Motel. For reservations call 352-542-7086. Suwannee has two restaurants within walking distance.

10. Anderson Landing River Camp to Shell Mound Park campground, 12 miles

From the campsite, it is a fairly straight shot to the lower Suwannee River via a canal. Paddle downstream to the river mouth through West Pass, being wary of strong currents and boat traffic. Continuing southeast along the coast, a good rest stop is the white sandy beach of Deer Island. One option for camping near Deer Island is the private Clark Island, where you can stay for a fee. Call Nature Coast Expeditions at 352-543-6463 for more information. As with many areas along the Big Bend, access at low tide can be tricky.

The county campground at the Shell Mound County Park is inexpensive and on the water, although the ramp can be difficult to reach at low tide and airboats use the ramp frequently.

The historic shell mound is a must see and several scenic Lower Suwannee National Wildlife Refuge Hiking Trails make this an interesting destination and chance to stretch your legs. This five-acre, 28-foot tall Timucuan Indian mound affords a panoramic view of a Gulf Coast wilderness. It was primarily built from discarded oyster and scallop shells over the course of generations that may have spanned 3500 years.

11. Shell Mound Campground to Hall Creek Campsite, 10 miles

The shortest route is to paddle close to the mainland and pass beneath the bridge to Cedar Key on your way to Hall Creek. You'll pass numerous small islands on your way. Hall Creek, Kelly Creek, Waccasassa River and Turtle Creek campsites are part of the Waccasassa Bay Preserve State Park and are available free of charge on a first-come, first-serve basis. The campsites are not exclusively for paddlers, so you may be sharing them with boaters.

Don't miss the historic town of Cedar Key which is well worth a day or two of exploration. Cross under the bridge and paddle around Scale Key to a cove on the southwest part of town where you can land at the Cedar Key Park (see map). This will add up to two miles to your day. At charming Cedar Key, you can buy groceries, eat in a variety of restaurants, visit a museum, and peruse numerous shops. In the late 1800s, Cedar Key was a major port city and processor of cedar logs for the pencil industry. Several factors contributed to its downfall: hurricanes, the emergence of Tampa as a major port, and the depletion of old-growth cedar trees. Today, tourism is a major industry although the popular destination is amazingly devoid of chain motels or restaurants and maintains a small town charm. Cedar Key has an important clam industry and is known for its tasty clams.

A good option is to stay at Cedar Key in one of many waterfront motels and kayak to the scenic islands of the Cedar Keys National Wildlife Refuge. All beaches along the islands are open for public access with the exception of Seahorse Key from March 1 through June 30 due to bird nesting. Atsena Otie Island, a half mile south of Cedar Key, is the only island where the interior is open for hiking year-round. Here, you can view an explanatory kiosk and the historic ruins of the Faber cedar mill near the dock and walk to the eastern end of the island to view the historic cemetery.

Seahorse Key is another must stop when the beaches are open. This former prison for Confederate soldiers has the highest elevation on Florida's west coast, rising 52 feet. Other nearby islands include Snake Key and North Key. The interiors of these islands are closed to the public, and for good reason. They have venomous snakes and thick undergrowth.

Find information on lodging, restaurants and other Cedar Key offerings and be sure to take the historic walking tour. Brochures can be purchased from the Cedar Key Historical Society Museum in the old downtown.

If paddling from the Shell Mound Campground to the spoil island campsite near Yankeetown and beyond, skipping Cedar Key, be sure to bring enough water for four to five days.

After entering Hall Creek, follow the winding main channel through the marsh to the first tree island on the left. You'll see a small side creek that takes you closer to this one-acre site. A thick area of cactus occupies the western side of the island.

12. Hall Creek Campsite to Kelly Creek Campsite, 8 miles

Kelly Creek is another unspoiled tidal creek along the marshy coast. The campsite is about a mile upstream from the mouth of Kelly Creek. After entering the mouth, stay in the main channel as you proceed up the creek. You'll begin passing through an area of bleached dead cedars and palms. The campsite is a large tree island on the right. Land on the backside (north) where you can more easily get out of the current. There's plenty of room to spread out and the island has a stone fire ring.

13. Kelly Creek Campsite to Waccasassa River Campsite, 7 miles

One option for this day is to paddle up the Waccasassa River, initially following channel markers that stretch into the bay.

The campsite is along a small side creek on the west side of the river called Double Barrel Creek. If you're not a thru paddler, you can access this area from a remote boat ramp along the upper Waccasassa River at the end of County Road 326 near Gulf Hammock, about 4 miles upriver from the river campsite.

Another camping option is along Turtle Creek, about 10 miles from Kelly Creek campsite. For locating this campsite, follow GPS coordinates into Turtle Creek Bay and proceed inland to an obvious fork. Take the left fork and follow the obvious channel less than a quarter mile to a small shell landing on a tree-covered peninsula on your right. Camp anywhere near the landing. There is a fire ring. You can stretch your legs by hiking along a nearby unpaved road. Turpentining and salt-making operations were once common in the area. Because the campsite is off the main route, it is still about 14 miles to the Cross Florida Greenway Spoil Island Campsite.

14. Waccasassa Campsite to Cross Florida Greenway Spoil Island Campsite, 15 miles

It may seem that the wild tidal creeks, marshy vistas and scenic tree islands will never end as you paddle to the boat ramp near Yankeetown at the mouth of the Withlacoochee River. The town itself is 3.5 miles up the Withlacoochee River where limited supplies can be obtained. B's Marina and Fish Camp in Yankeetown offers tent camping with showers, restrooms and a small grocery store (352-447-5888). Yankeetown is a picturesque fishing village with old-growth trees and stately homes.

The spoil island campsite is about two miles past the ramp (see map for GPS point). This island was created by dredging a channel for the now defunct Cross Florida Barge Canal. The old canal lands are now primarily managed for recreation as part of the Cross Florida Greenway. Primitive camping is on a first-come, first-serve basis.

Segment 7
Nature Coast

Emergency contact information:

911

Levy County Sheriff's Office: 352-486-5111

Citrus County Sheriff's Office: 352-726-4488

Pasco County Sheriff's Office: 727-847-5878

Hernando County Sheriff's office 352-754-6830

U S Coast Guard Station Yankeetown 352-447-6900 (North of Hernando Beach)

U S Coast Guard Station Sand Key 727-596-8666 (South of Hernando Beach)

Florida Fish and Wildlife Conservation Commission 24-hour wildlife emergency/boating under the influence hotline: 1-888-404-3922

Begin: Cross Florida Greenway spoil island near Yankeetown

End: Anclote Key State Park

Distance: 89 miles

Duration: 5-6 days

Special Considerations: Much of this segment is remote, where cell phone coverage can be spotty. Being properly equipped and prepared and leaving a float plan is very important. The coast here is shallow in places and low tides can present a problem for navigation and when seeking to land or launch. Keep a tide chart to help plan your trip. A GPS is necessary, especially when paddling the winding route between Crystal River and Chassahowitzka. There are also four straight days that require paddling more than 15 miles a day, so <u>long distance paddlers attempting this segment should be experienced and fit</u>.

Open water stretches around the Crystal River power plants and Anclote Key will prove challenging in high winds. Be sure to check the weather forecast before attempting to paddle these sections.

Introduction

Whether it is paddling through miles of winding tidal creeks or along unmarred beaches, or stopping at small coastal towns, this segment has much to offer the nature lover. Plus, wildlife abounds. Constant temperatures in the spring-fed Crystal and Homosassa rivers provide a winter refuge for numerous manatees. White pelicans, wading birds and a glimpse of endangered whooping cranes also add excitement to any excursion.

For cultural breaks, friendly trail towns spaced a day or two apart offer museums, restaurants, grocery stores, motels and campgrounds. Information on many of the local communities along the trail can be obtained by logging onto [Visit Nature Coast](), [Visit Citrus Coast]() and [Adventure Coast]().

Extensive public lands are the key to keeping the Nature Coast natural. Three coastal [state parks]() are featured: Crystal River Preserve, Werner-Boyce Salt Springs and Anclote Key. In addition, the Crystal River and Chassahowitzka [National Wildlife Refuges]() protect thousands of acres.

The [Chassahowitzka Wildlife Management Area]() is another large tract of public land just above Weeki Wachi, totaling nearly 34,000 acres.

This segment includes the 23,000-acre St Martins Aquatic Preserve, which helps to protect the marshy wilderness between Crystal River and Homosassa.

Near Inglis, paddlers will pass the outlet of one of Florida's largest public works projects—the Cross Florida Barge Canal. Before completion, this massive shipping channel was halted by President Nixon in 1971 and deauthorized by Congress in 1990. Now, the former canal lands constitute a world-class 110-mile recreational greenway, named after one of the major barge canal opponents, Marjorie Harris Carr.

Leave No Trace principles should be followed in camping at designated primitive sites in order to protect the environment and keep them open for paddlers.

1. Cross Florida Greenway spoil island campsite to Uncle Tom's Island campsite, 17 miles

To begin this segment, you can launch at the mouth of the Withlacoochee River near Yankeetown, at the end of Highway 40, and proceed a couple of miles to a spoil island that was created by dredging a channel for the now defunct Cross Florida Barge Canal (see map). Primitive camping is on a first-come, first-serve basis. You can also launch along the Cross Florida Greenway itself, either at the Highway 19 ramp or at various pullovers along the unpaved road leading along the canal to the Gulf.

After the campsite, you'll need to follow a GPS point on the map to a point where you can either cross (at high tide) or make a short portage over the jetty bordering a cooling canal for the Crystal River coal and nuclear power plants. This is about two miles from the campsite and more than three miles from the mainland. The jetty is wide and vegetated before this point and posted with no trespassing signs. If you want to see pods of manatees in the winter, you can paddle on the north side of the jetty towards the mainland where warm water is released from the power plants.

After crossing the jetty, you can aim for the mouth of Crystal River and pick up the channel markers. A straight shot is about five miles. Many boaters camp on the privately-owned Shell Island at the river mouth. Proceed up the river until you reach Pine Island and the mouth of the Salt River to the south, where you'll begin paddling the established 17-mile Nature Coast Paddling Trail, managed by Citrus County. This is a scenic and winding route along the Salt River and other waterways that requires a GPS and close attention to the maps. Signs along the route may aid navigation.

If you continue up the Crystal River into King's Bay, you'll have a good chance of encountering manatees. While some manatees live in the bay year-round, hundreds frequent the waters in winter as they are dependent upon the constant 72-degree temperatures of the springs. These manatees represent approximately 20 percent of the manatee population in the Gulf of Mexico. Please keep in mind that it is unlawful to chase or harass these gentle giants or to enter established manatee sanctuary areas. Some manatees may be curious enough to seek your company but keep your distance as they are capable of flipping a boat when their powerful tails thrust them in a downward dive to escape from harm. Numerous motels and restaurants are accessible from the water in the town of Crystal River. The Crystal River Archeological State Park, which features a museum and various Native American mound structures, is not accessible from the water. The closest access point is the Crystal River State Park Preserve ramp, where you will have to hike about two miles.

Along the Salt River, closely follow GPS points as you paddle through Dixie Bay and "The Narrows." About a half mile past "The Narrows" you'll see the north entrance to Salt Creek. Uncle Tom's Island is a remote tree island surrounded by marsh about a mile up Salt Creek on the left. You'll need to follow your GPS to find it. This campsite is ideally suited for a maximum of 8 people or 4 small tents and is available free of charge on a first come-first serve basis.

2. Uncle Tom's Island campsite to Chassahowitzka River Campground, 19 miles

From the campsite, you can exit Salt Creek at the south entrance (see map). Continue along the scenic Salt River where you can stop for a rest break at John Brown Park, just past the Highway 494 Bridge. You'll then proceed through Greenleaf Bay and Shivers Bay where you'll see numerous opportunities for rest stops.

Be wary of boat traffic and fast-moving airboats in this area, especially near the entrance of Battle Creek. For a lunch break or overnight option, you can travel up the Homosassa River a little over a mile to Homosassa Resort (352-628-2474), next to a public boat ramp. The resort offers food, lodging, a kayak outfitter, and the entertaining 'Monkey Island' observable from an outside bar.

As you proceed into the 31,000-acre Chassahowitzka National Wildlife Refuge through Porpoise Bay—where porpoises are frequently seen—follow your GPS to the entrance of Seven Cabbage Creek. This creek entrance is narrow and vegetated and can easily be missed. More than one paddler has mistakenly paddled up Rose Creek—very scenic, but there is no outlet. If you stay in the main channel of Seven Cabbage Creek, you should be fine, although a winter low tide can be problematic.

Leaving Seven Cabbage Creek, proceed up the Chassahowitzka River. A good spot for a break is the Dog Island Rest Area about 2.5 miles upriver along the northern bank. Managed by the refuge, this spot has a low dock, composting toilet, picnic tables and a pavilion. No camping is allowed in the refuge. The public ramp along the river is another 3.5 miles upriver. The river becomes increasingly shallow and clear as you proceed upstream. You'll pass several houses and fish camps that are only accessible by water. Numerous springs, often found along the many side streams, feed this scenic river. Just past the ramp, you can paddle through the small town of Chassahowitzka, which has a classic Old Florida look. About a mile past the public ramp, you can also paddle to a fish camp that offers cabins for rent and a restaurant.

You'll need to secure your kayak near the rental boats at the ramp and walk a quarter mile to the Chassahowitzka River Campground (352-382-2200). You'll find a snack bar and small store at the public ramp. Although out of the way, this is a scenic and interesting stop.

A primitive campsite along Ryle Creek (see map) in the Chassahowitzka Wildlife Management Area is available to paddlers in case of an emergency such as foul weather or injury. This campsite is remote and unimproved and is about a mile in from the creek mouth on the left side. Leave No Trace guidelines should apply. Access may be difficult during extreme low tide.

3. Chassahowitzka River Campground to Mary's Fish Camp, 20.5 miles

By following the suggested route through the refuge from the Chassahowitzka River and leading out South Blind Creek, you'll save some distance and there is a good channel, even at low tide. Otherwise, you may have to paddle a mile or so past the mouth of the Chassahowitzka River before you can proceed to the south. For several miles through the refuge, there are few if any accessible areas of dry land suitable for a rest break, so this will be one of the more challenging segments of the trail. Pine Island Park, with its water, restrooms and picnic area, will likely be a welcome sight. There is an unofficial campsite about 2 miles before the park known as 10 Palms (see data book).

You can take another rest break after about three miles at the Bayport fishing dock or nearby ramp as you proceed up the Weeki Wachee River and turn into the Mud River. Mary's Fish Camp, which rents cabins and tent space, is along the headwaters of the Mud River (352-597-3474). The Mud River is a tidal river with a mild current compared with the swift-flowing Weeki Wachee River.

Other overnight opportunities in the area include the Hernando Beach Motel, about three quarters of a mile in from the coast in Hernando Beach, 352-596-2527. Advanced reservations are recommended. Restaurants are within easy walking distance of all the overnight stops.

4. Mary's Fish Camp to Hudson, 16.5 miles

A good rest break is Norfleet Fish Camp in the Old Florida town of Aripeka, after about 9 miles (352-666-2900). Water, restrooms and snacks are available. Camping is possible on an emergency basis.

Hudson is a larger town where you can land at the city boat ramp just past the park (paddle around point and a short distance up canal) and access restaurants, water, restrooms and showers. Across the street from the park is the Inn on the Gulf, where you can rent a motel room. Call 727-868-5623 for rates and reservations.

5. Hudson to Werner-Boyce Salt Springs State Park campsite, 4.5 miles

Another overnight option is a primitive campsite at [Werner Boyce Salt Springs State Park](), less than a half mile up Hope Bayou. This scenic park primarily consists of open marsh and tidal creeks, protecting four miles of coastline. Be wary of airboats as they also use the park. The Salt Springs Alliance and the West Coast Airboat Club have recently completed a pavilion at the Hope Bayou primitive camp. The project was financed through fundraising by the CSO and constructed by volunteers. Be wary of airboats as they also use the park. Call park manager Adam Belden at 727-644-2085 or the park at 727-816-1890 if you plan to use this campsite. There is no charge.

6. Werner-Boyce Salt Springs State Park campsite to Anclote Key State Park, 11.5 miles

After a couple of miles, you can take a rest break at Brasher Park, which has restrooms and water. Here, you have a choice of hugging the coast and accessing other public parks such as Rees Park and Anclote Beach Park before paddling to [Anclote Key Preserve State Park](), or making a straight beeline across open water to the island. Weather will certainly be a determining factor. The closest point to the northern end of Anclote Key from the mainland is 4 miles, near the town of Tarpon Springs. Crossing at this point could add a couple of miles to your day's total. The famous sponge fishing town of Tarpon Springs is not very accessible by kayak, but you can paddle up the Anclote River to view it from the water or hike about 3 miles by road from the Anclote River Park. The town features a free museum, numerous restaurants and gift shops.

At Anclote Key, camping is allowed on the north end of the island. A series of hiking trails and a sandy beach offers great opportunities to explore this 3-mile long undeveloped island. Kayaking along the mangrove-lined bay side is inviting as well. The south end has picnic shelters, grill and a composting toilet for day users, while the north end has no facilities. At the south end, a 19th century lighthouse is still operational. Due to bird nesting, dogs are not allowed on the island.

Camping is free on Anclote Key, but you must first check in by calling 727-638-4447. Be wary of crossing open water stretches to and from the island as winds can cause dangerous paddling conditions.

Another more sheltered option along the coastline is to visit Eagle Point Park where local Eagle Scouts built a platform for an overnight stop. The platform has corner posts to hang tarps, tents etc., along with a fire ring and picnic table. There is a restroom on site, but visitors need to walk about 100 yards. Call and get confirmation to stay overnight and ask for the restrooms to be left unlocked/open. Phone number is 727-834-3278.

Segment 8
Pinellas

Emergency Contact Information:

911

Pinellas County Sheriff's Office: 727-582-6200

Florida Fish and Wildlife Conservation Commission 24-hour wildlife emergency/boating under the influence hotline: 1-888-404-3922

Begin: Anclote Key State Park

End: Fort De Soto Park

Distance: 45.5 miles

Duration: 3 days

Special Considerations: Open water stretches around Anclote Key may pose a hazard in windy or stormy weather. Currents and tidal influences in passes, especially Hurricane Pass, can pose a threat, too. As always, proceed with caution. Rats are known to inhabit some of the spoil islands and raccoons can always be problematic, especially at Fort De Soto Park, so do not leave food or fresh water unattended.

As with most South Florida segments, boat traffic can be heavy, especially on weekends.

Advance reservations are recommended for motels and campgrounds, especially during holidays and the spring season. The situation regarding motels may change as motels in some locations are being converted to condominiums and resorts that require multi-day rentals.

Introduction

The rich history of Pinellas County began thousands of years ago when Tocobaga Indians and their predecessors hunted, fished and later farmed the area. About 1,800 years ago, the area's native people created a more sophisticated social and ceremonial structure that was reflected in their art forms. This "Weedon Island culture," (sometimes spelled "Weeden") lasted about 800 years and was marked by exquisitely decorated pottery. The 3,164-acre Weedon Island Preserve on the west side of Tampa Bay protects a large shell midden and burial mound complex associated with this time period and is open to the public.

Panfilo de Narvaez landed along Tampa Bay with about 300 soldiers in 1528. The Spaniards treated the Indians cruelly in a futile search for gold and silver. Most of the Indians eventually died from European introduced diseases and Seminole Indians inhabited the area for a brief period before and during the Second Seminole War, before being driven south or removed to Oklahoma.

Odet Phillipe is credited with being the first white settler of the area, establishing a plantation and citrus grove in the 1830s. Philippe is believed to have spawned Florida's citrus industry. The area began to boom in the 1880s with completion of the Orange Belt Railroad to St. Petersburg. Large motels, such as the famous Belleview-Biltmore, were built to accommodate tourists. Many visitors who came for health reasons and balmy weather decided to stay. From a population of 13,000 during the county's inception in 1912, the residential population now stands at almost a million. In addition, more than four million tourists visit Pinellas County each year. The word "Pinellas" reflects the area's rich history, having been derived from the Spanish words *Punta Pinal*, and meaning "point of pines."

Although this segment marks the beginning of a long stretch of urbanized coastline as you head south, you'll be able to enjoy several scenic state and county parks reminiscent of original Florida. Three premier Florida state parks are situated along the route: Anclote Key, Honeymoon Island and Caladesi Island.

The Pinellas County park system, totaling more than 4,000 acres, is unrivaled. Several "green space" and beach parks are spaced out along the route. Some of the larger parks have viewing towers, hiking trails, paddling trails, kayak launches and unspoiled tracts of land. Birdwatching possibilities abound.

The paddling trail in this segment traverses the Pinellas County Aquatic Preserves. Established in 1972, the preserve's 336,265 acres of seagrass beds, hard and soft bottoms, oyster reefs, spoil islands and mangrove areas helps to protect wildlife species such as manatees, roseate spoonbills, bald eagles, sea turtles, indigo snakes and a host of fish and marine creatures.

Leave No Trace principles should be followed when camping on Anclote Key, or on any spoil island. Bear in mind that some spoil islands are bird colonies and should be avoided. These many spoil islands and their designations are described in the Boater's Guide to Clearwater Harbor and St. Joseph Sound. To obtain your free copy, call 727-893-2765 or 813-623-6826.

1. Anclote Key (north end) to spoil island # 13, 12 miles

At Anclote Key, three miles from the mainland near Tarpon Springs, primitive camping is at the north end of the island. There is a composting toilet, but no other amenities. You can explore this three-mile long undeveloped island on a series of hiking trails or along the Gulf side beach. Kayaking along the mangrove-lined bay side is inviting as well. The south end, open for day use, has picnic shelters, grill and a composting toilet, along with a 19th century lighthouse that is still operational. Due to bird nesting, dogs are not allowed on the island. Camping is free on Anclote Key, but you must first check in by calling (727) 469-5942.

Another more sheltered option along the coastline is to visit Eagle Point Park where local Eagle Scouts built a platform for an overnight stop. The platform has corner posts to hang tarps, tents, hammocks, along with a fire ring and picnic table. There is a restroom on site, but visitors need to walk about 100 yards. Call and get confirmation to stay overnight and ask for the restrooms to be left unlocked/open. Phone number is 727-834-3278.

Be wary of crossing open water stretches to and from the island as winds can cause dangerous paddling conditions.

Howard Park is directly east of Anclote Key and a good stopping point for water, restrooms and a picnic. The park also offers a paddling trail through sheltered mangrove areas, and the mainland section of the park covers an impressive live oak forest grove.

On your way south, be sure to stop at Honeymoon Island State Park and hike through the 80-acre old-growth slash pine forest. Viewing these majestic trees is worthy of a visit, but the forest also supports an unusually high density of active osprey nests.

After Honeymoon Island, you'll cross Hurricane Pass. Due to currents, tidal influence, boat traffic, and breakers on the Gulf side, crossing Hurricane Pass should only be attempted by experienced paddlers in favorable weather conditions along the bay side. If you cross under the Dunedin Causeway along the Intracoastal Waterway, you should be safe.

For camping, there are several spoil islands to choose from along the route, but the one near channel marker #13 is of good size and it features a marked interpretive trail, fire ring and picnic tables. The island has been impressively landscaped with native plants.

2. Spoil Island #13 to Island #BC 21, 17 miles

A cultural stop along the route is historic downtown Dunedin, which features a museum, shops, galleries and several restaurants. You can access this area by entering a sheltered marina of boat slips and hanging a right until you come to the Dunedin boat ramp (see map). Here, you can carry your kayak across the road and leave it at Edgewater Park.

Roughly a mile across from Dunedin is Caladesi Island State Park, accessible only by boat. Here, you can enjoy three miles of unspoiled beaches on the Gulf side and a three-mile round trip paddling trail on the bay side through mangroves. You can obtain maps for the trail at the marina near the boat docks, where you can land on a low kayak dock adjacent to the ferry dock. The park also has a snack bar and gift shop near the docks. Channel markers will lead you to the marina. Kayakers must pay a $1 admission fee.

Many paddlers access the park's marina from the Dunedin Causeway, where there are numerous launch points and a kayak concessionaire. From channel marker #14, just west of the Dunedin Causeway Bridge, take an approximate 212´degree heading on your compass for approximately one mile to the marked channel to the marina.

As you proceed south, you have the option of remaining on the bay side en-route to Island BC 21, or, if the weather is favorable, paddling on the Gulf side by traversing Clearwater Pass and arranging for a motel stay at a beachside motel along Indian Rocks Beach or other coastal communities to the south.

Advance reservations are recommended, especially in springtime beginning around February 1st.

It is about 13 miles from Island #13 to Indian Rocks Beach, and another 19 or so miles from there to Fort De Soto Park Campground along the Gulf, so plan accordingly. There are numerous public beaches along the route that make for ideal rest stops, most of which are listed on the maps. Supermarkets are located near the Memorial Causeway to Clearwater Beach on the north side and across the street from the St. Petersburg Beach Park (see map).

In the bottom half of the bay route, you will proceed through "The Narrows," where the width between the mainland and barrier islands is very narrow, thus the name. Be wary of boat traffic as there is not as much room for maneuvering. At the Bellair and Park Boulevard Causeways, you can find public boat ramps, restrooms and potable water. There are at least two marinas along this stretch as well. Numerous small spoil islands are available for rest stops all along the route.

As you leave the narrows and enter the first stretch of Boca Ciega Bay, Island #BC 21 will come into view. Campsites are on the southwest side of the island. For a break, you can land at Boca Ciega County Park near the viewing tower just to the east of the island. Stretch your legs on scenic boardwalks through mangrove forests. Restrooms are about 200 yards from the kayak launch area. The area is very shallow at low tide.

Another excellent island for camping is CB #9, about 3.5 miles farther south (see map). Camping is on the east side. Just northwest of the island campsite is another scenic county park--War Veterans' Memorial Park on Turtlecrawl Point. Restrooms and fresh water are near the kayak launch site.

3. Island #BC 21 to Fort De Soto Park Campground, 16.5 miles

As you head south, you may want to skirt around the end of Long Key to Pass-A-Grille Beach. Pass-A-Grille is an historic coastal village with a lot of charm. There is also a post office on 8th Avenue if you want to use it as a mail stop (zip code 33706). It is open Monday through Friday from 9-4 with a break for lunch. A downtown museum is open Thursday through Saturday from 10-4 and from 1-4 on Sunday.

The Spanish Explorer Panfilo de Narvaez was believed to be the first European in the area when he anchored off Pass-A-Grille Pass in 1528. Since then, the island was long used by fishermen to obtain fresh water and to grill their catch, thus the reason for the name (likely from the French *Passe aux Grilleurs)*. Beginning in 1857, John Gomez, a self-proclaimed pirate, opened the way for tourism by bringing in excursionists from Tampa. A section of Pass-A-Grille was declared a National Historic District in 1989.

Fort De Soto Park, your destination for the day and the end of this segment, also has a rich history. You can tour Fort De Soto, built to protect Tampa Bay during the Spanish-American War. The fort was named after Spanish explorer Hernando De Soto, who began his tumultuous three-year march from Tampa Bay in 1539 to find gold and subjugate the native population.

Fort De Soto Park is known for its birdwatching, one reason it is a featured stop on the Great Florida Birding Trail. Flocks of shore and migratory birds seem to pose for visitors as they feed or rest. Two hundred and ninety-six avian species have been sighted in the 1,136-acre park.

Exploring the park is easy. You can kayak through mangrove-lined lagoons in its interior to a kayak livery facility that also rents bicycles (see map). By bicycling or hiking, you can tour the park's off-road trails that lead to beaches, coastal hammock forests, a small museum, and the historic fort.

Numerous campsites at Fort De Soto Park are easily accessible by kayak, especially tent sites. A small seawall surrounds most of the RV campsites, which may prove difficult for kayaks, so make sure you reserve one of the tent sites (sites 1 through 85). Advanced reservations are highly recommended, so call (727) 582-2100 up to six months in advance of your trip or reserve online: https://public.co.pinellas.fl.us/parks/ParksMain.jsp.

Primitive camping is available at no charge on Shell Key, which is just offshore from North Beach in Fort De Soto Park (see map). This island is also managed by Pinellas County. Leave No Trace principles should be followed on the island. Campers must first obtain a Shell Key Preserve Camping Permit: http://www.pinellascounty.org/forms/shell-camp.htm.

Paddlers can take a break and rent a bike at Fort De Soto Park.

Segment 9
Ft. De Soto Park to Lido Beach

Emergency Contact Information:

911

Pinellas County Sheriff's Office: 727-582-6200

Manatee County Sheriff's Office: 941-747-3011

Sarasota County Sheriff's Office: 941-316-1201

Florida Fish and Wildlife Conservation Commission 24-hour wildlife emergency/boating under the influence hotline: 1-888-404-3922

Begin: Fort De Soto Park

End: Lido Beach

Distance: 30 miles, depending on route

Special Considerations: Crossing Tampa Bay can be hazardous and is recommended for experienced paddlers only, and only in good weather. Strong currents, large ships and wakes, sudden winds and waves can all be factors in the long passage across open water. Several options are given here, depending on weather, including taking a shuttle across the bay. South of Tampa Bay, paddlers have the choice of paddling on the Gulf side or inside the barrier islands, although motels for overnight stops are on the Gulf side. As with most South

Florida segments, boat traffic can be heavy, especially on weekends.

Introduction

For thousands of years, dugout canoes glided across Tampa Bay and nearby coastal waters, guided by skilled Native American paddlers. Sometimes, these early Florida sailors used small sails to help speed them along on trade journeys and fishing trips, utilizing landmarks, currents, stars and sun position to help with navigation.

Today, huge ocean liners and tankers can be seen chugging through Tampa Bay, along with numerous motorized pleasure crafts. Perhaps today's equivalent to the ocean-going dugout is a sea kayak, equipped with a foot-guided rudder, spray skirt and sometimes a sail to make passage easier. Navigation is usually by nautical maps, compass and gps, but that same sense of adventure early native paddlers must have experienced can be captured.

Historic Tampa Bay, abundant bird life, gleaming white beaches and a Native American temple mound are highlights of this segment of the Florida Circumnavigation Saltwater Paddling Trail. The trail passes through Boca Ciega Bay and Terra Ceia Aquatic Preserves. These preserves protect sea grass beds, hardbottom communities and other underwater habitats, and efforts are underway to restore sea grasses in places where pollution or boat dredging has damaged or destroyed them.

Another highlight of this segment is that paddlers can utilize alternative forms of transportation to explore areas of interest. Bicycle rentals are available at Ft DeSoto Park, and a free trolley system can be utilized on Anna Maria Island.

Paddlers have several options in crossing Tampa Bay, depending upon experience level and weather. One route traverses the historic Egmont Key State Park.

Along the Manatee County coast south of the bay, paddlers have the option of taking the Intracoastal Waterway or paddling the Gulf parallel to sandy beaches, depending again on weather conditions. The Paddle Manatee 75-mile network of paddling trails along the coast, bays, inlets and rivers has been developed by Manatee County.

The southern part of the trail runs parallel to Sarasota Blueways and a blueways guide for boaters has been developed by the Sarasota Bay National Estuary Program. Sarasota Bay is an important estuary for fish spawning and reproduction, and the outlying barrier islands support numerous loggerhead sea turtle nests each year.

1. Fort De Soto Park to Bradenton Beach, 15 miles

It is no wonder that Ft DeSoto Park is a featured stop on the Great Florida Birding Trail. Flocks of shore and migratory birds seem to pose for visitors as they feed or rest. Two hundred and ninety-six avian species have been sighted in the 1,136-acre park.

Exploring Pinellas County's Fort De Soto Park is easy. You can kayak through mangrove-lined lagoons in its interior to an outfitter that also rents bicycles (see map). By bicycling or hiking, you can tour the park's off-road trails that lead to beaches, coastal hammock forests, a small museum, and historic Fort De Soto, built to protect Tampa Bay during the Spanish-American War. The fort was named after Spanish explorer Hernando De Soto, who began his tumultuous three-year march from Tampa Bay in 1539 to find gold and subjugate the native population.

From the park, you can paddle about two miles or take a ferry to Egmont Key State Park, managed in cooperation the U.S. Fish and Wildlife Service and the U.S. Coast Guard. On the island, you can tour Fort Dade, built during the Spanish-American War, stroll along century-old brick roads, and tour an operating lighthouse that was built in 1848. Look for the mounds of soft sand that mark the burrows of gopher tortoises, a protected species abundant on the island's interior.

Numerous campsites at Fort De Soto Park are easily accessible by kayak, especially tent sites. A small seawall surrounds most of the RV campsites, which may prove difficult for kayaks, so make sure you reserve one of the tent sites (sites 1 through 85). Advanced reservations are highly recommended, so call (727) 582-2100 up to six months in advance of your trip or reserve online.

Primitive camping is available at no charge on Shell Key, which is just offshore from North Beach in Fort De Soto Park (see map). This island is also managed by Pinellas County. Leave No Trace principles should be followed on the island. Campers must first obtain a Shell Key Preserve Camping Permit online.

To traverse Tampa Bay from the campground, you have several options. For one, crossing the bay is recommended for experienced paddlers only in calm weather. Strong currents, large ships and wakes, sudden winds and waves can all be factors in the long passage across open water. In calm weather, the shortest distance is to Egmont Key (two miles from the tip of Ft. De Soto Park), and then across to Anna Maria Island. Then, the day's total is about 12 miles to motels at Holmes Beach or 15 miles to motels along Bradenton Beach.

Another passage is along the Skyway Bridge, where larger ships are funneled into a deep channel, although strong currents can be dangerous. Rest areas at the beginning and end of the bridge are accessible to kayakers. In rough weather, it is recommended that you either wait it out, paddle several miles along the interior of the bay to avoid long stretches of open water, or arrange a shuttle across the bay with a local outfitter. If you choose to paddle around the interior of Tampa Bay, you can utilize the Pinellas County Blueways guide for the Pinellas County portion of the bay.

If one paddles the Skyway Bridge and proceeds to Holmes Beach, the day's total is about 21 miles. Two points-of-interest along this route are accessible to paddlers. At Emerson Point Park, you can visit a large Native American temple mound on the south side of the park (see map). You can easily beach your boat and walk up a palm-lined walkway to the mound. The mound was used for centuries by Tocobaga Indians and later by a settler who built a structure atop the mound. The native people likely used the mound for ceremonies and as a place where chiefs or priests lived.

Almost directly across the mouth of the Manatee River from the temple mound is the De Soto National Memorial. Kayakers can land on the shore and explore the Visitors Center, try on heavy Spanish-style chain mail and armor, visit an historic Spanish camp--complete with living history interpreters--and marvel at mature gumbo limbo trees.

After crossing Tampa Bay, you have two route options at Anna Maria Island. In good weather, you can paddle around the island on the Gulf side, or you can paddle along the Intracoastal Waterway through Anna Maria Sound and Sarasota Bay. There are opportunities for bathroom breaks on both sides of the barrier islands as there are numerous public county beaches, boat launches, and private marinas. There is an option for primitive camping at scenic Robinson Preserve by reservation on Friday and Saturday nights only, call 941-742-5923. Access is limited to paddle craft only (canoe/Kayak) and there is no vehicle access to campsites. The historic Valentine

House is a visitors' center worth touring along with the Preserve's hiking trails, picnic pavilions, and observation tower. Paddlers can also find motel lodging at either Holmes Beach or Bradenton Beach on the Gulf side.

GPS points are given for Holmes Beach and the Club Bamboo South at Bradenton Beach for reference points. More information on these motels and others in this segment is available at online sites for Manatee and Sarasota counties. Since overnight opportunities are all on the Gulf side, one option is to paddle through Anna Maria Sound on the bay side, cut through Longboat Pass, and paddle north along Coquina Beach two to three miles to the motels at Bradenton Beach. On the bay side, you can stop at or cruise past the historic fishing village of Cortez, founded by fishermen from North Carolina in the 1880s. Being one of the last remaining fishing villages on Florida's Suncoast, Cortez is facing a number of pressures such as encroaching residential development and increased fishing regulation.

The beauty of staying on Anna Maria Island is the availability of a [free trolley](#) system that runs daily from 6 a.m. to 10:30 p.m., seven days a week. The trolley arrives at different stops about every 20 minutes and can take you to points of interest, shopping centers, restaurants, or simply on a sightseeing tour. Near Holmes Beach, it links to a bus that can take you to Bradenton and Palmetto for a small fee. Call 941-749-7116 for more information.

Accessible by trolley or kayak is a post office across the road from the historic Anna Maria Pier along the northern end of the island. The Anna Maria town post office is open from 8:30 a.m. to 4:30 p.m. Monday through Friday and from 9 a.m. to noon on Saturday. The zip code is 34216 in case you want to receive mail in care of general delivery.

2. Bradenton Beach to Lido Beach, 15 miles

Once again, you can take either the bay side or Gulf side for this stretch, depending on weather and preference. The bay side adds one to two miles.

On the bay side, one point of interest is the Joan Durante Park, where you can beach your boat (see map) and walk down several scenic trails and boardwalks. Bird life is abundant in the lagoons and coastal hammock of this wetlands restoration project, and restrooms are available near the parking lot.

If you land at the boat ramp on the south side of Ken Thompson Park, you can visit the Mote Marine Lab Aquarium, the Ann and Alfred Goldstein Marine Mammal Center, and Pelican Man's Bird Sanctuary. All of these interesting attractions charge entrance fees.

There is a canoe/kayak launch on the bay side in South Lido Beach Park (see map).

On the Gulf side, there are numerous lodging options choose from just south of Lido Beach. For a shorter day, you can stay at the Turtle Crawl Inn or other motels on the southern Gulf side of Longboat Key. The Gulf side includes several scenic county beaches for pleasant stops and bathroom breaks, most of which include outdoor showers and snack bars.

If you are paddling on the bay side, you can access the Gulf-side motels by either cutting through New Pass and heading south past Lido Beach, or by cutting through Big Pass and heading north along South Lido Beach about a mile. On your journey, look for some of the approximately 100 bottlenose dolphins that reside year-round in Sarasota Bay. In spring and summer, mothers and calves can be seen in shallow waters as newborns are more protected from deep-water predators such as bull sharks. Manatees can also be seen in the bay, especially during warmer months.

Whether paddling on the Gulf or bay side, this segment provides paddlers with a variety of bird life, scenic beaches and parks, fascinating attractions, and historic sites.

The De Soto National Memorial along the alternate route.

Segment 10
Sarasota/Venice

Emergency Contact Numbers:

911

Sarasota County Sheriff's Office: 941-861-5800

Florida Fish and Wildlife Conservation Commission 24-hour wildlife emergency/boating under the influence hotline: 1-888-404-3922

Begin: Lido Beach

End: Wanna B Inn near Stump Pass Beach State Park

Distance: 36 miles

Duration: 2-3 days

Special Considerations: As with most South Florida segments, boat traffic can be heavy, especially on weekends.

Advance reservations are recommended for motels and campgrounds, especially during holidays and the spring season. The situation regarding motels may change as motels are rapidly being converted to condominiums and resorts that require multi-day rentals. Also, the existing motels have a preference for multi-day rentals, especially during the busy spring tourist season.

Introduction

Whether paddling on the Gulf or bay side, this segment provides paddlers with a variety of bird life and scenic beaches and parks. Sarasota Bay and numerous other small bays are highlights of this segment, with their rich marine life. On your journey, look for bottlenose dolphins that reside year-round in Sarasota Bay and other waters. In spring and summer, mothers and calves can be seen in shallow waters as newborns are more protected from deep-water predators such as bull sharks. Manatees can also be seen, especially during warmer months.

This segment includes Oscar Scherer State Park along scenic South Creek, where a large tract of scrubby flatwoods is home to the threatened Florida scrub jay, a species found only in Florida. For camping reservations visit Reserve America or call at 1-800-326-3521.

The Lemon Bay Aquatic Preserve is in the southern end of the segment. Two Gulf passes and seven tributaries have helped to create a diverse network of mangroves, marsh grass, and vast expanses of seagrass meadows. The diversity includes more than 150 species of birds, 100 species of invertebrates, and 200 species of fish.

1: Lido Beach to Oscar Scherer State Park, 13 miles

You can begin this segment either at a canoe/kayak launch on the bay side in South Lido Beach Park (see map), or by launching at Lido Beach on the Gulf side. If you are a long-distance paddler, simply continue from one of several motels just south of Lido Beach on the Gulf side. For more information visit Manatee County lodging or Sarasota Lodging.

You can paddle along the Gulf side or the bay side, depending on winds, weather and preference, although there are more parks on the Gulf side that are ideal for rest breaks. There is also the Turtle Beach Campground, about 8 miles from Lido Beach. The campground is accessible from the Gulf or from a lagoon about a half mile in from the bay side (see map). Advance reservations are highly recommended: 941-349-3839 or reserve online. Restaurants are within walking distance.

Since [Oscar Scherer State Park](#) is on South Creek along the mainland, you'll either need to paddle to the bay side just after Lido Beach through Big Sarasota Pass or portage to the bay across a 100-foot stretch of sand in between Siesta and Casey Keys at a spot known as Midnight Pass (see map for GPS point). The pass filled with sand in the early 1980s.

If you want to stay on the Gulf side past Midnight Pass, you can stay at the [Gulf Surf Motel](#), about 11 miles from Lido Beach (call 941-966-2669 for reservations).

Along the bay side, you'll pass several bird rookeries and birding hot spots such as Skiers Island in Roberts Bay and the Neville Preserve in Little Sarasota Bay. To stay at the state park, paddle up South Creek a short distance and stop at the small beach landing near the entrance station to register for a site at the campground (see map for GPS coordinates). Then, paddle to the park canoe launch site (a total of about a mile from the bay). You'll have to leave your boat here and walk a nature trail along the creek less than a half mile to the campground, which is accessible by bridge on the south side of the creek.

For an overnight alternative, you can paddle another 4 miles from South Creek to the Venice Inlet where you can primitive camp on Snake Island, a popular spot for boaters. Parks are on either side of the inlet, and a marina and restaurant are along the south bank. This will shave off 4 miles from your paddle the next day.

2: Oscar Scherer State Park to Wanna B Inn, 23 miles

Paddle down South Creek to Blackburn Bay and continue south along the mainland. At Venice, you'll have a choice of paddling out the Venice Inlet and into the Gulf or paddling the

Intracoastal Waterway, which snakes its way inland for more than five miles. Along the Gulf, you can either stay at the small Beach Croft Motel at Englewood Beach after 20 miles (941-474-6509 for reservations) or circle through Stump Pass to the larger Wanna B Inn on the bay side, 24 total miles from Oscar Scherer State Park. Be wary of strong currents in Stump Pass. An outgoing tide will make paddling through the pass to the bay side difficult.

If paddling the Intracoastal route, it is about 23 miles from Oscar Scherer to Wanna B Inn. Wanna B Inn is a large resort conveniently located on the bay and Gulf adjacent to Stump Pass Beach State Park. Paddlers can use the ramp right at the motel, check in, and secure kayaks on shore. Like most motels in the area, there is a two-night minimum stay for weekends and three nights for holidays. Call 941-474-3431 for reservations. Spring is considered the busy season.

If staying at the Wanna B Inn, you can walk to Stump Pass Beach State Park and hike a mile or so to Stump Pass, either along the undeveloped beach or down the park's nature trail through the interior. Look for shells and shark teeth along the beach, especially after a storm.

Segment 11
Charlotte Harbor

Emergency Contact Numbers:

911

Charlotte County Sheriff's Office: 941-639-2101

Lee County Sheriff's Office: 239-477-1000

Florida Fish and Wildlife Conservation Commission 24-hour wildlife emergency/boating under the influence hotline: 1-888-404-3922

Begin: Wanna B Inn near Stump Pass Beach State Park

End: Cayo Costa State Park

Distance: 18.5 miles

Duration: 2 days

Special Considerations: Extreme caution should be taken in crossing Stump Pass and Boca Grande Pass. Due to currents, boat traffic and breakers on the Gulf side, these crossings should only be attempted by experienced paddlers in favorable weather conditions along the bay side. As with most South Florida segments, boat traffic can be heavy, especially on weekends. Boca Grande Pass can be packed with boats during the peak tarpon season, from April through June.

Advance reservations are recommended for motels and campgrounds, especially during holidays and the spring season. The situation regarding motels may change as motels are rapidly being converted to condominiums and resorts that require multi-day rentals.

Introduction

Developed and pristine barrier islands contrast each other in this segment, which spans Charlotte Harbor. Paddlers have the option of cruising the bay side or the Gulf side, depending on weather. This guide will focus on the bay side since most of the camping and lodging opportunities are inside the barrier islands, and it is considered safer. The centerpiece for this segment is Charlotte Harbor, an area with a rich history.

Early Calusa Indians built canals and temple mounds in the region. Houses can be seen on some of their early shell middens along Pine Island. Ponce de Leon is believed to have visited in the early 1500s, and he was followed by various European explorers. Cattle was king in the 1800s, with cattle being shipped through the harbor to Cuba and other points. Sports fishing became popular by the turn of the last century, especially for tarpon in Boca Grande Pass, a trend that continues.

Five contiguous Charlotte Harbor Aquatic Preserves cover most of Charlotte Harbor: Lemon Bay, Cape Haze, Gasparilla Sound-Charlotte Harbor, Matlacha Pass and Pine Island Sound. Altogether, they total more than 150,000 acres. Besides serving as a valuable nursery grounds for both recreational and commercial species of fish, crabs and shrimp, the Charlotte Harbor region harbors 86 endangered or threatened species. They include five species of sea turtle, the Florida manatee, and numerous birds such as roseate spoonbills, peregrine falcons and bald eagles.

Four scenic state parks are featured in this segment: Stump Pass Beach, Don Pedro Island, Gasparilla Island and Cayo

Costa. All of the parks offer sandy beaches, hiking trails, restrooms, fresh water and picnic facilities.

Only one state park, Cayo Costa, offers cabins and camping. For reservations visit Reserve America or call at 800-326-3521.

For day paddling opportunities in and along the bay's many tributaries, download the Charlotte County Blueways Guide.

1: Wanna B Inn to Dog Island, 9 (miles) or Hoagen Key (12 miles)

Wanna B Inn is a large resort conveniently located on the bay and Gulf adjacent to Stump Pass Beach State Park. Paddlers can use the ramp right at the motel, check in, and secure kayaks on shore. Like most motels in the area, there is a two-night minimum stay for weekends and three nights for holidays. Call 941-474-3431 for reservations. Spring is considered the busy season.

If staying at Wanna B Inn, you can walk to Stump Pass Beach State Park and hike a mile or so to Stump Pass, either along the undeveloped beach or down the park's nature trail through the interior. Look for shells and shark teeth along the beach, especially after a storm.

Proceeding from Wanna B Inn along the paddling trail, paddle along the state park on the bay side and be watchful of heavy currents, boats and breakers as you cross Stump Pass. You can take a rest stop/bathroom break on the mainland land base of Don Pedro Island State Park, landing just to the left of the dock. For a longer break, make sure to visit Don Pedro Island. Look for a shallow channel and state park sign off the Intracoastal Waterway at green marker #35. This channel leads to a small cove and the island's dock. Before state acquisition in 1985, this property was used as a private beach for people who owned land in the Rotunda Development on the mainland, seen from the air as a huge wagon wheel. The park boasts about a mile of unspoiled beach and five distinct natural communities.

From the park, paddle through Little Gasparilla Sound, heading east toward the Intracoastal Waterway. Dog Island, your destination for the night, is near the mainland just on the other side of the Boca Grande Causeway (S.R. 771) to Gasparilla Island. An adjacent island, Little Dog Island, is a bird sanctuary so be sure to keep a distance to avoid disturbance.

A permit is not required to camp on Dog Island although it was in the past. To reach it proceed northeast and enter Coral Creek. There are no facilities on the island which is maintained by FPTA volunteers who visit it frequently to keep the island pristine. Leave No Trace principles should be followed on the island, meaning that all trash and human waste should be packed out.

Near Dog Island, you can enjoy the winding Woolverton Kayak Trail through a scenic mangrove forest.

Another option for primitive camping is Hoagen Key, a privately owned site that is maintained by the Florida Paddling Trails Association and only accessible by small watercraft. Camping is free and on a first-come, first-serve basis. A maximum number of 8 people (4 small tents) can stay on the island. Leave No Trace guidelines should be followed. There are no facilities.

2: Dog Island or Hoagen Key to Cayo Costa State Park, 9.5 or 6.5 miles respectively

If you land on Gasparilla Island on your way to Cayo Costa, look for some of the many naturalized geckos that roam the island. Some are an impressive three-feet long and look like mini Komodo dragons. You have the option of extending your trip by staying at The Innlet (941-964-4600) a motel accessible by kayak from the bay side. From the motel, you can more easily check out the restaurants, shops and culture of Boca Grande.

A must stop is Gasparilla Island State Park, along Boca Grande Pass. You can land along the bay side and stroll along scenic beaches. Be sure to visit the historic Boca Grande Lighthouse, built in 1890. The lighthouse contains an informative museum and visitor's center. Learn more about the Calusa civilization and early European and American settlers, and how tarpon gather in the waters around Gasparilla Island to prepare for their journey to offshore spawning grounds (the reason why Boca Grande Pass is known as the Tarpon Capital of the World).

Carefully cross Boca Grande Pass along the bay side to Cayo Costa Island. This island is only accessible by boat. After roughly two miles, you'll see the Cayo Costa State Park boat dock. Paddle up the small inlet to the right of the dock to a kayak landing spot on a tiny beach in the mangroves. Pull up your boat and keep it separate from the rental boats.

Even if you have a camping reservation, you must check in at the office near the dock. Until five p.m., a shuttle can take you and your gear (not your kayak) to the campground and cabins about a mile away on the beach side.

If you happen to land on the Gulf side near the campground, you must register at the park office (on the bay side) before setting up. You can carry your boat to your campsite or cabin. Periodic shuttles can give you a lift to the office, or you can hike.

Advanced reservations for campsites or cabins are highly recommended, especially on weekends and holidays and during the spring. Visit Reserve America (800) 326-3521. Restrooms, water and cold showers are available at the park.

In the 1800s, four Spanish fishing "ranchos" were once located on Cayo Costa, places where fish were caught, dried and shipped to Cuban markets. In the early twentieth century, the island was a small fishing village for about 20 families, with a school, post office and grocery store. Most of the island is now owned by the Florida Park Service.

If visiting or staying on Cayo Costa, take time to hike the several miles of beach and interior trails. Numerous wildflowers may be blooming in spring, such as the deep red coral bean. Look for wild pigs of many different color varieties. Mosquitoes can be pesky in warm weather. Along the beaches, you'll see numerous bleached tree trunks, victims of hurricanes and rising sea levels. Being remote and scenic, Cayo Costa will likely be a highlight of this segment.

Segment 12
Pine Island/Estero Bay

Emergency contact information:

911

Lee County Sheriff's Office: 239-477-1000

Florida Fish and Wildlife Conservation Commission 24-hour wildlife emergency/boating under the influence hotline: 1-888-404-3922

Begin: Cayo Costa State Park

End: Lovers Key/Bowtie Island

Distance: 57.5 miles

Duration: 5 days

Special Considerations: Extreme caution should be taken in paddling to and from Cayo Costa and in crossing the various passes. Due to currents and boat traffic, these open water crossings should only be attempted by experienced paddlers in favorable weather conditions along the bay side. As with most South Florida segments, boat traffic can be heavy, especially on weekends. Advance reservations are recommended for motels and campgrounds, especially during holidays and the spring season.

Introduction

Paddlers will have the option of utilizing one of two main routes as part of the Great Calusa Blueway. One route extends east from Cayo Costa and runs around Pine Island through Matlacha Pass. The other hugs the inside of North Captiva, Captiva and Sanibel islands. Both routes are highly scenic, providing opportunities to view numerous species of wading birds and other wildlife. For the purposes of this guide, we will focus primarily on the Matlacha Pass option for long-distance paddlers because overnight accommodations are reasonably priced and the waters are generally more sheltered once you reach Pine Island.

Early Calusa Indians built canals and temple mounds in the region. Houses were built atop some of their early shell mounds on Pine Island. Ponce de Leon is believed to have visited in the early 1500s, and he was followed by various European explorers. Cattle were king in the 1800s, with cattle being shipped through Charlotte Harbor to Cuba and other points.

Three Aquatic Preserves cover part of the segment: Matlacha Pass, Pine Island Sound, and Estero Bay. The preserves serve as valuable nursery grounds for both recreational and commercial species of fish, crabs and shrimp, harboring over 100 species of invertebrates, 200 species of fish and 150 species of shore and wading birds. Protected animals include five species of sea turtle, the Florida manatee, and numerous birds such as roseate spoonbills, peregrine falcons and bald eagles.

Several scenic state parks are featured in this segment. Cayo Costa and Lover's Key state parks feature hiking trails, restrooms, fresh water, and picnic facilities. In addition, Cayo Costa offers camping and cabins. Camping is also available at the Koreshan State Historic Site fronting the Estero River. Mound Key Archeological State Park features hiking and large Calusa middens and, like Cayo Costa, is only accessible by boat or kayak. Estero Bay Preserve State Park features unique scrub sand ridges -- remnants of historic dune systems.

Advance reservations at Reserve America are highly recommended for overnight stays. Call 800-326-3521.

1. Cayo Costa to Jug Creek Cottages, 11 miles

Cayo Costa is only accessible by boat or kayak. The park's boat dock and kayak landings are on the interior side of the island. Pull up your boat and keep it separate from the rental boats. Another option is to take the park shuttle boat and either rent kayaks at the park or bring your kayak on the shuttle boat.

Even if you have a camping reservation at Cayo Costa, you must check in at the office near the dock. Until 5 p.m., a shuttle can take you and your gear (not your kayak) to the campground and cabins about a mile away on the beach side.

If you happen to land on the Gulf side near the campground, you must register at the park office (on the bay side) before setting up. You can carry your boat to your campsite or cabin. Periodic shuttles can give you a lift to the office, or you can hike.

From Cayo Costa, paddle to Pine Island between Patricio and Useppa islands. Fascinating points-of-interest include the historic village of Pineland and the Randell Research Center -- site of a Calusa Indian village for more than 1500 years. The center features a self-guided trail through an extensive Calusa mound and canal complex. Open 10 a.m. to 4 p.m. daily except Christmas and Thanksgiving. A donation is requested. If you skip the research center and Pineland, you'll shave off about 3 miles from your day's total.

Jug Creek Cottages are part of the Cayo Costa State Park land base. The cottages, built in the 1940s, help to give visitors the feeling of a slower, earlier time. The cottages are available for single night rentals except on weekends and holidays, when there is a two-night minimum. Call 239-283-0015 for reservations.

Alternate route: From Cayo Costa, you can stop at Cabbage Key, where there is a restaurant, lodge and picturesque cottages. Hug the inside of Captiva and Sanibel islands and stay at the Castaway Cottages near Blind Pass after about 17 miles (239-472-1252). As you near Blind Pass, look for a marked channel through the mangroves to Castaway Cottages. A general store with groceries is next door. It is about 12 miles from Castaway Cottages to Picnic Island. This route will enable you to view the famed J. N. Ding Darling National Wildlife Refuge, home to almost 300 species of birds. The islands are also known for their strict ordinances regarding building heights, signs and landscaping; there are no big box stores and very few chain restaurants.

2. Jug Creek Cottages to Matlacha, 9.5 miles

To reach Matlacha (pronounced Mat-lah-shay), paddle along Pine Island and enter Matlacha Pass. Matlacha offers several small motels, restaurants, outfitters and a small store. A GPS point is given for one motel as a reference point.

3. Matlacha to Picnic Island, 12 miles

Leave Matlacha with enough fresh water for two days. From Matlacha, continue hugging Little Pine Island and Pine Island to Picnic Island. You can take a rest break at Tropical Point Park, although there are no facilities. There are no facilities either on Picnic Island; primitive camping is required. Follow Leave No Trace guidelines.

4. Picnic Island to Koreshan State Park, 17.5 miles

From Picnic Island, you'll head toward the mainland. You can stop at the Punta Rassa Boat Ramp and replenish your fresh water supply. About 3 miles past the ramp is Bunche Beach, once the beach for African Americans during the Jim Crow days. Just across Matanzas Pass from the beach—about a mile--is the 17-acre Bowditch Point Regional Park where you can access restrooms, a snack bar and outdoor showers.

You can follow the signs for the Great Calusa Blueway on the inside of San Carlos Island or you can shorten your day by about 1.5 miles by paddling on the inside of Estero Island. A point of interest along this route is the Mound House, a cultural museum and environmental center originally built in 1906. The center is converting an old swimming pool on the site into an underground room that is part of the large Calusa shell mound that the house was built on.

Koreshan State Park is almost 4 miles up the Estero River from the river mouth. After a mile or so, the extreme tidal influence wanes and the current is fairly slack, making for easy paddling. Along the way, you can land at the Estero River Scrub, part of Estero Bay Preserve State Park, and hike through 1,260 acres of mostly dry scrub habitat ridges. These remnant dune systems are home to gopher tortoises and other unique animals.

At Koreshan State Park, you can land and secure your kayak at the boat ramp next to the rental canoes. It is about 300 feet to the campground via the nature trail along the river. You must first register at the entrance station, which is less than a half mile along the paved entrance road from the ramp. Advanced reservations are highly recommended; the campground frequently fills up.

The park encompasses the Koreshan Unity Settlement site where about 200 religious utopian followers of Dr. Cyrus R. Teed first settled in 1880. The Koreshans believed that the universe existed within a giant hollow sphere. Not surprisingly, their beliefs were often at odds with the surrounding society. The Koreshans built their own stores, schools, sawmill, cement works, hostelry, boat works and printing house. Dr. Teed died in 1908, and in 1961, the four remaining members of the community donated the land and settlement to the state. You can hike to the historic settlement on the park nature trail along the river.

5. Koreshan State Park to Lovers Key/Bowtie Island, 7.5 miles.

After leaving the Estero River, it is less than a mile to Mound Key Archeological State Park. Kayak landings are at trail heads on the northwest and southeast portions of the island. Interpretive trails lead one through the island and to shell middens that rise up to 32 feet.

The romantic sounding Lover's Key State Park is an ideal place to end this segment. Once the possible hideout of the pirate Black Augustus, and later the site of numerous fish camps, this cluster of four scenic barrier islands was slated for development before the state of Florida and Lee County stepped in to the create the state park. You can hike or bike miles of interior trails or launch your kayak at a landing along Estero Bay. If on a long-distance paddle, you can land on either the bay side or Gulf side for a picnic, to obtain fresh water, and to use the restrooms. There is a small store and kayak rental near the boat launch. No camping is allowed in the park, but if you wish to primitive camp in the area, Bowtie Island is available on a first-come-first-served basis free-of-charge. Managed by the Florida Paddling Trails Association, the island is about two miles south of the Lover's Key wayside picnic area and is accessed on the southeast corner (see map).

Segment 13
Rookery Bay/Ten Thousand Islands

Emergency contact information:
911
Collier County Sheriff's Office: 239-774-4434
Everglades National Park 24-hour search and rescue: 305-247-7272
Florida Fish and Wildlife Conservation Commission 24-hour wildlife emergency/boating under the influence hotline: 1-888-404-3922

Begin: Lovers Key/Bowtie Island
End: Everglades City
Distance: 68 miles, although distances will vary depending on route taken

Special Considerations: Paddlers have the option of taking the Gulf side of the many islands in this area, making for easier navigation and shorter distances between campsites. In windy or inclement weather, however, paddlers should travel inside the islands through more sheltered bays and waterways. Advanced reservations are recommended for motels, and for campsites within Everglades National Park. NOAA charts and/or a Top Spot map, along with a GPS unit, are highly recommended in the Ten Island Islands as stories abound about lost boaters.

Introduction

Rookery Bay and Florida's Ten Thousand Islands are steeped in history and mystery. The area is a watery maze of mangrove keys where Calusa Indians once dug canals and built land with their discarded shells. Seminole Indians and outlaws sought refuge along the sometimes bewildering, twisting waterways. Men once eked out a living by hunting alligators and crocodiles, killing egrets for their plumes, and making moonshine.

Historic landmarks still remain such as Chokoloskee's Smallwood Store where the proprietor once traded with dugout-paddling Seminole Indians. The Indians swapped pelts and silver money for tools, guns and staples. Today, kayakers can land at the cracker-style landmark and peruse the museum and gift shop.

In 1896, Marco Island, then called Key Marco, yielded some of the most astounding Native American artifacts ever found in Florida. Digging in the island's mangrove muck, Frank Hamilton Cushing and his Smithsonian expedition crew uncovered an incredible array of perishable objects—carved and painted wood animal heads, masks, clubs, bowls and atlatls (spear throwing devices). They also found nets, fishhooks, cord, ropes, floats and shell jewelry. Cushing later wrote of these early people, "… their art is not only an art of the sea, but is an art of shells and teeth, an art for which the sea supplied nearly all the working parts of tools, the land only some of the materials worked upon."

Environmentally, more than 150 species of birds frequent these unique southwest Florida habitats. Mangrove forests predominate the landscape, the leaves of which fall and create a rich detritus that is the base of the estuarine food web. Look for the nearly impenetrable walls of prop roots created by red mangrove trees. Black and white mangroves are generally farther inland on higher ground.

Numerous fish, dolphins and manatees frequent the channels, bays and coves of the area. Rich seagrass beds are nursery grounds for a variety of fish, shellfish and crustaceans, and they also provide food for manatees and sea turtles. The area's sandy beaches, mostly along the mainland and barrier islands, provide invaluable nest sites for endangered sea turtles. These beaches are also famous for their shelling opportunities.

Learn more about the Rookery Bay National Estuarine Research Reserve and Everglades National Park Information. This segment also covers several premier Florida state parks: Lover's Key, Delnor-Wiggins Pass, and Collier-Seminole, although Collier-Seminole is off the main route.

There are numerous other paddling opportunities in this segment. The northern part (in Lee County) is part of the Great Calusa Blueway. The rest of the segment, which lies in Collier County, will be phased in as part of the Paradise Coast Blueway: These blueways offer diverse paddling trips along the coast and associated waterways.

1. Lovers Key/Bowtie Island to Lighthouse Inn or Vanderbilt Beach Resort, 10.5 miles

Lover's Key... this romantic sounding state park is an ideal place to begin this segment. Once the possible hideout of pirate Black Augustus, and later the site of numerous fish camps, this cluster of four scenic barrier islands was slated for development before the state of Florida and Lee County stepped into the create the state park. You can hike or bike miles of interior trails or launch your kayak at a landing along Estero Bay. If on a long-distance paddle, you can land on either the bay side or Gulf side for a picnic, obtain fresh water, and use the restrooms. There is a small store and kayak rental near the boat launch. No camping is allowed in the park.

If you wish to primitive camp in the area, Bowtie Island is available on a first-come, first-served basis free-of-charge. Managed by the [Florida Paddling Trails Association](), the island is about two miles south of the Lover's Key wayside picnic area (see map).

From Lover's Key, you can take a more sheltered inside passage about nine miles to Wiggins Pass, if you wish. On the Gulf side, it is about eight miles to Wiggins Pass and you can take breaks at two lovely county parks—Barefoot Beach and Bonita Beach (see map). Along the south shore of Wiggins Pass you can enjoy [Delnor-Wiggins Pass State Park](), partly named after Joe Wiggins, the area's first homesteader who ran an apiary and trading post. Here, you can take a break and enjoy a picnic, take a shower, or grab a snack at a beachside concession.

If you're planning to stay at the Lighthouse Inn, you'll need to keep on the inside channel for more than two miles to reach the motel. The motel docks are high so a high tide would make it easier to disembark and pull your boat onto the dock. Reservations are recommended, so call (239) 463-9392 or book online. The motel is adjacent to a restaurant and it is a short walk to Vanderbilt Beach. If you have wheels for your kayak, you can portage to Vanderbilt Beach (about 900 feet). Otherwise, you'll need to add about 5 miles to your next day's paddle.

Another option for overnight lodging, directly on the beach, is the [Vanderbilt Beach Resort](), just before the public beach. This option will be more expensive but you will not have to portage or paddle extra distance. Again, reservations are recommended, so call (800) 243-9076. Restaurants and a small convenience store are in the area.

2. Lighthouse Inn or Vanderbilt Beach Resort to Keewaydin Island, 19.5 miles (add 5 miles if staying at Lighthouse Inn and not portaging to Vanderbilt Beach)
Hug the Gulf shoreline as you head south. This is a long stretch of paddling, but you can break it up with stops at county parks and at the Naples City Pier. At Gordon Pass, you can take the inside passage along Key Island (also referred to as Keewaydin Island) and avoid much of the boat traffic, but this will add more than a mile to your day.

The reward for all of your efforts is Keewaydin Island. Accessible only by boat, the Gulf side of this barrier island has some of the best shelling opportunities in Florida. Note that a 3.5-acre portion of the southern end of the island may be closed from mid-April through mid-August for Least Tern nesting. Look for signs. Primitive camping is available on the southern end of Key Island when birds are not nesting, or just north of the nesting area. The western side of Sea Oat Island has good camping as well.

If heading south, Keewaydin Island marks the point where there are several primitive camping options in the Rookery Bay National Estuarine Reserve (see maps). These campsites are unimproved and can be used on a first-come, first-serve basis by paddlers and other boaters. Leave No Trace guidelines apply.

3. Keewaydin Island to Cape Romano, 11.5 miles
The mileage listed is for the Gulf side. However, you may need to take the inside channel in inclement weather, which will add about four miles. If paddling on inland waterways, Johnson Bay is recommended as motorboats are required to travel at

slow speeds. The area can be busy with boats on weekends and holidays. If paddling through Johnson Bay, you may want to land at one of the kayak friendly restaurants along the Isle of Capri.

NOTE: if you are a long-distance paddler set on continuing through the Ten Thousand Islands and Florida Bay to the Keys, Marco Island offers the last opportunity to stock up at a supermarket. For this supply run, you'll need to paddle about 3.5 miles on the inside of Marco Island to the Highway 951 Bridge. You can land at a small beach and hike almost a mile down Collier Boulevard to the town center, where there is a large supermarket and other stores and restaurants. There is no supermarket at the south end of Marco Island. Once the site of major clam digging operations and a clam cannery in the first half of the 1900s, Marco Island boomed in the 1960s with plush developments for those attracted to island living.

If you take the Gulf side to Cape Romano, you can take a break at Tiger Tail Beach, which has restrooms, a kayak rental, and a restaurant. Along the bay side, you can stop at a marina and restaurant along the Highway 92 Bridge. The town of Goodland offers a small store and restaurants. This small fishing village has struggled to keep its rural identity in the face of a booming coastal real estate market.

Cape Romano is an isolated point that is fully exposed to the elements, so proceed with caution. You may see the ruins of unusual dome structures in the water near your campsite. The elements are slowly claiming them. If you take the inside passage and the weather is inclement, you may want to proceed to Whitehorse Key.

4. Cape Romano to Whitehorse Key, 7.5 miles
Here, you will be entering the heart of the Ten Thousand Islands. If you hug the outside of the islands, you'll have no

problem finding your way. You can easily get lost if you travel through the inside passages. It is best to follow marked channels.

Whitehorse Key is situated between Gullivan Key and Hog Key and you can camp on these two islands as well.

Just to the east of your campsite is Panther Key. This was where one of the area's most colorful characters once lived—Old John Gomez. Born in the 1770s, Gomez claimed to have met Napoleon, served with the pirate Jose Gaspar (Gasparilla), fought in the Second Seminole War, and operated as a blockade-runner during the Civil War. He named his home Panther Key because panthers would swim to the island and eat his goats. Old John Gomez attracted many visitors and writers to Panther Key until his death in 1900 at age 122.

While the Ten Thousand Islands contained some harmless hermits, it also harbored numerous fugitives, such as Ed Watson, who allegedly killed the outlaw Belle Starr, among other people. An early account of seven unwritten laws for the area reads like something out of the frontier West: suspect every man; ask no questions; settle your own quarrels; never steal from an Islander; stick by him, even if you do not know him; shoot quick, when your secret is in danger; cover your kill.

About a century later, it is unlikely you will need to follow this code when paddling through the Ten Thousand Islands.

5. Whitehorse Key to Everglades City, 14 miles
After Whitehorse Key, you will soon enter Everglades National Park, a vast watery wilderness of islands, sawgrass, mangroves and forests. Its life-giving fresh water supply, unfortunately, is largely controlled by pumps, floodgates and retention ponds outside the park, a man-made system that has been detrimental

to the Everglades' natural ecological balance. A multi-billion dollar restoration plan may fix some of the problems.

Before you can camp in the national park, you must obtain a permit at the visitor's center in Everglades City (see map). Indian Key Pass is the most direct route to Everglades City. Follow the marked channel. An incoming tide will be a big help.

Everglades National Park takes no advance reservations by phone; you must arrive in person up to 24 hours in advance of your planned first night's campsite. Since it is 14 miles from Whitehorse Key to Everglades City, it would be best to spend the night in Everglades City. There are numerous motels and cabin rentals, some of which are accessible by water. Advanced reservations are recommended. The [Museum of the Everglades](#) in downtown Everglades City is worth a visit, open from 10 a.m. to 4 p.m. Tuesday through Saturday.

From Everglades City, you'll have your choice of taking the 99-mile [Wilderness Waterway](#) to Flamingo, or the Gulf route. Weather may be a deciding factor. Campsites range from chickees that have been built on pilings in rivers and bays, ground sites that have been cleared within the mangrove forests, and beach sites. Campfires are only allowed at the beach sites (below high-tide line). The ground sites tend to have more insects, but be prepared for insects anywhere in this region at any time of year.

For local information visit or call the [Gulf Coast Visitor Center](#) at Everglades City, (239) 695-3311. The lobby at the [Flamingo Visitor Center](#) can be accessed 24 hours for backcountry site self-registration during the summer season. Call 239-695-2945.
IMPORTANT: The segment from Everglades City to Flamingo is the longest stretch along the circumnavigation trail without a fresh water supply. At Everglades City, you'll need

to obtain a gallon of water per day per person for seven to eight days. That is a lot of weight and bulk. Some groups contract with a boat guide in Everglades City or Flamingo to resupply them with water en-route.

Raccoons are the biggest threat to your food and water. Raccoons have been known to chew through thin plastic water jugs. When camping, secure your food and water in your kayak compartments and flip your boat upside down if necessary. Campers have unintentionally contributed to larger raccoon numbers near campsites. In turn, hungry raccoons destroy an estimated 90 percent of sea turtle nests in the park.

Kayaks on Rabbit Key in the Ten Thousand Islands.

Segment 14
Everglades/Florida Bay

Emergency contact information:

911

Everglades National Park 24-hour search and rescue: 305-247-7272

Collier County Sheriff's Office: 239-774-4434

Monroe County Sheriff's Office: 305-289-2430

Florida Fish and Wildlife Conservation Commission 24-hour wildlife emergency/boating under the influence hotline: 1-888-404-3922

Begin: Everglades City

End: Long Key State Park

Estimated Mileage: 99.5 miles via the Gulf side; 126.5 miles via the Wilderness Waterway

Special Considerations

It is possible now (Fall 2015) to select an alternate route from Flamingo to Miami that hugs the mainland shoreline for the most part. If weather conditions are inclement with winds out of the west or north, this may be a more sheltered option. If weather conditions improve then you can consider rejoining the original CT route of Segments 14-16. This option may be found on page 207.

MPORTANT: The segment from Everglades City to Flamingo is the longest stretch along the circumnavigation trail without a fresh water supply. At Everglades City, you'll need to obtain a gallon of water per day per person for seven to eight days. That is a lot of weight and bulk. Some groups contract with a boat guide in Everglades City or Flamingo to resupply them with water enroute.

Raccoons are the biggest threat to your food and water. Raccoons have been known to chew through thin plastic water jugs. When camping, secure your food and water in your kayak compartments and flip over your boat if necessary. Campers have unintentionally contributed to larger raccoon numbers near campsites. In turn, hungry raccoons destroy an estimated 90% of sea turtle nests in the park.

For backcountry permits and local information visit or call the Gulf Coast Visitor Center at Everglades City, (239) 695-3311. The lobby at the Flamingo Visitor Center can be accessed 24 hours for backcountry site self-registration during the summer season. Call 239-695-2945. These two visitor's centers are currently the only places where camping permits can be obtained.

A GPS unit and good navigational maps are essential in this segment as many unprepared boaters have become lost in the maze of mangrove islands in the Ten Thousand Islands. A compass is essential, too, in case thick mangroves interfere with your GPS unit or your unit malfunctions.

Introduction

Everglades National Park and Florida Bay are two of Florida's natural treasures that attract visitors from throughout the world. This vast watery wilderness of islands, sawgrass, mangroves, forests, waterways and open water often appears little different than when dugout travelers fished the waters and set up villages and camps on the islands.

In this segment, you'll see a unique combination of subtropical and tropical plants, marine creatures from both marine and estuarine environments, and the only place in the world where alligators and crocodiles co-exist. Bird life includes roseate spoonbills, ospreys, white pelicans and wood storks. Sea turtles can often be seen poking up their heads in the Gulf and Florida Bay. If fortunate, you might glimpse a rare sawfish. Its long, flat snout contains 24 or more pairs of sharp teeth that resembles a two-bladed crosscut saw.

Unfortunately, to the detriment of many native creatures in Florida Bay, pumps, floodgates and retention ponds outside the park now largely control the Everglades' life-giving fresh water supply. A multi-billion dollar restoration plan may fix some of the problems, along with improved timing of water releases.

From Everglades City, you'll have your choice of taking the 99-mile Wilderness Waterway to Flamingo, or the Gulf route. The Gulf route is shorter and generally has fewer bugs, but weather may be a deciding factor. Campsites range from chickees that have been built on pilings in rivers and bays, ground sites that have been cleared within the mangrove forests, and beach sites. Campfires are only allowed at the beach sites (below high-tide line). The ground sites tend to have more insects, but be prepared for insects anywhere in this region at any time of year.

This guide will focus on the Gulf route across the Ten Thousand Islands to Flamingo since it is shorter and less known. There are two routes now from Flamingo to the Keys or an alternate route from Flamingo to Miami, where campsites are spaced a reasonable distance apart.

As always, Leave No Trace principles and practices should be followed for primitive camping.

1: Everglades City to Rabbit Key, 9 miles

Before you can camp in the national park, you must obtain a permit at the Visitor's Center in Everglades City (see map) and pay a small fee. Everglades National Park takes no advance reservations by phone; you must arrive in person up to 24 hours in advance of your planned first night's campsite. Plan to have alternate campsites in mind in case your first choices are full. Some campsites have portable toilets while others do not, so plan accordingly.

Since camping at the Flamingo Campground is not part of the permit system, you'll need to make separate reservations or call The National Park Reservation Service at 1-877-444-6777.

For the long distance paddler arriving from Whitehorse Key, it is 14 miles to Everglades City so you'll need to spend the night in Everglades City. There is a grocery store and numerous motels and cabin rentals, some of which are accessible by water. Advanced reservations are recommended. The historic Rod & Gun Club is worth visiting for a meal or overnight stay, there is no website so call (239) 695-210. The Museum of the Everglades in downtown Everglades City is worth a visit, open from 10 a.m. to 4 p.m. Tuesday through Saturday.

Tides can greatly influence paddling to and from Everglades City. If you can time it properly, take the incoming tide to the Visitor's Center and the outgoing tide to Rabbit Key through Rabbit Key Pass. Park rangers often check for permits, so have it handy in your kayak and tie it onto your tent after you set up camp. Stick to your permit itinerary unless there are extenuating circumstances such as injury or a big storm.

Paddling to Rabbit Key, you'll cross the open Chokoloskee Bay to the small hamlet of Chokoloskee, originally a massive shell mound built by Calusa Indians and now linked to the mainland by a causeway. Take a break at fascinating Smallwood's Store (see map). Established by Ted Smallwood in 1906, this store was the main trading outpost in the region. Residents and nearby Seminole Indians would paddle or boat to the store to trade or sell hides, furs and produce for dry goods, guns and ammunition. It remained open until 1982 and is now a museum. For a small fee, you can tour the exhibits and view many of the items that were once for sale or trade.

From Chokoloskee, you can wind through a maze of mangrove inlets to Rabbit Key Pass or choose less direct routes. Rabbit Key is perched on the edge of the Gulf, so you'll have the best of both worlds: a view of mangrove islands on one side and open water on the other.

2: Rabbit Key to Turkey Key, 11.5 miles

You can take a direct open water route to Pavilion Key and beyond, or you can duck behind mangrove islands in order to find shelter from winds and waves. Some of the water will be very shallow at low tide, however. Proceed cautiously across the open water from Pavilion Key to Mormon Key as unfavorable winds and tides have caused numerous small crafts to capsize, some say the highest number of capsizes in the park.

The approach to the beach campsite at Turkey Key is shallow, so a high tide is best. The key was once the site of a commercial fishing operation.

3: Turkey Key to Highland Beach, 12 miles

In the latter part of this segment, you'll be leaving the Ten Thousand Islands and moving along a more continuous shoreline of mangroves, beaches and bays.

Highland Beach, your destination, is a natural beach with a long shell ridge formed by wave action. Once farmed by the Rewis family, it has a grass prairie, cabbage palms and other plants to break up the mangrove forests. Highland Beach is best accessed at high tide as the water is very shallow near the beach.

4: Highland Beach to Graveyard Creek, 9 miles

Along this route, you'll paddle through the mouths of the North and South Harney rivers, named for Colonel William Harney, who used the river to cross the Everglades in a surprise raid on the Indian leader Chekika and his band in 1840. The raid was, in part, retaliation for Chekika's raid on Indian Key, in which seven settlers were killed. By 1842, with most Seminoles killed, imprisoned or removed to Oklahoma, hostilities ceased until re-igniting again in the 1850s.

This shorter day will allow you to explore Graveyard Creek and the many other tributaries along Ponce De Leon Bay. The bay is also known for its good fishing.

Graveyard Creek campsite has characteristics of both a ground and beach campsite. It is best to land at the campsite along Graveyard Creek as the water is deeper.

5: Graveyard Creek to Northwest Cape Sable, 11 miles

At low tide, the mouth of Graveyard Creek can be a mud flat, so you may want to paddle up Graveyard Creek and wind around into Ponce De Leon Bay, where the water is deeper, allowing you to continue your journey south.

On this day you'll begin your approach of Cape Sable, one of the finest natural shorelines remaining in Florida. A grassy plain borders the sandy beach in most places, with occasional clumps of sable palms, Jamaica dogwood and hardwood hammocks. Gopher tortoises and Cape Sable seaside sparrows are among the protected species here, with the Cape Sable seaside sparrow being the only bird restricted entirely to the Everglades environment. They depend upon prairies that both periodically flood and burn.

Before the national park was established in 1947, many attempts to farm, ranch and develop Cape Sable were short-lived due to its remoteness, insect life, and killer hurricanes.

Because of the remoteness of the Northwest Cape campsite, you'll likely see few other visitors. The extensive beach and prairies make for excellent hiking.

6: Northwest Cape Sable to East Cape Sable, 9.5 miles

The sharp point at Middle Cape, roughly the halfway point, was once the site of a 1850s Army fort established as a base to hunt down Seminole Indians. In the 1880s, a coconut farm once flourished nearby until a 1935 hurricane destroyed the coconut palms. Few signs of human inhabitation are seen here today.

This segment can be very windy. There is an interior route through a series of creeks and canals and across Lake Ingraham that is heavily influenced by tides. With luck, you can paddle towards the lake on an incoming tide and leave the lake on an outgoing tide.

The East Cape campsite is the southernmost point in the mainland United States. Fort Poinsett was erected here in the 1830s in an effort to prevent Seminole Indians from obtaining arms from Spanish fishermen, but traces of the log fort have vanished.

7: East Cape Sable to Flamingo, 10 miles

Flamingo will likely be a welcome break after six or seven days of paddling. The park service manages a campground and a small store is adjacent to the landing. Canoe and kayak rentals are also available. The campground is about a mile before the marina and accessible by water at high tide. At low tide, you might have to wade through mud. Reservations should be made ahead of time online or by calling 1-855-708-2207.

Flamingo, named in 1893 for the colorful flamingo birds that once arrived in great number from Cuba and the Bahamas, is an isolated town and was formerly only accessible by water. It is notorious for flying insect life during the warm months and early residents relied upon smoldering smudge pots inside their homes and even under baby carriages. When a scarcely passable road was built to Flamingo in 1922, one resident joked, "There were fewer people than ever at Flamingo. They had found a way to get out."

8: Flamingo to Little Rabbit Key, 13 miles

At this point it is possible to select the Mainland Alternate Route from Flamingo to Miami that for the most part hugs the mainland shoreline. If weather conditions are inclement with winds out of the west or north, this may be a more sheltered option. If weather conditions improve then you can consider rejoining the original Segment 15 route skirting along the 'outside' of the Keys.

Make sure to check the weather forecast at the Flamingo Visitor's Center before embarking. Even though Florida Bay is shallow, you'll be entering the most expansive stretch of open water on the entire trail. For a safer and slightly longer passage, you might want to follow the banks and shallow flats outlined on your navigational charts. Avoid getting too close to fishing boats poling in the shallows as anglers are often sight-fishing for bonefish, permit and tarpon on these flats.

A chickee campsite on stilts with a portable toilet near Johnson Key is available about halfway to Rabbit Key, a half mile off the route (see map). There is also a chickee campsite on stilts near Shark Point 7.5 miles east of Flamingo. From this campsite, it is about 20 miles to Tavernier or Nest Key if following the Alternate Mainland Route. These chickees are attractive to a number of bird species and as a result the platforms may be covered with their droppings. Bring along a piece of plastic or tarp to establish your tent site.

The clarity of the water around Little Rabbit Key has been described as stunning, and you'll be able to glimpse numerous fish, crabs and other aquatic creatures. There is no sandy beach at Little Rabbit Key. Tent sites are behind a small dock on the northwest side.

9: Little Rabbit Key to Long Key State Park, 14.5 miles

From Little Rabbit Key, you'll have a long stretch of open water paddling broken only by small mangrove islands. Long Key sticks out like a huge boot. Early Spaniards called it "Cayo

Vivora," which means Viper Key because its shape is said to resemble a snake with open jaws. At Long Key Point, you'll connect with the Florida Keys Overseas Paddling Trail (Segment 15).

Camping is on the Atlantic side of Long Key State Park where you can reserve one of the park's 60 scenic campsites in the campground (all bordering the Atlantic Ocean). You must make reservations well in advance for the regular campground, but you can call the park headquarters for reserving one of the primitive sites: (305) 664-4815. The park also offers nature trails, an observation tower, and a marked paddling trail through a mangrove paradise (just over a mile in length).

Note: due to Hurricane Irma, Long Key State Park campsites are closed for reconstruction through 2019 and possibly beyond. Check state park website for updates.

Segment 15
Florida Keys Overseas Paddling Trail

Emergency contact information:
911
Monroe County Sheriff's Office: 305-853-3266
Florida Fish and Wildlife Conservation Commission 24-hour wildlife emergency/boating under the influence hotline: 1-888-404-3922

Begin: John Pennekamp State Park, Key Largo
End: Fort Zachary Taylor Historic State Park, Key West
Estimated Distance: 111 miles
Duration: 9-10 days
Special Considerations: The Keys are unlike any other segment in that you can paddle up and back and choose paddling on the Florida Bay/Gulf of Mexico side or along the Atlantic Ocean. Distance and duration will be determined by which side is chosen. The Bay side is longer as the shoreline is more sinuous and there are numerous opportunities to explore a multitude of islands, especially in the Lower Keys. You can also weave in and out between the bay and ocean through several creeks and channels, taking advantage of prevailing winds and weather conditions. Many of the same campsites can be utilized since they often border channels between the main islands. All mileage estimates in this guide are for the Atlantic side of the keys; they are measured in statute miles, not

nautical miles. A GPS unit and good maps are highly recommended to find campsites and points of interest. For long-distance circumnavigation paddlers arriving from Everglades National Park and Florida Bay, the current point of connection to this trail is to come in from a primitive campsite at Rabbit Keys to the Indian Key Channel between Upper and Lower Matecumbe Keys. If you selected the 'Alternate Mainland' route between Flamingo and Miami to avoid bad weather you may want to consider joining this segment whenever conditions improve to experience the delights of paddling the Keys.

Introduction
Paddling in the Keys is a great way to experience both tropical splendor and unique culture. The Overseas Highway is busy, powerboats abound on weekends and holidays, and some of the island towns can become congested during the peak winter tourist season, but by paddling just a short distance to lush, uninhabited islands or down winding tunnels through mangrove forests, it is easy to taste wildness and to experience solitude. Paddlers can enjoy viewing a rich diversity of marine life, ranging from manatees and sea turtles to lobsters, fish and stingrays. An array of bird life can also be spotted, from migrating hawks to magnificent frigate birds to brightly-colored warblers. Conversely, civilization in the form of great restaurants, lodging, and evening entertainment is often within easy reach of the water. Thus, the best of both worlds can be experienced!

History, too, is a strong part of the keys experience. Visual reminders of Henry Flagler's overseas railroad of the early 1900s can be seen in the arching concrete columns of several old bridges, including the original Seven Mile Bridge between Knight's Key and Ohio Key. Remnant railroad depots still exist, and the Flagler Station Over-Sea Railway Historeum can be visited at the Key West Seaport. The Labor Day Hurricane of 1935 destroyed much of the railroad.

Historic sites such as Indian Key Historic State Park and Fort Zachary Taylor Historic State Park can be visited from the water. Shipwrecks can sometimes be spotted in the gin-clear waters, testament as to how treacherous the Keys' waters were for navigation. Salvaging shipwrecks, known as wrecking, was once the main industry in the Keys.

Because the Keys are a popular winter destination for tourists and snowbirds, advanced reservations for desired motels and public or private campsites are highly recommended. There are some primitive campsites specifically for paddlers at several state parks, details follow in the text below. Please keep these sites clean and follow all regulations in order for them to remain open for paddlers. Most of these sites are "pack-it-in, pack-it-out" only, with campers following Leave No Trace principles.

Lodging is available in all of the Keys' towns, and there are numerous private campgrounds. Several outfitters in the Keys can also assist you in renting or selling equipment or in guiding trips.

Many important land areas and water bodies in the Keys are in the public domain, to be carefully managed for ecological, historical or recreational purposes. There are some wonderful State parks in the Keys that offer delightful camping options for paddlers. There are two Aquatic Preserves, Lignumvitae Key and Coupon Bight, that conserve underwater habitat. The Florida Fish and Wildlife Conservation Commission manages the Florida Keys Wildlife & Environmental Area. Federal land and waters include Everglades National Park, National Key Deer Refuge, Great White Heron National Wildlife Refuge, Crocodile Lake National Wildlife Refuge, Key West National

Wildlife Refuge , and the Key Largo, Looe Key and Florida Keys National Marine Sanctuaries. The Florida Keys Marine Sanctuary covers most waters in the keys, encompassing 2900 square miles, and kayakers should be aware of regulations if planning to fish or snorkel.

A large number of shorter paddling adventures are available in the Keys other than the sections outlined here. To learn more, check out *The Florida Keys Paddling Atlas* by Bill and Mary Burnham (Falcon Press), *The Florida Keys Paddling Guide* by Bill Keogh (Backcountry Press) and *Kayaking the Keys* by Kathleen Patton (University Press of Florida). Up-to-date trail information can also be obtained by calling or visiting local outfitters. Whether you are planning to paddle an hour or a week or more, seeing the keys by kayak offers many rewards.

1: John Pennekamp State Park to Tavernier, 12 miles
John Pennekamp Coral Reef State Park is an appropriate beginning point for the Keys trail. Dedicated in 1960 and named after the late John D. Pennekamp, a Miami newspaper editor and strong supporter of establishing the park, this was the first undersea park in the United States. While the famed coral reefs are considered too far offshore for a kayak, the park offers several types of tours in which to safely view the reefs and rich marine life. Call 305-451-6300 for more information on these tours. The park also boasts a large aquarium and visitor's center, two nature trails, full facility camping, and 2.5 miles of marked mangrove wilderness trails for canoes or kayaks. Approximately 100 feet offshore from Pennekamp's Cannon Beach, you can snorkel or glide over the remnants of an early Spanish shipwreck.

You can begin this section at Pennekamp's kayak and canoe launch along Largo Sound. Be watchful of boat traffic as you make you way to the Atlantic along the park's canoe and kayak trail, heading south along a tidal creek through the mangroves.

Paddle along Key Largo to Tavernier. Many paddlers camp on Tavernier Key, but this island is private and formal approval for camping has not been granted.

Tavernier Creek can take you to the bay side, if so desired. Accessible motels along the bayside include Coconut Palm (305-852-3017), Island Bay (305-852-4087) and Lookout Lodge (305-852-9915). See map for GPS points. During the peak spring season, some of these motels may require a two or three night minimum stay.

2: Tavernier to Islamorada, 9 miles
In his *History of Tavernier,* Jerry Wilkinson writes, "In early writings, the harbor between Tavernier Key and Key Largo is mentioned as a rendezvous area for Bahamian wreckers. It offered a haven from Atlantic gales and a good view of the Upper Keys reefs. In the early 1820s it is believed that slaves were gathered on Key Tavernier to be smuggled into the Bahamas by wreckers, but this has never been documented. It was used as a relay point for some escaped slaves enroute to the Bahamas."

The Keys history website, along with several good books, can inform you more about fascinating aspects of Keys history such as the wrecking industry, sponging, early native inhabitants, Flagler's railroad, devastating hurricanes and more.

Leaving historic Tavernier Key, it is a fairly straight shot along Plantation Key, once the site of a large Native American village. A huge Indian mound that stood on the island for centuries was leveled for construction in 1958.

When you reach the town of Islamorada, you can arrange for Islamorada Lodging at one of several resorts and motels. Waterfront motels that are considered kayak friendly include:

Conch On Inn Motel (mm 89.5) 305 852-9309; Lookout Lodge (mm 88) 305-852-9915; Coconut Cove Motel (mm85) 305 664-0123. The Whale Harbor Channel in Islamorada is a link to the bay side. Islamorada has often been called the fishing capital of the world.

3: Islamorada to Long Key State Park, 15 miles
The first of many long bridges separate Upper and Lower Matecumbe Keys in this section. On the Atlantic side of the bridge is Indian Key, famous for a Seminole raid in 1838 on the family of Dr. Henry Perrine. Perrine and several others were killed, though many family members successfully hid in a turtle kraal beneath the house. The island is now a state park and can be visited seven days a week from 8 AM to 5 PM. Tours are available at 9 AM and 1 PM Thursday through Monday. Just to the southwest of the park is the San Pedro Underwater Archeological Preserve State Park. In good weather, you can glide over or snorkel the remains of a 1733 Spanish treasure ship, which lies in 18 feet of water. Look for the five white mooring buoys marking the site approximately 1.25 miles south of Indian Key. You can tie your kayak to these while snorkeling.

On the other side of the bridge is Lignumvitae Key, famed for harboring now rare lignum vitae trees. Meaning "wood of life" in Latin, the tree was used to treat diseases ranging from syphilis to gout, and its dense wood was used for submarine propeller shafts and other specific uses. Rare orchids, tree cacti and an historic homestead can also be seen on this state botanical area. Note that the park is also open from Thursday through Monday, from 8 AM to 5 PM. Tours are available at 10 AM and 2 PM.

Surrounding the island is the Lignumvitae Key Aquatic Preserve and the Lignumvitae Key Management Area. Encompassing 10,000 acres of seagrass meadows, deep-water channels and hard-bottom communities, look for tarpon, bonefish, permit, sea turtles, lobster and other marine creatures in the clear waters. Most of the seagrass areas are zoned off limits to combustion engines.

Past Lower Matecumbe Key, Long Key sticks out like a huge boot. Early Spaniards called it "Cayo Vivora," which means Viper Key because its shape is said to resemble a snake with open jaws. On Long Key, you'll see remains of coral reefs formed 100,000 years ago, when sea level was 20 to 300 feet higher than today. When sea levels dropped during the last Ice Age, the reefs died and formed the islands of the keys. The highest point in the Keys is 18 feet above sea level, while the average is less than 10 feet above sea level, a main reason why the Keys are so vulnerable to hurricanes.

Long Key is famous for Henry Flagler's Long Key Fishing Club, which attracted such notables as western author Zane Grey. Grey summed up his time spent on Long Key: "Into my memory had been burned indelibly a picture of a sunlit, cloud-mirroring, green and gold bordered cove, above the center of which shone a glorious fish-creature in the air." The original fishing resort was destroyed in the 1935 hurricane.

Camping in [Long Key State Park](#) is on the Atlantic side where you can reserve one of the park's 60 scenic campsites in the campground (all bordering the Atlantic Ocean). You must reserve through Reserve America well in advance. The park also offers nature trails, an observation tower, and ranger-led interpretative programs.

Note: due to Hurricane Irma, Long Key State Park campsites are closed for reconstruction through 2019 and possibly beyond. Check state park website for updates.

4. Long Key State Park to Curry Hammock State Park, 13 miles

In this section, you'll pass several small islands and cross a long section of open water. Duck Key, which was bypassed by both the railroad and overseas highway, is the first large island you'll encounter. In the early 1800s, Charles Howe utilized the tidal creeks and pools of Duck Key for making salt. At that time, salt was the main element used in preserving meat.

You have the option of paddling to the inside (along the Overseas Highway) or outside of Duck Key to Tom's Harbor Keys and Grassy Key. Just past Grassy Key is Little Crawl Key and Curry Hammock State Park. Use Reserve America to reserve a site in advance at <u>Curry Hammock State Park</u> or call the park at least 24 hours in advance to check walk-in availability (305) 394-3330. Take a walk through the hardwood hammocks and view one of the largest populations of thatch palms in the United States.

5. Curry Hammock State Park to Molasses Key, 15 miles

Take your time paddling through this section. First, you can take a break at Sombrero Beach in Marathon. <u>Make sure to use the kayak launch site on the west side of the swimming beach.</u>

As a side trip, you can take Sister's Creek (just west of Sombrero Beach) and then paddle through a labyrinth of shallow mangrove tunnels that wind through Boot Key, but be careful not to become lost! Once on the trail again, you'll cruise alongside a famous Keys landmark—the Seven Mile Bridge just past Marathon. You can view the new bridge, built in 1982, as well as the longest surviving bridge segment of Flagler's railroad. Imagine the work that went into the original bridge. Top quality cement was imported from Europe. Huge floating concrete mixers had to be used. Dams were built around each column to keep out water, as workers labored to bridge the span. Several hurricanes dealt serious blows to men and machines during the overall project. The fact that the bridge remains is a testament to the quality of workmanship and materials. The new bridge is also acclaimed as a major architectural and engineering achievement.

A little over two miles down the old bridge from Knight's Key, you can stop at <u>Pigeon Key Marine Science Center</u> and tour through a restored village and museum. Pigeon Key originally housed workers for the Flagler Railroad. What survives are eight restored Flagler-era buildings. <u>Be sure to land on the beach on the north side of Pigeon Key.</u> There is an entrance fee.

Primitive camping is on Molasses Key, a private island just over half way down the Seven Mile Bridge on the Atlantic side, but far enough away from the highway to avoid most of the traffic noise. The smaller of the two islands of Molasses Key is recommended. Be mindful of swift currents and the potential for strong winds when crossing these open spans of water.

6. Molasses Key to Bahia Honda State Park, 7 miles
Some places just seem more graced with beauty than others. <u>Bahia Honda State Park</u> is one of them. Arching palms frame sandy beaches and coves alongside sparkling clear water. An old section of the Flagler railroad bridge (the only trestle bridge along the route) across the Bahia Honda Channel gives the park an historic flavor.

This is a very popular state park, considered one of the top beaches in the world, so reserve campsites early. There is camping near the bridge in the Buttonwood Camping Area (sites 12 through 25 are electric sites along the water) and eight non-electric sites (cheaper) along Florida Bay in the Bayside Camping Area. You may want to access the park on the north side of the abandoned railroad bridge along the west end of the key if the surf is strong along the Atlantic beaches.

Campsite #80 on the bay side is available to paddlers on a first-come, first-serve basis. Paddlers must first register at the park's ranger station. If you plan to use the site, call the park at (305) 872-2353 on the morning of your planned arrival to ensure that the site will not be released for use by the general public. The site is held by the park until 3 p.m. each day to allow for paddlers to get a first shot.

At the far end of Sandspur Beach, don't miss the nature trail that follows the shore of a tidal lagoon. Here, you can see two national champion trees: the silver palm, a threatened species, and the yellow satinwood. The endangered lily thorn can also be seen. The park boasts one of the largest stands of silver palms in the United States.

If Bahia Honda is booked, try camping at the [Big Pine Key Fishing Lodge](#) just across the Bahia Honda Channel (305 872-2351). You can land at the boat ramp via the inlet parallel to U.S. 1. Sites 10 through 14 and 40 through 46 are tent sites right on the water. The campground has a convenience store, pool, and laundry. Bicycles can often be rented if one wants to ride the two or so miles to restaurants and a larger grocery store in Big Pine.

Be on the lookout for endangered key deer, which roam freely on Big Pine Key. The Key deer is the smallest subspecies of the Virginia white-tailed deer, having become isolated in the middle keys about 4,000 to 10,000 years ago when sea levels rose. Big Pine Key also contains a high level of biodiversity, with 466 documented plant species.

If you stay at Big Pine Key Fishing Lodge, you can cut about 3.5 miles off your next day's paddle to Sugarloaf Creek.

Another option on Big Pine Key is Camp Sawyer, owned and operated by the Boy Scouts of America. It is available for camping based on availability with advanced confirmed reservations. Please adhere to Camp Sawyer rules so it remains available. Contact Cliff Freiwald, Program Director, 305-364-0020 x 213; Cliff.Freiwald@Scouting.org.

7. Bahia Honda State Park to Sugarloaf Key KOA, 17 miles
Part of the beauty of paddling this stretch is that once you pass Spanish Harbor, you can paddle alongside several remote islands more than two miles from the main highway, so traffic noise is minimized. You'll also cruise through the 6,000-acre Coupon Bight Aquatic Preserve, located on both sides of Newfound Harbor Keys. On the Atlantic side of the keys, look for circular domed formations which are living coral patch reefs. By snorkeling, you can spot brightly-colored tropical fish along with larger grouper, snapper, snook and barracuda. Besides providing necessary habitat for marine life, patch reefs such as these baffle wave energy, thus helping to provide storm protection for the islands.

Coupon Bight itself is a shallow tropical lagoon where you can spot numerous wading birds and possibly key deer along the shore. Sea turtles nest on the preserve's beaches. These waters are known for harboring large numbers of tarpon in the spring.

Camping is at the Sugarloaf Key KOA, 305-745-3549. This full facility commercial campground is located on the Atlantic side of Sugarloaf Key along a well-marked channel. GPS on map is for the boat ramp. Kayakers can stay in a spacious primitive tent area for less than the regular fee. Some paddlers stay at an unauthorized campsite near a collapsed bridge along Tarpon Creek.

NOTE: Due to damage from Hurricane Irma, Sugarloaf Key KOA is closed until further notice. Check website or call for updates.

For another option, you can camp on Picnic Island (see map MM 39-27 on website) about 5 miles past Big Pine Fishing Lodge and almost 9 miles from Bahia Honda. This island is less than ideal since it is popular with boaters, but there is room for a few tents. From Picnic Island, it is about 23 miles to Boyd's Campground if taking a direct route.

8. Sugarloaf Key KOA to Boyd's Key West Campground, 20-21 miles

On your way to Boyd's, you'll paddle along Sugarloaf Key. An 1850 census reveals only three males residing on Sugarloaf Key. One was known as "Happy Jack." Believed to have a fondness for whiskey, he survived by trapping deer and raising fruit. Other colorful Keys hermits of the time included Paddy Whack, Jolly Whack, Red Jim and Lame Bill.

Sugarloaf Key is better known for a 35-foot tower that remained unoccupied. In 1929, trying to control the hefty mosquito population, R.C. Perky called in outside help to build a giant bat house. Stocked with imported bats, the bats promptly flew away and the tower failed to attract new bats. Nevertheless, tourists continue to flock to this national historic landmark. The tower is located on the west side of Sugarloaf Sound on the bayside.

A good rest stop and launch site is [Sammy Creek Landing](), on the east side of Sugarloaf Creek (see map) where there are picnic tables and a pavilion.

Paddle alongside Boca Chica Key through the [Western Sambos Ecological Reserve](), believed to contain the greatest habitat diversity in the Lower Keys. Nearshore patch reefs are accessible to kayakers while bank reefs and other coral formations may be too far offshore.

Proceed to Key West, the largest of the Keys' towns and one that boasts a culture all its own. Boyd's Campground is located on the east side of Stock Island about a half-mile south of the main highway. It boasts several waterfront tent sites along with a heated pool, laundry facilities, game room and convenience store. You can email for reservations or if you are planning to arrive within two days, you can call directly at (305) 294-1465. There are also several oceanside resorts and motels in Key West.

The old part of Key West is about five miles west of Boyd's Campground. Buses or taxis, or your own two feet, can take you to numerous museums, restaurants and other attractions. Don't miss the sunset celebration at Mallory Square, where people-watching is an added bonus.

10. Boyd's Key West Campground to Fort Zachary Taylor Historic State Park, Key West, 7 miles

Cruise along several scenic beaches, such as the renowned Smathers Beach. You may want to stop for a photo at the southernmost point in the continental United States, identified by a huge red-topped metal marker just past South Beach. The end of this segment is Fort Zachary Taylor Historic State Park. You can only land at the designated kayak launch spot on the eastern end of the park's beach if you notify the park in advance and state that you are a long-distance paddler in need of a rest stop or being picked up: (305) 292-6713. You need to check in at the admissions gate before using the park and touring the fort and/or the person picking you up will need to pay park admission. Normally, only those day users who have launched from the park are allowed to land at the park.

Construction of Fort Taylor began in 1845. Union forces occupied it during the Civil War to control blockade-running ships. This helped Key West to prosper during the war since numerous ships from several nations were seized and brought into Key West's harbor for disposition. The fort was used again during the Spanish-American War. Today, Fort Taylor is noted for containing the largest buried arsenal of Civil War cannons in the United States.

You can end (or begin) your journey here, or turn around and head back to Boyd's Campground. Another option is to circumnavigate Key West, but beware of large ships (such as cruise liners) entering or leaving Key West harbor just past the fort. Taking this route will add three to four miles to your return trip to Boyd's Campground.

Note: if you are doing the entire circumnavigational trail in one swoop, you are welcome to shuttle back to the point where you entered the Keys. No need to paddle the same water twice.

Segment 16
Biscayne Bay

Emergency contact information:

911

Monroe County Sheriff's Office: Lower Keys (305) 296-2424. Middle Keys (305) 289-2430. Upper Keys (305) 853-3266

Miami-Dade Police Department: 305-4-POLICE

Florida Fish and Wildlife Conservation Commission 24-hour wildlife emergency/boating under the influence hotline: 1-888-404-3922 or *FWC

Begin: John Pennekamp Coral Reef State Park

End: Oleta River State Park

Distance: 72.5 miles

Duration: 5-6 days

Special Considerations: Heavy winds and storms may prove challenging in open water areas. Weekend boat traffic can be heavy, especially in the more narrow northern section of the bay. Day two will be a highly interesting though challenging day in terms of mileage.

Introduction

Paddlers can follow in the wake of Tequesta Indians, Bahamian tree-cutters, pirates, wreckers, smugglers, fortune hunters, millionaires and several United States presidents who have utilized Biscayne Bay for their livelihood or as their playground. The numerous islands and keys reveal a surprising wildness, especially due to their close proximity to Miami, and several spoil islands have been restored and turned into tropical oases. Much of the bay is shallow, so paddlers can largely avoid boating lanes and hug the shorelines, being wary of large wakes.

Since the heart of Biscayne Bay is a wide watery expanse, paddlers should pay close attention to weather conditions. To quote from the Biscayne National Park website: "Some days, Biscayne Bay's shallow waters are glassy smooth, a window on another world. Other times, the wind whistles and whips, creating white waves that bite like teeth at an angry sky."

Several routes can be taken through this segment, depending upon desire and prevalent winds. This draft will focus on one main route since campsites are currently limited to just a few sites.

Three Florida state parks are included in this segment: John Pennekamp, Bill Baggs Cape Florida, and Oleta River. The route traverses the Biscayne Bay Aquatic Preserve, an area that includes extensive mangrove forests, seagrass meadows, estuarine and hard-bottom communities, and a diverse array of marine life. At least 512 fish species occur in the bay and more than 800 benthic organisms. Manatees, sea turtles and a wide variety of birds can be seen.

Paddlers will also enjoy Biscayne National Park, the largest marine park in the national park system, with more than 180,000 acres of islands, mangrove shorelines and undersea life.

Regarding primitive campsites outlined in this guide, users are required to keep these sites clean and follow all regulations in order for them to remain open for paddlers. All human waste must be packed out and properly disposed according to Leave No Trace Principles. A reliable GPS unit is a must to safely follow the route and find campsites. Bug repellent is essential even in winter, although biting insects are more prevalent in warm months. Temperatures can be surprisingly cold in the winter months also.

1: John Pennekamp Coral Reef State Park to Garden Cove campsite, 4.5 miles

In this section, you'll begin paddling through one of the most pristine areas in coastal South Florida. Green mangrove-lined shorelines greet paddlers along with shallow patch reefs with their colorful fish.

From the Pennekamp kayak launch site (just over the wooden bridge on your left along Largo Sound), paddle north through North Sound Creek and skirt the inside of Rattlesnake Key. The Garden Cove campsite at [Dagny Johnson Key Largo Hammock Botanical State Park](#) has a composting toilet and fire ring. Paddlers wanting to camp must pack everything in and out; there is limited access to Key Largo. Arrangements must be made in advance by calling the Ranger Station at John Pennekamp Coral Reef State Park, 305-676-3777. The site is only available to paddlers.

The name of Garden Cove dates back to the 1830s. A Keys ship captain, John Whalton, and his crew maintained a garden of fruits and vegetables in the area to augment their intermittent supply shipments. When Whalton and four crew members paddled ashore to tend the garden on June 26, 1837, Seminole Indians surprised them and killed Whalton and one crew member.

2: Garden Cove campsite to Elliott Key, 24.5 miles (Carysfort campsite will shorten distance by 6 miles when available)

Paddling along the shore, you'll eventually pass the Ocean Reef Club, an exclusive member's-only community that does not allow uninvited guests by sea or land.

For an ideal rest stop, follow the channel markers into Palo Alto Key and take the first tidal creek on the right. The rest stop is a short ways up the creek on the right in a tiny cove. Use your GPS unit to verify. Please do not explore the area as this is a protected hammock site. Poisonwood trees in the area are distinguishable by black splotches of poisonous sap on the smooth trunks. Most people are sensitive and can develop skin rashes.

As you pass Old Rhodes Key, you'll notice the bleached bones of mangroves as this area received a direct hit from Hurricane Andrew in 1992.

Porgy Key is an interesting point of interest as this is the home site of the Jones family. Of African descent, they settled the key in 1897 and raised pineapples and limes to sell in Key West. Eventually, only one member of the family remained on the island, Sir Lancelot Jones. He worked as a sponger and fishing guide, having the distinction of taking four different United States presidents bonefishing. Known fondly as "the philosopher of Porgy Key," Sir Lancelot was moved from the island at age 94 when Hurricane Andrew was bearing down. Today, visitors can view concrete foundations of his house and that of his family, and picture the life they once lived.

The 550-acre Jones Lagoon just south of the house site is worthy of exploration since it is a shallow and clear marine wonderland. The non-profit Biscayne National Park Institute leads [daily guided paddling trips](#) through the lagoon.

Across from Porgy Key is a Biscayne National Park day-use area on [Adams Key](#) where you can have a picnic and use the restrooms.

Overnight camping is on the bay side roughly halfway up [Elliott Key](#) . You can tie up your kayaks on the low docks that are generally reserved for dinghies. Regulations forbid kayakers to land on the swimming beach.

Elliott Key has restrooms, picnic tables, grills, cold showers and fresh water. A group camping site is on the ocean side about half a mile across the island. You can stretch your legs on numerous trails, exploring this scenic island. One seven-mile trail cuts lengthwise through the center of the island through a tropical hardwood hammock. Originally, this trail was a 150-foot wide swath cut by a former landowner just before the National Park Service took control of the island. Known as Spite Highway, the swatch has since grown back to become a pleasing canopied trail. A nature trail on the ocean side will enable you to view sea grape, black mangrove, bay cedar, buttonwood and other subtropical plants. Camping on both Elliott Key and Boca Chita Key is on a first-come, first-served basis for a modest fee.

3: Elliott Key to Boca Chita Key, 5 miles

This is a short day, certainly optional, to a premier campsite on Boca Chita Key, also managed by the National Park Service. The landing site is on the north side of the 32-acre island. There are picnic tables, grills and restrooms, but no fresh water. Take time to explore "the little lighthouse that isn't," a lighthouse built illegally from native coral rock by Mark Honeywell in the 1940s for his own personal navigation landmark. He was forced to permanently extinguish the beacon when it was deemed an uncharted hazard to navigation in the area.

4: Boca Chita Key to Teacher's Island, 21 Miles (10 miles to Bill Baggs State Park)

Paddlers have several options to reach Teacher's Island, which is near the mainland. The most direct route in calm weather is to head straight north and explore tiny Soldier Key, Stiltsville, followed by the Cape Florida Lighthouse at Bill Baggs Cape Florida State Park, and then cut across. It is possible to stay at the State Park at the youth camp and reduce the distance by about ten miles if you make prior arrangements by calling 305-361-8779, M-F 8-4:30. The camp site is primitive with no

restrooms, shelters or power. When the park is closed (between sunset and 8:00 a.m.), campers must remain in the youth camp. No after-hours access to the park will be granted during sea turtle nesting season - May 1st though October 31st.
If arriving from the beach side go to the northern end where warning flags are posted. A long boardwalk leads to restrooms and showers. To access the campsite cross the parking lot and go west 0.5 miles on Harbor Rd. You can also access the park from No Name Harbor, but you'll have to climb over a seawall. You can secure kayaks to the bike rack near the restaurant and then carry gear 0.2 mile east to youth camp.

The Cape Florida lighthouse was first built in 1825, destroyed by Seminole Indians in 1836, and rebuilt in 1846. The 95-foot lighthouse is the oldest standing structure in Miami-Dade County. Ponce de Leon was believed to have landed in this area in 1513 during the first Spanish expedition in Florida.

Depending on winds, the safest route is by way of the channel along Featherbed Bank, which is largely bordered by shoals, and then follow the mainland. Taking this route, however, will add 4-5 miles to your day.

You can take a break at the Black Point Park & Marina, and look for sea cows in this high manatee use area. Heading north along the shore, you will pass a distinct Florida landscape feature, Mount Trashmore, more than six stories tall. This is where Dade County's solid waste is disposed.

Take your time to explore some of Miami's shoreline culture by stopping for restaurant breaks near Matheson Hammock Park and the Dinner Key area. If you have time, walk about a mile through the park to the fantastic Fairchild Tropical Botanic Gardens to enjoy the lush landscape and Butterfly Conservatory. After Matheson Hammock, the bay will gradually narrow toward the Rickenbaker Causeway.

It is possible to paddle along the increasingly developed coastline to Teacher's Island. If staying on the traditional Segment 16 route it is recommended that you skirt around Virginia Key on the Atlantic coastal (east) side and slide between Fisher Island and the Port of Miami, avoiding the Intracoastal Waterway. Be wary of large ships as you cross Government Cut. A large offshore zone on the northwest side of Virginia Key is a restricted area.

A great rest stop and point of interest is the 82.5-acre Virginia Key Beach Park, located on the east side of the key along the recommended route. Kayakers need to land on the northeast corner of the park beach (see map). At the park, you can access restrooms, fresh water, picnic pavilions and an interpretive trail. In 1945, Virginia Key Beach was established as Dade County's only public beach and recreation facility for "the exclusive use of Negroes." It is now on the National Register of Historic Places and a popular off-road cycling destination. The key also features several native plant communities that are scarce in Dade County, and it harbors the state endangered Biscayne prickly ash.

Another point of interest is the Flagler Monument Island just offshore from Miami Beach on the bay side. This is a tiny island that harbors a 60-foot obelisk dedicated to Henry Morrison Flagler, builder of the Florida East Coast Railroad. Carl Fisher, the major developer of Miami Beach, built the monument in 1919. Allegorical statues representing pioneering, education, industry and prosperity are located on each side of the monument's base.

Teacher's Island, just past the Venetian Causeway near the mainland, is the first of several spoil islands that Dade County has restored into tropical paradises with native vegetation. Most are nearly surrounded by riprap (large rocks) to stem erosion, but small beaches or docks on each island offer handy landing spots. With the exception of Bird Key, which is a bird rookery and off limits, each island has a picnic area, and some have nature trails and shelters. No long-term camping is permitted, but the islands make great stopovers for circumnavigation paddlers as long as No Trace Principles are utilized. Nearby parks on the mainland, such as Morningside Park near Morningside Island, offer public restrooms. Bear in mind that on most weekends, the islands are very popular with boaters.

In exploring the islands, try to identify native species that have been planted on these once barren isles of sand. Species may include bay cedar, sabal and coconut palm, sea lavender, sea grape, sea oats, gumbo limbo, Jamaica dogwood and mahogany.

5: Teacher's Island to Oleta River State Park, 10.5 miles

The bay gradually narrows as you head north until you'll see the huge area of mature mangrove forests, framed by large buildings. This is Oleta River State Park, resembling a coastal Central Park in an urban setting. Exceeding a thousand acres, this is the largest urban park in the state. The upland areas were built from spoil material from dredging and are now best known for premier mountain biking. Wet areas mostly consist of mangroves, though it is interesting to note that sawgrass once dominated these sites. A 1926 hurricane opened a channel across from the park, allowing more salinity into the northern bay, enabling salt-tolerant mangroves to take hold. Dredging now keeps the Baker's Haulover Inlet open.

Paddlers can enjoy the park by landing at a designated spot along a tidal creek near the beach. It is against park regulations to land a craft on the beach as it may pose hazardous for bathers swimming underwater. Visitors need to pay a day-use fee in the iron ranger near the landing spot, or they can hike to the entrance station. You can enjoy the luxuries of one of the park's cabins for a fee. Advanced reservations are recommended, especially on weekends.

Across the road from the park headquarters are restaurants and a movie theater. A supermarket is one block east. Along the river at the bridge is the park's visitor services provider—Blue Moon Outdoor Center and Blue Marlin Fish House. Kayak rentals are available.

As you enjoy Oleta River State Park, it is difficult to imagine that millions of people live within a 20-mile radius. Like many parts of this segment, Oleta is a natural oasis in an urban setting.

Segment 17
Hollywood/Ft. Lauderdale

Emergency contact information:
911
Miami-Dade Police Department: 305-576-9900
Broward County Sheriff's Department: 954-764-4321
Florida Fish and Wildlife Conservation Commission 24-hour wildlife emergency/boating under the influence hotline: 1-888-404-3922

Begin: Oleta River State Park
End: Hugh Taylor Birch State Park
Distance: 16 miles
Special Considerations: Given the narrow Intracoastal Waterway (ICW), lengthy stretches of seawalls, and sometimes heavy boat traffic, this is a challenging segment and recommended for paddlers who have sufficient expertise in paddling over large and high energy wakes that often rebound off sea walls. Boat traffic is higher on weekends and holidays and should be avoided if possible. Paddlers should take special precautions in passing large ships moving and docking at Port Everglades.

During favorable weather, paddlers may opt to paddle along the Atlantic, with rest stops at area beaches. Both routes are included in this guide and on the maps. After the primitive campsite at Oleta River State Park, there is no camping in this segment, so advance motel reservations are recommended in Fort Lauderdale or Lauderdale-By-The-Sea.

Introduction
From a quiet area where Tequesta Indians lived for thousands of years, the Miami-Dade/Broward County region began its boom in 1896 when Henry Flagler's East Coast Railroad reached Miami. New towns and cities sprung up, quickly encompassing the small settler towns of Coconut Grove and Lemon City. From an 1890 population of about 2,000 people in Miami-Dade County, which then included most of Broward County, today's combined population for the two counties is around four million.

Even though this is a short and urbanized segment, paddlers will enjoy several scenic state and local parks. State parks include Oleta River, Mizell/Johnson and Hugh Taylor Birch. In addition, Oleta River and Mizell/Johnson have restaurants and canoe/kayak rentals. Hugh Taylor Birch State Park rents canoes on an interior lagoon.

A highlight of the segment is the West Lake Park and Anne Kolb Nature Center, among other Broward County parks.

1. Oleta River State Park to Holland Park, 7 miles
If choosing the ICW route, proceed north from Oleta River. Seawalls may prevent opportunities for rest breaks until you reach Hollywood, where there are places to land near the Hollywood Marina and at Holland Park. Holland Park would make for the better lunch break since it has picnic shelters and a viewing tower that offers impressive views of the area.

One luxurious overnight stop in Hollywood is The Diplomat on the ICW. The high-rise motel has a floating dock and storage space for paddlers.

An option to taking the ICW is to paddle along the Atlantic shore, but only in good weather with mild winds. To reach the

Atlantic from Oleta River State Park, you'll need to backtrack to the Baker's Haulover Canal, then proceed north. Your next opportunity to reenter the Intracoastal Waterway is the busy entrance to Port Everglades.

Several city and county beaches along the Atlantic offer opportunities for restroom breaks and picnicking. You can land anywhere at the Hallandale City Beach, but be watchful of swimmers. There, you can witness Italian-Americans playing their traditional bocce ball games. At Hollywood Beach, you must land or launch at the east end of Meade Street (see map for coordinates) and remain 100 yards offshore when traveling north or south.

2. Holland Park to Mizell/Johnson State Park boat ramp, 4.5 miles
A must stop is the Anne Kolb Nature Center, a site on the Great Florida Birding Trail. Here, you can land at the canoe/kayak rental area, parking your boat to the side so it won't be confused with the rental craft. You can't launch a boat here, but kayaking visitors are welcome to land. Tour the exhibit center, view displays of art, sculptures, marine ecology and aquariums. Several trails and boardwalks run through the park, and you can climb a three-story viewing tower.

Proceeding north, you have the option of taking scenic Whiskey Creek through Mizell/Johnson State Park, a quiet refuge for birds, manatees and paddlers. The tidal creek was believed to have figured prominently in "Prohibition Era" liquor running from the Bahamas. Some shallow areas in the creek may not be navigable at low tide, however.
The park's 2.5-mile beach was part of the 68-mile route of the "Barefoot Mailman," named for the carriers who walked barefoot at water's edge from 1885 to 1892. The almost week-long route consisted of 28 miles by small boat and 40 miles by beach from Palm Beach to Miami. Prior to 1885, a letter from

Palm Beach to Miami would first make its way to New York and then Cuba, for a total of 3,000 miles and up to two months. The barefoot service was discontinued in 1892 when a rock road was completed from Jupiter to Miami.

3. Mizell/Johnson State Park boat ramp to Hugh Taylor Birch State Park, 4.5 miles

Take special care when proceeding past Port Everglades, where gargantuan cruise ships and other boats frequently dock. Fort Lauderdale boasts of being the "Yacht Capital of the World," and if you're paddling on a weekend or holiday, you might realize why. Be wary of large ships in the ICW and their wakes.

A good rest stop is the Fort Lauderdale South Beach Park. The kayak launch spot is located at the northern end of the park across from the Oasis Restaurant (see map).

Hugh Taylor Birch State Park was named for the gentleman who settled in the small village of Fort Lauderdale in 1893 and eventually bought a subtropical paradise along the coast for about a dollar an acre. Witnessing the rapid development growing up around his estate, Birch donated the land for public use and the park was officially opened in 1949. The main problem with Hugh Taylor Birch State Park is that high seawalls prevent access from the ICW. The only access by water is from the Atlantic side, where visitors take an underpass beneath A1A to reach the main body of the park. The underpass closes at 5 p.m. Canoe rentals are available along an interior landlocked lagoon.

A point of interest just south of the park is the Bonnet House Museum and Gardens, the former home of artists Frederic and Evelyn Bartlett. For a fee, you can tour this 1920s era oceanfront estate with its elaborate architecture, art collections and 35-acre green oasis. A quote from Evelyn Birch Bartlett reveals how much the surrounding area has changed: "When I first came to Fort Lauderdale in 1931, it wasn't a town, just a village. When we drove up the long driveway to Bonnet House, we might see a wildcat, raccoons,...even a panther was seen on the property..." Mrs. Bartlett was determined to preserve the estate and donated it to the Florida Trust for Historic Preservation in 1983. The estate is closed on Mondays. From Bonnet House, it is possible to access Hugh Taylor Birch State Park through the main gate.

If paddling on the Atlantic side, there is no access to the ICW until the Hillsboro Inlet, roughly 12 miles north of Port Everglades. You can stay at a motel along the Atlantic in Fort Lauderdale or Lauderdale-By-The-Sea 1 to 2 miles north of the park. You can find several accessible motels to choose from through the Greater Fort Lauderdale Convention and Visitor's Bureau website. Since most motels do not have secure storage space for paddlers, you may want to secure your boat with a cable to a fence or post.

The Doubletree Gallery One Motel is along the ICW near the park on the west side (954-565-3800). If staying at the Doubletree, the dock can be 3-4 feet high at low tide, so landing at high tide is preferable. After landing, make sure to pull your kayak completely out of the water as large wakes can swamp your craft.

 The beaches of Ft. Lauderdale

Segment 18
Pompano/Lake Worth

Emergency contact information:

911

Broward County Sheriff's Department: 954-831-8900, 954-765-4321

Palm Beach County Sheriff's Department: 561-995-2800

Florida Fish and Wildlife Conservation Commission 24-hour wildlife emergency/boating under the influence hotline: 1-888-404-3922

Begin: Hugh Taylor Birch State Park

End: Lake Worth

Distance: 34 miles

Special Considerations: For most of this segment, paddlers have the option of either paddling the Intracoastal Waterway (ICW) or the Atlantic shore, depending on wind and weather. In calm weather, the Atlantic side might be safer until the ICW becomes wider north of the Boynton Inlet. However, the Boynton Inlet is exceptionally hazardous even in optimum conditions and paddlers should consider the Hillsborough Inlet or Boca Raton Inlet as a safer option to access the ICW. Where the ICW is narrow and lined with seawalls, paddlers must be wary of large boats and their wakes, and there are limited spots to land. Boat wakes often rebound off sea walls. Boat traffic is higher on weekends and holidays. Do not tie kayaks to docks along the ICW as boat wakes may cause swamping or damage; always lift them out of the water. Note: this stretch of the Atlantic coast and ICW has the highest number of boat accidents in the state.

On the Atlantic side, there are numerous public parks and beaches, and these offer restrooms, water and cold showers. However, kayakers must land outside of the "guarded" section of public beach, meaning that you must land before the first lifeguard tower or after the last lifeguard tower and walk to the public facilities.

There is no camping available in this segment, so advance motel reservations are recommended for motels outlined in this guide. Paddlers on the Atlantic shore will need to access the ICW at Hillsborough Inlet, Boca Rotan Inlet or Boynton Inlet (see above) in order to reach motels for day two. As with all narrow inlets, be wary of boat traffic and strong currents.

Introduction

Even though this is a short and urbanized segment, paddlers will enjoy several small scenic local parks and one state park, Hugh Taylor Birch.

1. Hugh Taylor Birch State Park to Stratford Motel, 7 miles

The campground at Hugh Taylor Birch State Park is not accessible by kayak, so a motel stay in the area is necessary. The Doubletree Gallery One Motel is along the ICW near the park. The dock can be 3-4 feet high at low tide, so landing at high tide is preferable. Call 954-565-3800 for reservations or more information. Other motels are along the Atlantic Shore in Lauderdale by the Sea 1 to 2 miles north of the park.

The Stratford Motel is along the east side of the ICW; it has another challenging dock for the kayaker. As stated before, kayaks should be taken out of the water due to high boat wakes. Call the motel at 954-943-2781 for more information and reservations.

2. Stratford Motel to Delray Sands Resort, 13.5 miles

Highlights along the ICW in this stretch are the Gumbo Limbo Nature Center and the Spanish River Park. Before landing at the nature center beach, you must first obtain permission by calling 561-338-1473. The center features aquariums, interpretive displays, nature trails through a tropical hardwood hammock, a viewing tower and a butterfly garden. Spanish River Park features nature trails and plenty of welcome shade. Camping is allowed for organized youth groups only.

The Delray Sands Resort is accessible on both the Atlantic side and along the ICW. GPS points are given for both access points. Along the ICW, land on a small beach just before the paved parking lot and secure your kayak to a nearby tree. The motel is directly across the highway. For reservations, call 561-278-6241.

Another overnight option from the Atlantic side is the Comfort Inn Oceanside, about a half block from the beach. For reservations and to check on securing your kayak, call 954-428-0650. It is about 5.5 miles north of the Stratford Motel (see map 1B).

3. Delray Sands Resort to Fairfield Inn or Sabal Palm House B&B, 13.5 miles

Several parks are situated along the ICW and along the Atlantic shore, so there are ample opportunities for rest breaks. If you are paddling along the Atlantic shore, move into the ICW at the Boca Raton Inlet or Boynton Inlet (see above). It is at this point where the ICW widens into the Lake Worth Lagoon. Once a freshwater lake, the creation of two permanent inlets to the ocean has transformed the lagoon into an urban estuary that contains important habitats for a variety of sea life.

The Fairfield Inn is accessible along the ICW by way of a small sandy rise in the corner of the seawall near the Highway 802 Bridge. You can secure your kayak either on a nearby tree or on the outside of the pool fence after obtaining permission from the front desk. For reservations, call 1-800-347-5434.

The kayak-friendly Sabal Palm House Bed and Breakfast is adjacent to the Snook Islands Natural Area kayak launch (see map) on the north side of the Highway 802 Bridge. Call 1-888-722-2572

Paddling Kitching Creek off the Loxahatchee River.

Segment 19
Palm Beach/Loxahatchee

Emergency contact information
911

Palm Beach County Sheriff's Department: 561-688-3000

Martin County Sheriff's Department: 772-220-7000

Florida Fish and Wildlife Conservation Commission 24-hour wildlife emergency/boating under the influence hotline: 1-888-404-3922

Begin: Lake Worth
End: Jonathan Dickinson State Park
Distance: 29 miles
Special Considerations: Since the route follows the Intracoastal Waterway (ICW), special precautions should be taken in the narrow portions of the ICW regarding boat traffic; be wary of large boats and their wakes. Boat wakes often rebound off sea walls. Boat traffic is higher on weekends and holidays. Do not tie kayaks to docks along the ICW as boat wakes may cause swamping or damage; always lift them out of the water.

Introduction
In 1867, Almeda Armour, new wife of Jupiter Inlet Lighthouse keeper Captain Armour, learned to her chagrin that the nearest doctor lived 120 miles away, and that occasional roving bands of Seminole Indians and visiting ship crews would be their main company. Still, Almeda Armour bore seven children during her family's 40 year stay. They saw many changes, and certainly many more changes occurred since their departure, but the Jupiter Inlet Lighthouse still

stands. It is one of many interesting points of interest in this segment for the paddler to investigate.

Besides historical sites, this segment features two premier state parks and several county parks and islands, offering a diverse experience for the paddler. The state parks are John D. MacArthur and Jonathan Dickinson. John D. MacArthur Beach State Park features up to 1,500 annual sea turtle nests on only 1.8 miles of beach, and Jonathan Dickinson State Park, at 11,500 acres, boasts 13 different plant communities and miles of hiking and paddling trails. Be sure to reserve a site at the River Campground on-line or call Reserve America at (800) 326-3521.

Two Florida Aquatic Preserves are part of this segment. The Loxahatchee River-Lake Worth Creek and Jenson Beach to Jupiter Inlet Indian River. Both preserves contain seagrass beds, marshes, mangroves, oyster bars and tidal flats—vital nursery habitat for a variety of fish and marine creatures.

1. Fairfield Inn or Sabal Palm B&B to Peanut Island, 11 miles
As you paddle north through the Lake Worth Lagoon, you may notice that this urban estuary supports a variety of habitats such as mangroves, tidal flats, seagrasses and oyster bars. Hard to believe that this water body was once a freshwater lake until the Lake Worth Inlet was created in 1877. Later, in 1915, the Port of Palm Beach created a permanent inlet at the northern end of the lagoon, completing the transformation to a brackish estuary. Water clarity will often change with the tides. The majority of shoreline that you'll pass has bulkheads, although restoration and enhancement projects are ongoing.

The Palm Beach Maritime Museum in Currie Park (Map 1B) is worth a stop since it showcases artifacts and exhibits about the regional marine environment along with artifacts from the bunker that was built for President John F. Kennedy on Peanut Island. The bunker was constructed as a temporary command post during the Cuban Missile Crisis of 1962.

If you are a camping enthusiast and coming from the south through the lagoon, the 86-acre Peanut Island will be a welcome sight. This county park offers fee sites at a full-service campground on the island's east side. The west side once offered free primitive beach camping but the area is now closed due to erosion. Reservations are required, so call 561-845-4445 up to three months in advance. One tent is allowed per site. The park also features a nature trail and an observation deck.

Peanut Island was originally created from dredged spoil material in 1918 and was enlarged with subsequent dredging. The island is not peanut shaped; its name came about from an early plan to store and ship peanut oil. In more recent years, managers have created tidal channels and lavishly landscaped the island with native vegetation, part of a $13 million environmental enhancement project completed in 2005. The tall sides of a mound in the island's center are actually borders for a huge crater that is still used to store dredged material.

2. Peanut Island to Jonathan Dickinson State Park, 18 miles
In a little less than 3 miles, a good rest stop and point of interest is Munyon Island, part of John D. MacArthur Beach State Park. Accessible only by boat, the island was once the site of James Munyon's lavish five-story resort hotel, "The Hygeia," named for the Greek goddess of health. Paw-Paw elixir, a tonic Munyon concocted from sulphur water and papaya juice, was featured at the resort and billed as a cure-all. The hotel burned down in 1917. More recently, wetlands and native vegetation have been restored on the island, helping to reverse the detrimental effects of past dredging and filling.

The main body of the state park can best be accessed along the Lake Worth Cove. The park features a kayak launch, a long boardwalk and nature trails, as well as an unspoiled beach. From early May through late August, large numbers of leatherback, green and loggerhead sea turtles nest on the beach.

Soon after Munyon Island, the ICW bears left and narrows for a long stretch. Fortunately, three local parks—Juno, Bert Winters and Burt Reynolds--will provide welcome rest breaks before the ICW opens up into the Loxahatchee River. If you have time, two points of interest along the Jupiter Inlet are worth visiting (see map for access points). On the inlet's south side is Dubois Park, site of the Dubois Pioneer home which sits atop a tall Indian midden. Open Tuesday and Wednesday afternoons, the spot is also the site of the Indian village of Jobe or Hobe (Hoe-Bay) where Jonathan Dickinson and his shipmates were held captive in 1697 after being shipwrecked along the coast.

On the north side of the inlet, you can tour the impressive Jupiter Lighthouse and museum. Built in 1860, the lighthouse stands 105 feet tall and continues to warn approaching ships of treacherous reefs near the Gulf Stream. The beam also marks the point where northbound ships can catch the northern flowing current. On a clear night, the beam can be seen for about 18 miles.

You have two choices for overnight stays. You can proceed northward up the ICW about two miles and stay at the Jupiter Waterfront Inn (888-747-9085) on the west side of the ICW, just across from the Blowing Rocks Preserve. This will lessen your distance by 3 miles and lessen your mileage by 7 miles for the next day if proceeding north.

The other option is to camp at Jonathan Dickinson State Park. Be sure to make a reservation at the River Campground. You'll need to paddle about 5 miles up the Loxahatchee River to the park boat ramp. You can leave your kayak and walk about 200 yards to the campground. Normally campers must register for their campsite at the Ranger Station. However, since the Ranger Station is five miles from the River Campground, paddlers should have a prepaid reservation for a specific site, and then call the Ranger Station for check-in upon arrival at 772-546-2771.

The state park features several miles of hiking trails, and it is worth paddling upriver to an old homestead known as the Trapper Nelson Interpretive Site. The 11,500-acre park is named for Jonathan Dickinson, a Quaker merchant whose vessel shipwrecked nearby in 1696. During World War II, the land the park now occupies was home to Camp Murphy, a top-secret radar training school with over 6,600 men. The land became a state park in 1950. Trapper Nelson came to this area in the 1930s and lived off the land, trapping and selling furs. He became famous as the 'Wildman of the Loxahatchee,' opening his 'Trapper's Jungle Gardens and Wildlife Zoo' to the public.

The upper 9.5 miles of the Loxahatchee includes the designated Loxahatchee River Paddling Trail. This is the first of two federally designated wild and scenic rivers in Florida and a favorite among paddlers. Kitching Creek, about a mile upriver, is also worth exploring by kayak where you can marvel at giant leather ferns that can reach impressive heights of 12 feet. Both of these popular waterways are encompassed by the Jupiter Waterway Trails.

Segment 20
Hobe Sound/Ft. Pierce

Emergency contact information:
911

Martin County Sheriff's Department: 772-220-7000

St. Lucie County Sheriff's Department: 772-462-7300

Florida Fish and Wildlife Conservation Commission 24-hour wildlife emergency/boating under the influence hotline: 1-888-404-3922

Begin: Jonathan Dickinson State Park
End: Ft. Pierce
Distance: 44.5 miles
Special Considerations: Special precautions should be taken in the narrow portions of the Intracoastal Waterway (ICW) regarding boat traffic; be wary of large boats and their wakes. Boat wakes often rebound off sea walls. Boat traffic is higher on weekends and holidays. Do not tie kayaks to docks along the ICW as boat wakes may cause swamping or damage; always lift them out of the water. Lack of camping opportunities and the erosion of some spoil islands are the reasons for the 20-plus miles that need to be covered each day. Leave No Trace guidelines should be followed for all primitive camping. Staying at the Jupiter Waterfront Inn instead of Jonathan Dickinson State Park can shave off about 7 miles from the day one total.

Introduction
In 1696, Quaker merchant Jonathan Dickinson became shipwrecked along the coast near Peck Lake. He and his crew were captured by Jobe or Hobe (Hoe-Bay) Indians, later released, and they walked to St. Augustine. In his book *God's Protecting Providence*, Dickinson writes of first setting foot on the coast: "the wilderness country looked very dismal, having no trees, but only sand hills covered with shrubby palmetto, the stalks of which were prickly, that there was no walking amongst them."

Later, Dickinson's group was marched south by the native inhabitants to their main village along Jupiter Inlet. "After we had traveled about five miles along the deep sand, the sun being extremely hot, we came to an inlet," Dickinson wrote. "On the other side was the Indian town, being little wigwams made of small poles stuck in the ground, which they bended one to another, making an arch, and covered them with thatch of small palmetto-leaves." The shipwreck survivors learned to bury themselves in sand to avoid the mosquito hordes while the Indians often used bear grease and fish oil. Eventually, they were released, whereupon they walked north to St. Augustine.

Much has changed in this part of Florida since Dickinson's day. The Jobe and other area Indians became extinct, and the human population growth in the area has skyrocketed. But thanks to the efforts of state and local officials and private citizens, several premier parks provide a glimpse into seventeenth century Florida.

This segment features four state parks: [Jonathan Dickinson](), [St. Lucie Inlet Preserve](), [Seabranch Preserve]() and [Fort Pierce Inlet](). All are accessible from the ICW and are good spots to explore natural Florida. Only Jonathan Dickinson, at the beginning, has a regular family campground. Ft. Pierce Inlet has a primitive youth/group campsite.

Two Aquatic Preserves are part of this segment. The Loxahatchee River-Lake Worth Creek and Jensen Beach to Jupiter Inlet Indian River. Both preserves consist of seagrass beds, marshes, mangroves, oyster bars and tidal flats—vital nursery habitats for a variety of fish and marine creatures.

1. Jonathan Dickinson State Park to Spoil Island MC3, 23.5 miles, (Other options reduce distance)

From the park boat ramp, proceed almost five miles downriver to the ICW. Since the ICW makes a sharp bend here, keep heading east to Jupiter Inlet and make a sharp turn north. The inlet marks the beginning of the 155-mile Indian River Lagoon. See segment 19 text for information about Jonathan Dickinson State Park and points of interest along the Jupiter Inlet. If beginning at the Jupiter Waterfront Inn along the ICW, it will be about 16.5 miles to Spoil Island MC3.

Numerous points of interest in this stretch will help to break up the day's paddling. Coral Cove Park is a short ways north of Jupiter Inlet along the east side of the ICW. This natural area provides walking access to the beach side and to the Blowing Rocks Preserve, managed by the Nature Conservancy, just to the north. The beach here boasts uniquely shaped Anastasia limestone outcroppings that consist of coquina shells, other seashells and sand.

Continuing north on the ICW, you'll enter the 1000-acre Hobe Sound National Wildlife Refuge, home to over 70 endangered species. You can access the refuge's nature center on the west side of the ICW and learn more about the area's wildlife and ecology.

About 5 miles farther north, Peck Lake Park features a quarter-mile boardwalk with impressive interpretive panels about the area's history and environment. In summer, you may spot the elusive mangrove cuckoo or hear its sweet song.

St. Lucie Inlet Preserve State Park on the eastern side of the ICW also features a long boardwalk, this one to a 2.7-mile public beach. A winding tidal creek through the park is also an inviting kayak trail. St. Lucie was named for an early blockhouse built by Spaniards in 1565. They were searching for survivors of a lost Spanish treasure fleet and built the blockhouse when the area's Native Americans proved to be hostile. Failing to convert the Indians to Christianity, constant attacks prompted the Spanish to abandon the area within two years.

Spoil Island MC3 is large with high and dry camping and some shade. Best access is on the south and west sides.

2. Spoil Island MC3 to Ft. Pierce, 21 miles
The Indian River is up to two miles wide in this stretch, so it is easy to avoid the sometimes busy boat channel. Only a mile and a half from the island along the east side of the waterway is the Gilbert's Bar House of Refuge Museum on Hutchinson Island. This fascinating historical site is worth a stop. The building, located on a rock outcropping that provides a commanding view of the Atlantic shore, is the last of ten houses built along this once remote East Florida coast in the 1800s to provide comfort and shelter to shipwreck survivors. It fulfilled its mission on several occasions.

Besides taking a museum tour, you may want to walk the beach here as it is lined with Anastasia limestone outcroppings similar to those found at the Blowing Rocks Preserve to the south. Hurricanes uncovered Native American artifacts near the museum that date back several thousand years. It is also fascinating to note that black bears once frequented Hutchinson Island and were shot and eaten by early pioneers.

A mile north of the museum, just before the bridge, is a motel opportunity, the Hutchinson Island Marriott Beach Resort and Marina. Call 772-225-3700 for more information.

Take advantage of the parks near Jensen Beach for water and restroom breaks because few opportunities exist until Ft. Pierce. Just north of the Hutchinson Island nuclear power plant, several local park preserves along the eastern shore offer a scenic unspoiled view and rest stop opportunities, but no facilities. Wetlands in these parks are being restored by ditch removal and re-flooding with salt water. Some small spoil islands in the area, once open for primitive camping, have disappeared due to storms and erosion. Fort Pierce Inlet State Park has a primitive youth/group campsite, but for regular primitive camping, you'll need to proceed north of the inlet to a recommended spoil island (see segment 21).

Segment 21
Indian River/Pelican Island

Emergency contact info:
911

Indian River County Sheriff's Office: 772-569-6700

Brevard County Sheriff's Office: 321-264-5100, 321-633-7162

Florida Fish and Wildlife Conservation Commission 24-hour wildlife emergency/boating under the influence hotline: 1-888-404-3922

Begin: Ft. Pierce Inlet State Park

End: Front Street Park in Melbourne

Distance: 47.5 miles

Duration: 3.5 days

Special Considerations: Boat traffic can be heavy along the Intracoastal Waterway (ICW), especially on weekends and holidays. Paddling along the high energy East Coast shoreline is not recommended due to safety considerations. While some calm periods may make it suitable for paddling the coastal shoreline, conditions can change abruptly and few inlets allow paddlers to move to more sheltered waters.

Introduction
Covering the middle section of the Indian River Lagoon, considered to be North America's most diverse estuary, this segment incorporates premier state and county parks, federal land, numerous spoil islands, and a traditional fish camp. Paddlers are almost guaranteed to spot sea turtles, manatees, dolphins and a wide variety of bird life.

A highlight is the Pelican Island National Wildlife Refuge, where paddlers can cruise along the small island rookery that marked the beginning of the National Wildlife Refuge System. Two scenic state parks are covered, Ft. Pierce Inlet and Sebastian Inlet. Both of these parks link the Indian River Lagoon with the sparkling Atlantic Coast. Paddlers can land in safe waters and visit sandy Atlantic beaches on foot if desired

This segment also covers the Indian River - Malabar to Vero Beach and the Indian River - Vero Beach to Ft. Pierce Aquatic Preserves. A purpose of both preserves is to highlight the ecological and economic importance of the Indian River Lagoon since the entire natural system is estimated to generate more than $800 million in annual revenue to the local economy. Preserve efforts have helped to reconnect mangrove marshes and seagrass beds that act as nursery grounds to recreationally and commercially important species, such as snook, grouper, snapper, seatrout, tarpon, and lobster. Also, many species of migratory waterfowl winter in the Indian River Lagoon.

Of special benefit to the paddling trail, aquatic preserve staff and volunteers work from October through April of each year to enhance the numerous spoil islands along the ICW by creating campsites, installing fire rings and picnic tables, blazing trails, stabilizing shorelines, removing trash and exotic species, and building informational kiosks. Many groups have adopted spoil islands and regularly remove debris and do enhancement work. Some of the recommended campsites in this guide have been enhanced through these efforts. Leave No Trace principles should be utilized for any primitive camping outlined in this guide.

This guide covers some of the spoil islands available for camping, but for free comprehensive guides to spoil islands in the Indian River Lagoon, call the Florida Inland Navigation District: 561-627-3386. Also, for maps and information about current spoil island enhancement projects, check out the Indian River Lagoon Spoil Island website.

1. Ft. Pierce Inlet State Park to Gifford Point, 15.5 miles
Once a place where U.S. Navy Frogmen trained for the D-Day invasion in World War II, Ft. Pierce Inlet State Park offers a great rest stop and beach. You can launch or land along a sandy stretch on the north side of the inlet near Dynamite Point, named for the activities of the Navy Underwater Demolition Team (see map). From here, you can access restrooms, the picnic area, beaches and a short nature trail.

Several islands near the park along the ICW are available for camping. Many local paddlers recommend Island #SL2, otherwise known as Run-a-Muck Island. This is about a mile from Round Island, a popular place for paddlers and a good place to spot bottlenose dolphins and manatees. There is a county-run kayak launch at Round Island along with restrooms and water.

2. Gifford Point to Island #IR5, 11.5 miles
As you head north, you can follow the narrowing ICW on the east side of Pine Island, or you can paddle on the shallower west side and avoid most of the boat traffic.

North of the Wabasso Causeway, where you can take a rest break with full amenities, hug the shallower eastern side of the lagoon along several scenic islands. Eventually, you'll come to tiny Pelican Island, part of the Pelican Island National Wildlife Refuge. This island was the last known brown pelican rookery along the east coast at the turn of the twentieth century. Diligently defended by German immigrant Paul Kroegel, he convinced President Theodore Roosevelt to formally protect the island in 1903, helping to spawn the national wildlife refuge system. Today, the system is comprised of 540 units in all 50 states and includes American Samoa, Puerto Rico, Virgin Islands, Johnson Atoll, Midway Atoll and several other Pacific islands.

While you can't land on Pelican Island, you can observe the birds from a safe distance. Use a camera zoom lens or binoculars to keep a football field distance between you and wildlife when possible. Besides pelicans, you may also spot wood storks, anhingas, cormorants, American oystercatchers and several types of wading birds. The Great Florida Birding Trail has many sites along this coastline where the quiet, observant paddler can see a multitude of bird species, especially during spring and fall migration.

From Pelican Island, curve around to the ICW where Island #IR5 is located. A nearby boat ramp in the town of Sebastian will enable you to access several restaurants and paddler-friendly Captain Hiram's Resort within easy walking distance. Biologists have noted that the area between Pelican Island and Sebastian Inlet is a nursery ground for juvenile green sea turtles.

Another choice for camping, or a good rest stop, is Sebastian Inlet State Park. If camping, the best place to land is opposite the boat ramp where you can carry or wheel your kayak a hundred yards or so to a campsite. Reservations on-line are recommended, especially in late winter/early spring. Or call Reserve America at 1-800-326-3521.

In 1715, a Spanish fleet laden with gold and silver from Mexico and Peru wrecked in the vicinity of the park. More than a thousand sailors made it to shore. Some died from exposure to the elements, but many more would have perished if not for the generosity of Ais Indians. When salvagers from Havana finally arrived, they recovered only half the treasure. Modern-day treasure hunters found a sunken ship laden with gold and jewelry. The McLarty Treasure Museum is located within the Sebastian Inlet State Park off A1A, and highlights the shipwreck and treasure salvage. A second museum, the Sebastian Fishing Museum tells the history of the area's fishing industry.

Just past the state park is another campground with full amenities, Long Point County Park (see map). Reserve a site on-line or call 321-952-4532.

Yet another camping option in the vicinity is Donald MacDonald County Park, less than two miles up the Sebastian River. Camping at the shaded campground is on a first-come, first serve basis. Call 772-589-0087 for more information.

3. Island #IR5 to island #BC38, 13 miles

Besides Sebastian Inlet State Park (see previous section) an interesting stop along the way is the Honest John's Fish Camp, one of the last of the Old Florida style fish camps along the east coast. An 1890s pioneer home and a vintage train depot exist on grounds. Kayak rentals, snacks and cold drinks are available. Fishing in the area is legendary.

The camp was named for Honest John, otherwise known as the Cracker of all Crackers. He was best known for his fishing exploits and for his aversion to wearing shoes. At his funeral, all of his pallbearers were in bare feet.

For a grocery stop, your best bet is a Winn Dixie supermarket on the mainland about a mile north of the mouth of the Sebastian River. You can land along the shore, climb the bank to U.S. 1, and the supermarket is across the road (see map).

The Island #BC38 campsite is on the southwest side.

4. Island #BC38 to Front Street Park in Melbourne, 7.5 miles

In this stretch, several parks on the west bank offer good rest stops, while a point of interest is the Melbourne Beach Park on the eastern shore. Melbourne Beach was founded in the 1880s when Captain Rufus Beaujean began sailing people to the island from the mainland. A railroad was soon built from the pier to the beach. Several historic buildings exist within easy walking distance of the park.

At the Front Street Park boat ramp in Melbourne, you can easily access restrooms and water along with nearby businesses and restaurants.

For a scenic day trip, many paddlers enjoy wildlife-rich Turkey Creek in Palm Bay. The upper portions of the creek wind beneath a hardwood forest canopy and along steep sandy bluffs.

Segment 22
Space Coast

Emergency contact info:
911

Brevard County Sheriff's Office: 321-264-5100, 321-633-7162

Volusia County Sheriff's Office: 386-423-3888

Florida Fish and Wildlife Conservation Commission 24-hour wildlife emergency/boating under the influence hotline: 1-888-404-3922

Begin: Front Street Park in Melbourne

End: Smyrna Dunes Park

Distance: 81-82 miles

Duration: 5-6 days

Special Considerations: Boat traffic can be heavy along the Intracoastal Waterway, especially on weekends and holidays. Paddling along the high energy East Coast shoreline is not recommended due to safety considerations. While some calm periods may make it suitable for paddling the coastal shoreline, conditions can change abruptly and there are few inlets to allow paddlers to move to more sheltered waters.

This is an area where large populations of manatees congregate. Manatees can become skittish at times, especially in dark water, throwing up a large amount of water and having the potential of capsizing a kayak. Be respectful and keep a good distance from manatees and other wildlife for their protection and yours.

Introduction
This segment continues along the Indian River Lagoon, considered to be North America's most diverse estuary. Overlapping boundaries of tropical and subtropical climates have helped to create a system that supports 4,300 plants and animals, 72 of which are endangered or threatened. Paddlers are almost guaranteed to spot sea turtles, manatees, dolphins and a wide variety of bird life, from roseate spoonbills to bald eagles, depending on the season.

A highlight of the segment will likely be the Mosquito Lagoon, an inviting place of unspoiled islands and a labyrinth of tidal creeks that is sheltered from the Atlantic by Cape Canaveral and Merritt Island. This estuary is a vital nursery for fish, oysters, clams, shrimp and other sea life and, not surprisingly, it's one of Florida's most famous fishing grounds.

The abundant life of the Indian River and Mosquito Lagoon estuaries have attracted people for thousands of years. Timucuan Indians annually migrated to these shores from inland areas to gather clams, oysters and to catch fish. They left behind giant shell mounds, two of which can be seen today—Seminole Rest and Turtle Mound, both of which are managed by the Canaveral National Seashore.

The adjacent Merritt Island National Wildlife Refuge, like the national seashore, was established as a buffer zone for nearby National Aeronautics and Space Administration (NASA) activities. It covers 140,000 scenic acres of brackish estuaries, marshes, coastal dunes, scrub oaks, pine forests and flatwoods, and palm and oak hammocks.

This segment covers two aquatic preserves, Banana River and Mosquito Lagoon. An optional route through the wildlife rich Banana River is highly recommended. The preserves help to maintain and restore water quality along with mangrove marshes and seagrass beds that act as nursery grounds for recreationally and commercially important species such as snook, grouper, snapper, seatrout, tarpon, and lobster. Also, many species of migratory waterfowl winter in the Indian River and Mosquito lagoons.

This guide primarily covers the western shore of the Indian River Lagoon as it offers more parks and boat ramps that can be used as rest areas and water stops. Plus, between Cocoa and Titusville, much of the western shore is a shallow manatee protection zone where boaters must observe slow speeds.

1. Front Street Park in Melbourne to Island #35, 18 miles
Front Street Park has a boat ramp, restrooms and water and is a good launch site for this segment. Proceed north along the Indian River Lagoon. Bear in mind that although this stretch involves paddling in a relatively straight and wide water body, this is an estuary teeming with life. You may want to hug the shore to see more bird life and to view original Victorian homes, especially in Rockledge, an enclave founded in 1867.

Island #35 is one of numerous spoil islands created from the dredging of the Intracoastal Waterway in the 1950s. Primitive camping is allowed. No amenities are provided. Other islands have been designated for educational purposes and a few are designated as conservation, generally because they are active bird rookeries. Paddlers should keep at least 100 yards from the shore of conservation islands and observe birds quietly.

Island #35 is located 500 yards east of channel marker 80, a mile and half south of the Highway 520 Bridge. Access is on the east side.

Alternate Route: Paddlers can enter the Banana River Aquatic Preserve just past the Highway 518 Bridge in Melbourne. The Banana River has many notable features. Almost every East Coast manatee comes through the river due to its abundant sea grasses. Not surprisingly, the river is the site of the largest manatee aggregation ever documented outside of a warm water site (700). It boasts one of three diamondback terrapin sites on the East Coast, counting the Keys. It has the largest known brown pelican rookery, a large great blue heron rookery, and it is a major place for dolphins. Just north of Port Canaveral, a manatee protection zone exists where no motorized watercraft are allowed.

To break up this stretch, the 53-acre Samsons Island is available for primitive camping in the southern end of the Banana River near Satellite Beach. It lies about 6.5 miles from the launch in Melbourne. Free permits must be obtained from the city prior to camping, either in person or by fax. Contact info: City of Satellite Beach, 1089 South Patrick Drive, Satellite Beach, FL 32937; (321) 773-6458; Fax: (321) 779-1388. There are fire pits, grills and a port-a-let on the island, but no water or other facilities. Leave No Trace principles should be utilized for any primitive camping outlined in this guide. The permit holder must be 18 years old or older and must remain on the island for the duration of the permit.

The next campsite is on Ski Island near Port Canaveral. Ski Island is about 23.5 miles from Front Street Park in Melbourne, or about 17 miles from Samsons Island. From Ski Island, you may want to spend a day exploring the no-motor zone of the Banana River north of the power lines. Thousands of alligators and other wildlife frequent this area. Canine companions should be left at home as they will attract alligators. Fishing is considered excellent. Port Canaveral offers numerous restaurants and opportunities to view manatees, dolphins and large fish going through the locks. Past the locks, there is a full-service campground at Jetty Park; (321) 783-7111.

Sykes Creek, between Banana River and Indian River Lagoon, is a popular waterway for day kayak trips. Sykes Creek can also be used as an alternate route in windy conditions, although camping options are limited.

From Ski Island, head east on the barge canal to reenter the Indian River Lagoon. It is about 13 miles from Ski Island to Manatee Hammock Campground.

2. Island #35 to Manatee Hammock Campground, 13.5 miles

In proceeding north, you can land at Lee Wenner Park at the Highway 520 Bridge after about two miles. Restrooms and water are available and several restaurants and shops are easily accessible just to the west in historic Cocoa Village.

The Port St. John Boat Ramp is the only other public landing spot to the north. This is about two miles before the campground. A city park with restrooms and water is a hundred yards north, but you may want to walk there as landing is difficult. Across the highway are several restaurants. A supermarket is one half mile north on U.S. 1.

The Manatee Hammock Campground, managed by Brevard County, offers shaded sites, water, showers, a swimming pool, a laundromat, volleyball and shuffleboard courts, and horseshoes. A supermarket is 1.3 miles south on U.S. 1. The park has a narrow landing for small boats south of the fishing pier. You may want to reserve tent sites 163 through 168 as these are closest to the water.

3. Manatee Hammock Campground to Titusville Spoil Island, 9.5 miles

Make sure to stock up on fresh water in Titusville, either at Kennedy Point Park or at the Highway 406 Bridge boat ramp, as there may not be another opportunity until late the next day. Camping is on a spoil island just north of the Highway 406 Bridge in Titusville. There are also two islands closer to the bridge. Note that the spoil islands in a direct line to the Haulover Canal are managed by the Merritt Island National Wildlife Refuge and are off limits to camping. Refuge lands also extend into Mosquito Lagoon. Camping is prohibited on all islands and shoreline to marker 19 in the Intracoastal Waterway.

4. Titusville Spoil Island to County Line Island, 17 miles

In this section, you will proceed toward the Haulover Canal. Before the canal was dug, fishermen used to haul their boats over this short spit of land to the Mosquito Lagoon, thus the name. Two of the spoil islands before the canal have since become bird rookeries. Keep your distance as you observe these active bird colonies. Adult birds will be tending young, defending territories, and retrieving food and nest materials.

In the canal, be sure to pull into the little cove for the Bair's Cove Boat Ramp. Manatees frequent this spot along with other parts of the canal.

Once in the Mosquito Lagoon, proceed north along a series of spoil islands. You can stay on the west side of the islands to keep out of boat traffic if you wish. Next available water stop is at Lefils Fish Camp (a.k.a. Oak Hill Fish Camp), two miles past County Line Island. Islands managed by the Canaveral National Seashore that are available for camping begin at County Line Island about two miles south of Lefils Fish Camp. You can adjust your mileage with several island campsite choices. There are 14 total primitive campsites at Canaveral National Seashore that can be reserved on-line or by calling 1-877-444-6777. Sites 1 thru 5 are generally reserved for paddlers, but boaters can take them if not used.

Next available water stop is at Lefils Fish Camp (a.k.a. Oak Hill Fish Camp), two miles past County Line Island, so if you are heading north and stay at County Line Island, make sure you have enough water until the next day.

5. County Line Island to Smyrna Dunes Park, 18 miles

This will be a very scenic paddle through the upper half of Mosquito Lagoon, winding around several uninhabited islands that provide numerous opportunities for rest breaks. You can take an old channel called Ship Yard Channel or the locals call "Government Cut" just east of the Intracoastal Waterway for most of the way (see map). Callalisa Creek is also a scenic option, passable by kayak. This winding route may add a mile or so to your day. The town of New Smyrna Beach has a lively historic downtown worth visiting and a matrix of local paddling trails between Edgewater and New Smyrna Beach.

Be sure to stop at the Seminole Rest Mound, one of the few remaining shell mounds along the Atlantic Coast. Two pioneer houses stand atop the mound. The Snyder family protected this Timucuan built mound early in the last century, while a nearby mound suffered the fate of most ancient shell mounds—it was hauled away for fill material. There is a restaurant about a quarter mile north of the mound.

A good rest stop is River Breeze Park, operated by Volusia County. The park offers shaded picnic tables, water and a short hiking trail. It is the site of a Colonial-era plantation. According to the West Volusia Audubon Society, the park and its environs are great for birdwatching. This is from their website: "Here, up close on a sandbar, Marbled Godwits doze and preen and luxuriate in the sunshine, shoulder to shoulder with handsome Black Skimmers. In the brackish waters of the lagoon, the birder may spot a wintering American White Pelican or a Common Loon. Reddish Egrets and Red-breasted, Common and Hooded Mergansers visit this spot and you may see American Oystercatchers. Check the area for migrating warblers before you leave."

In order to more fully explore the unique and scenic Mosquito Lagoon area, proceed west from River Breeze Park along Slippery Creek, paddling around several islands. Once along the main peninsula of the Canaveral National Seashore, you can dock and stroll around the historic two-story house visible from the water. This is the restored Eldora Statehouse, a vestige of a waterway community that once thrived on these shores. When location of the Intracoastal Waterway shifted, and a railroad was built on the mainland, Eldora slowly declined. You can hike a short nature trail through the scenic Eldora Hammock.

From Eldora, cruise about a mile along the peninsula to the ranger station where there is water and picnic tables.

Just after the ranger station, be sure to visit Turtle Mound, a huge midden built by Timucuan Indians for more than 600 years. These early people would visit coastal lagoons every winter to harvest abundant marine resources, staying in camps of one or more families—25-30 people. Don't miss the panoramic view of the lagoon and coast from atop the 50-foot mound.

Just past Turtle Mound, you can take a scenic paddling trail to campsites 2 and 3, which are on the west side of Shipyard Island.

Smyrna Dunes Park, operated by Volusia County, is a coastal treasure. You can land near the park entrance where the Intracoastal Waterway veers northwest and hike on a long boardwalk that spans a pristine dunes ecosystem. You can view the scenic Ponce Inlet and access some fine beaches along the Atlantic Ocean. If you paddle Ponce Inlet, proceed with caution as currents are strong and breakers will likely be encountered as you near the Atlantic.

Camping is on spoil islands just north of the park. These will be described in segment 23.

The Indian River Lagoon is known for its manatees.

Segment 23
Tomoka/Pellicer

Emergency contact info:

911

Volusia County Sheriff's Office: 386-254-4689

Flagler County Sheriff's Office: 386-437-4116

Florida Fish and Wildlife Conservation Commission 24-hour wildlife emergency/boating under the influence hotline: 1-888-404-3922

Begin: Smyrna Dunes Park

End: Faver-Dykes State Park/Mellon Island

Distance: 48 miles

Duration: 4 days

Special Considerations: Boat traffic can be heavy along the Intracoastal Waterway (ICW), especially on weekends and holidays. Paddling along the high energy East Coast shoreline is not recommended due to safety considerations. While some calm periods may make it suitable for paddling the coastal shoreline, conditions can change abruptly and few inlets allow paddlers to move to more sheltered waters.

Introduction

Rich in history, ecology and scenic beauty, this segment invites paddlers to enjoy scenes that have changed little since

Timucuan Indians plied these waters in dugout canoes. The village of Nocoroco, perhaps the largest Timucuan town, thrived in an area now contained in Tomoka State Park, a point of interest along the route. Once numbering about 40,000, the tribe's population quickly dropped after European contact due to disease and war. The last Timucuans fled with the Spanish as they retreated from the peninsula in 1763.

After Spain's withdraw, English planters developed several large plantations in the area, such as Bulow and Mount Oswald. Boosted by skilled slave labor, the plantations raised cotton, indigo, various vegetables and rice. The plantations also exported timber, hides, molasses, rum, sugar and oranges. Indigo, valuable for blue dye, became a primary cash crop and some indigo plants can still be found in area forests today. Most of the plantations and associated sugar mills and other structures were burned by raiding Seminole Indians and black warriors during the Second Seminole War and were never rebuilt.

Along Ponce Inlet, paddlers will have the opportunity to visit the Ponce de Leon Inlet Lighthouse Museum and climb Florida's tallest lighthouse for panoramic views in all directions. Paddlers can explore numerous islands and shallow creeks around Ponce Inlet and enjoy wide scenic stretches and numerous islands along the Tomoka Basin and Pellicer Flats.

Five outstanding Florida state parks are within reach of paddlers for exploration and enjoyment: Tomoka, Northern Peninsula, Gamble Rogers, Faver-Dykes and Washington Oaks State Gardens.

The Tomoka Marsh and Pellicer Creek Aquatic Preserves are part of this segment. These preserves are valuable nursery areas for shrimp, crabs and fish. They are utilized by more than 120 species of fish and more than 180 bird species. The Pellicer Creek preserve, largely buffered by public lands, is one of the most pristine estuarine/riverine systems along Florida's east coast.

Leave No Trace principles should be utilized for any primitive camping outlined in this guide.

1. Smyrna Dunes to Port Orange Causeway (Highway A1A bridge), 7 miles

Heading north from Smyrna Dunes Park, on the south side of Ponce Inlet, numerous spoil and natural islands within the wide Halifax River basin are available for primitive camping. We have provided GPS coordinates for two islands on the map, but most islands are available unless they are obvious bird rookeries. There are two such rookeries near the A1A Bridge. Roosting birds should be viewed from a safe distance (100 yards). Spruce Creek is also a state designated paddling trail and popular kayaking spot in the area. The wide nature of this section enables paddlers to utilize side channels and creeks and avoid the sometimes busy ICW.

On the north side of the Ponce Inlet, you can land on a small beach at the county park and hike to the Atlantic shore if you wish. High waves breaking over the jetty can be impressive. Due to currents and heavy wave action, it is not recommended that you paddle through the inlet to the Atlantic.

A must stop is the Ponce de Leon Inlet Lighthouse Museum. You can land at a public ramp (see map), enjoy an adjacent restaurant, and walk less than a hundred yards to your left (facing the lighthouse) to the museum entrance. For a fee, you can explore the historic buildings on the grounds, view various Fresnel Lenses on display (used for lighting the lighthouse) and climb the spiraling staircase of the redbrick lighthouse, the tallest in Florida and second tallest in the United States. The lighthouse is still in use and has had the unintended effect of limiting high-rise condominiums and motels from being built in the immediate area. Just south of the boat ramp is Volusia County's Marine Science Center, which includes exhibits, aquariums, nature trails, an observation tower and facilities to rehabilitate sea turtles and seabirds. The Port Orange

Causeway Park, a site on the Great Florida Birding Trail at the A1A Bridge can be a welcome rest stop.

2. Port Orange Causeway to Tomoka Basin islands, 16 miles

While this long stretch through the urban setting of the Daytona Beach area lacks suitable islands or other lands available for camping at the moment, it offers other options such as numerous shaded riverfront parks with docks for picnics and respite and many popular waterfront restaurants with docks. Also, the River Lily Inn B&B, (386-253-5002) is easily accessible directly across from Ross Point Park in Holly Hill (just over 7 miles from Port Orange Causeway). Check for paddler discounts. You can access the shops, restaurants and events of Daytona Beach from the downtown Riverfront Park (see map) at the docks at Halifax Harbor Marina shops and Manatee Island paddling docks near Main Street Bridge (sunrise/sunset hours).

Near the Tomoka Basin, you'll see the first of several spoil and natural islands that stretch for a couple of miles. Since the ICW is on the narrow east side of these islands, you may want to paddle on the west side and enjoy an unfettered view of the Tomoka Basin. Most of these islands are open for camping. Try to pick a spot on the western side of the islands, out of view of houses that line the eastern shore of the river.

A visit to Tomoka State Park is highly recommended. You can access the park via a boat ramp and walk a short distance to a museum, which includes displays of the park's Timucuan and European history, as well as its ecology. You can also learn more about artist Fred Dana Marsh, creator of the park's huge statue depicting Chief Tomoka and maidens and warriors. The statue will likely be removed at a future date due to deterioration, but a replica is on display in the visitor's center. Canopied nature trails allow you to enjoy the park's renowned live oak hammocks. The park store next to the boat ramp offers snacks, some supplies, and canoe rentals.

3. Tomoka Basin to Silver Lake spoil islands, 11 miles

After the Tomoka Basin, the Halifax River suddenly narrows and morphs into Halifax Creek, then into Smith Creek, and finally into the Matanzas River. Along the way, you can stop at Northern Peninsula State Park and access the two-mile Coastal Strand hiking trail. A short distance later, you can land at Gamble Rogers State Park and enjoy a short hike to an unmarred Atlantic beach.

Several spoil islands are available for camping near Silver Lake, although be wary of cacti in open areas. The GPS point on the map is for a suitable campsite that has been cleared. There is a tiny kayak launch on the east side of Silver Lake along a mangrove-lined canal. The launch can be muddy, especially at low tide. No facilities are available.

4. Silver Lake spoil islands to Mellon Island, 14 miles

As the river widens in the Pellicer Flats, numerous spoil and natural islands appear. Most are suitable for camping. You will likely want to paddle on the western side of the islands through the flats, where numerous oyster reefs keep out most motorized crafts. You can also paddle up the unspoiled Pellicer Creek, a state designated paddling trail, to Princess Place Preserve and visit Faver-Dykes State Park.

Princess Place Preserve is named after previous owner Angela Sherbatoff, who was married to an exiled Russian prince. This spacious property of more than 1500 acres features numerous hiking trails and historic buildings and is definitely worth a visit.

Faver-Dykes State Park is accessible about 2.5 miles up Pellicer Creek and is known for its pristine looking pine and hardwood forests. It was once part of the Buena Suerte (Good Luck) Plantation in the early 1800s and was occupied by federal troops during the Second Seminole War. Restrooms and water are available at the park ramp.

Two scenic natural islands are also available for primitive camping along the river, Jordan and Mellon Islands, managed by Faver-Dykes State Park. You'll notice that the predominant mangrove shorelines just to the south have given way to mature forests of cedar, sable palm and live oak. A half-mile nature trail runs the length of Mellon Island. There are three primitive campsites on each island and they are available free of charge on a first-come, first-serve basis.

A must stop in this section is the Washington Oaks State Gardens, once owned by a relative of George Washington. You can land near the picnic area and access a nature trail. The picnic area is a short distance to the south and the picturesque gardens and historic interpretive center begin about a half mile to the north. The creator of the gardens envisioned a manicured exotic landscape "in the jungle" with numerous fountains and reflective pools. Arching live oak limbs festooned with Spanish moss and resurrection ferns provide a natural garden dome.

Another interesting stop is Marineland, a short distance before Mellon Island along the eastern shore. You can land at the River to Sea Preserve kayak launch and walk a short distance south along A1A to the world's first "oceanarium." Opened in 1938 by an eclectic group that included members of the Vanderbilt and Tolstoy families, the park fell on hard times with the advent of central Florida's theme parks. The facility has since been revived, with a special emphasis on dolphin interactions.

Segment 24
St. Augustine

Emergency contact info:

911

St. John's County Sheriff's Office: 800-346-7596

Florida Fish and Wildlife Conservation Commission 24-hour wildlife emergency/boating under the influence hotline: 1-888-404-3922

Begin: Faver-Dykes State Park/Mellon Island

End: Palm Valley Road (Highway 210)

Distance: 35.5 miles

Duration: 3 days

Special Considerations: Boat traffic can be heavy along the Intracoastal Waterway (ICW), especially on weekends and holidays. Paddling along the high energy East Coast shoreline is not recommended due to safety considerations. While some calm periods may make it suitable for paddling the coastal shoreline, conditions can change abruptly and few inlets allow paddlers to move to more sheltered waters. Even in the ICW, there is often a strong easterly shore breeze.

Introduction

St. Augustine is the oldest European-founded city in the United States. For centuries, Spain, France, England, a young United States and various Native American tribes wrested for control of Florida through the historic town. Paddlers on the circumnavigational trail can touch the past by visiting the historic section of St. Augustine and other historical sites in the area.

The St. Augustine segment is also blessed with scenic beauty. The trail skirts county parks and large tracts of public land. These include the Guana Tolomato Matanzas National Estuarine Research Reserve (GTM). The reserve encompasses more than 60,000 acres of wetlands, upland habitats and offshore areas.

The Matanzas State Forest, along the western shore of the Matanzas River in the beginning of this segment, is part of a 16,000-acre conservation corridor linking protected lands along Pellicer Creek to the Moses Creek Conservation Area. A significant wood stork rookery is located in the forest. Moses Creek Conservation Area is managed by the St. Johns River Water Management District and features scenic primitive camping along the sandy bluffs of Moses Creek, along with miles of hiking trails.

Anastasia State Park and its white sand beaches and campground are accessible near the end of the Salt Run east of St. Augustine, just past the St. Augustine Lighthouse and Museum (also accessible by kayak). Much of the coquina rock used to build Castillo de San Marcos in St. Augustine was quarried here by the Spanish. Two historic Spanish-built forts can be accessed from the trail, Fort Matanzas and Castillo de San Marcos. Both are national monuments.

Guana River Wildlife Management Area covers nearly 10,000 acres along the eastern shore of the Tolomato River in the northern part of this segment. An estimated 3000-4000 migratory waterfowl winter at Guana Lake, a site on the Great Florida Birding Trail. The area is known for being an ideal place to spot peregrine falcons during April and October.

1. Mellon Island to Moses Creek Conservation Area, 7 miles

Take your time paddling this section for there is much to see and explore. By taking the old channel of the Matanzas River just past Mellon Island, you'll not only avoid busy boat traffic, you can also access the Fort Matanzas National Monument. Land near the dock along the east side of the river to tour the visitor's center and hike the nature trail. Do not land at the fort itself. To reach the fort, you must take a free ferry ride across the river, where you will be treated to a guided tour by a person in character as a Spanish infantryman. The panoramic view of a relatively unspoiled terrain from atop the fort is worth the trip alone. If you are taller than 5'7", duck your head through the doorways.

The ferry boat leaves every hour from 9:30 am to 4:30 pm, seven days a week every day except Christmas. Ground-shaking cannon firing demonstrations occur Saturday through Monday. The fort, built from 1740-1742, was needed by the Spanish to guard the Matanzas Inlet to St. Augustine. The Spanish had good reason to fear a raid since the English repeatedly harassed St. Augustine, beginning in 1586 when Sir Francis Drake burned the city. The fort proved to be an adequate deterrent. Gunners fired upon British vessels soon after completion, and never saw military action thereafter.

The Matanzas Inlet was named for a Spanish slaughter of about 250 Frenchmen who had surrendered to Pedro Menendez de Aviles in 1564. Matanzas is the Spanish word for "slaughters."

About a mile past the Highway 206 Bridge along the western shore is the Moses Creek Conservation Area. Two primitive campsites atop sandy bluffs overlooking Moses Creek are hard to beat anywhere. The first shaded site beneath arching live oak and cedar trees is only a quarter of a mile in from the Matanzas River near Murat Point. This campsite has picnic tables, a fire ring and a hand pump for washing dishes (not potable). Each site can accommodate up to four tents; they are available free of charge on a first-come, first-served basis. From this first campsite, you can access several miles of marked hiking trails, or you can paddle up Moses Creek.

2. Moses Creek Conservation Area to St. Augustine, 9.5 miles

To access the historic section of St. Augustine, land your kayak at the low dock at the St. Augustine Municipal Marina alongside numerous small dinghies, just south of the Bridge of Lions. Make sure you have a bowline to tie up. You'll need to register at the marina office at the end of the dock and pay a small fee. The marina has restrooms, showers, a laundromat, small store, and there is a motel across the street. Various other motels and bed and breakfasts are within easy walking distance, including an inexpensive hostel with an all-you-can-eat pancake breakfast, The Pirate Haus Inn—954-567-7275. You can also walk to shops, museums, restaurants and to the historic Castillo de San Marcos, or you can paddle to the fort and land on the north side at a small beach. Learn how Seminole Indians achieved their great escape from the fort's jail during the Second Seminole War. Downtown ghost tours are available after dark. If you don't want to walk, you can take a sightseeing train or a horse drawn carriage.

If not staying in St. Augustine, about four miles north on the east side of the Tolomato River is the North Beach Camp Resort. You can land at the boat ramp near a bait and tackle shop (see map) and walk to the office to register for a tent site. The campground has restrooms, showers and a laundromat. Advanced reservations are recommended. Call 800-542-8316.

Though a bit off the route, you can also camp at Anastasia State Park by paddling up the Salt Run to the park's launch area. The campground is a short walk across the road. Make reservations on-line well in advance or call 1-800-326-3521.

3. St. Augustine to Palm Valley Road (Highway 210), 19 miles

As you head north, you'll be passing alongside several large tracts of public land, mostly along the eastern shore.

To access the GTM Reserve's Guana River site, you can land at Shell Bluff, the site of a coquina well remaining from a Minorcan farm in the early 1800s. There are 10 miles of hiking/biking trails and it is about a 1.5-mile walk from Shell Bluff to the GTM Environmental Education Center (small fee for entry) where there are exhibits, aquariums, an orientation video, and a nature shop. The Guana River and lake east of the Tolomato River is a popular destination for day paddlers.

The next large chunk of public lands is the Guana River Wildlife Management Area (WMA). While there is no camping allowed on WMA land on the east side of the ICW, you can paddle through several adjacent coves and side channels that will allow you to separate yourself from the sometimes busy ICW and enjoy unspoiled marshy vistas and rich bird life.

Several spoil areas along the ICW are often used for primitive camping by boaters, but permission has not been granted to include them in this guide. Leave No Trace principles should be utilized for any primitive camping outlined in this guide.

Kayaker at Moses Creek Campsite

Segment 25
Jacksonville

Emergency contact info:

911

St. John's County Sheriff's Office: 800-346-7596

Duval County Sheriff's Office: 904-630-0500

Florida Fish and Wildlife Conservation Commission 24-hour wildlife emergency/boating under the influence hotline: 1-888-404-3922

Begin: Palm Valley Road (Highway 210)

End: Sister's Creek Marina

Distance: 21 miles

Duration: 2 days

Special Considerations: Boat traffic can be heavy along the Intracoastal Waterway (ICW), especially on weekends and holidays. Paddling along the high energy East Coast shoreline is not recommended due to safety considerations. Plus, there are no inlets in this segment connecting the ICW to the Atlantic with the exception of the St. Johns River. Jetties that extend almost two miles into the Atlantic along the mouth of the St.

Johns make this option prohibitive. Tides will begin to have a stronger influence as you head north. Paddlers in the ICW must often contend with a strong easterly shore breeze.

Introduction
The city of Jacksonville, chartered in 1832, was named after Florida's first territorial governor, Andrew Jackson. An important seaport, the city figured prominently in the Civil War, being occupied by Union forces on four separate occasions. In 1901, a devastating fire left almost 9,000 homeless, but the city was quickly rebuilt and today Jacksonville is a thriving urban center and port. Paddlers may spot numerous fast-moving helicopters along the ICW as Jacksonville is home to the United States Coast Guard Helicopter Interdiction Tactical Squadron, commissioned to interdict high-speed drug-running vessels and helping to ensure homeland security.

While this segment covers one of the largest urban areas in the state, paddlers will be pleasantly surprised. Numerous unspoiled areas provide optimal paddling opportunities. Vast stretches of marsh, islands and coastal forest have been protected largely through the efforts of the City of Jacksonville, the Timucuan National Preserve, and private landowners. The Preservation Project Jacksonville was begun in 1999 by then mayor John Delaney after voters approved a bond issue. Since then, more than 50,000 acres have been protected. The goal of the project is to help to guide growth, protect environmentally sensitive lands, improve water quality, and to provide more outdoor recreation opportunities.

Four main preserves are accessible along the trail: Cradle Creek, Castaway Island, Dutton Island and Tideviews. The scenic network of these preserves has helped to create the Jacksonville Intracoastal Salt Marsh Paddling Guide. Access to all of these preserves except for Dutton Island is limited at low tide.

This segment also traverses the southern part of the Timucuan Ecological and Historic Preserve. Managed by the National Park Service, it is named for a large Native American tribe that once inhabited the area. The 46,000-acre preserve encompasses wetlands, upland forests, and historic sites. Paddling trails for day trips are available in the preserve.

Leave No Trace guidelines should be followed for primitive camping in this segment.

1. Palm Valley Road to Dutton Island, 16 miles
The landing at the Palm Valley Road Bridge is on the eastern shore, with a restaurant adjacent to the landing. Although the ICW becomes long and narrow for about nine miles north of the bridge, the west bank is relatively unspoiled and primarily consists of a mature hardwood forest. A private landowner owns the property. Two restaurants can be seen along the eastern shore, but access from the water is difficult.

The ICW widens after the Highway 202 Bridge and becomes more natural looking, with numerous tree islands, tidal creeks and unbroken expanses of marsh. Cradle Creek, along the eastern shore, is the first of three Jacksonville preservation lands that are ideal for kayaking. The next city preserve, Castaway Island, is along the western shore just past the Beach Boulevard Bridge.

To access nearby restaurants, a drug store and a supermarket within easy walking distance (about a half mile), you can land at the Palm Cove Marina (see map). Check in at the marina service station first. There is also a restaurant at the marina. Directly across the ICW on the eastern shore is Beach Marine where you can also access restaurants.

Proceeding north in the ICW, past the Atlantic Boulevard Bridge, the Tideviews and Dutton Island Preserves will be along the eastern shore. This unspoiled area of islands and tidal creeks features a kayak launch dock and a mile-long marked paddling trail through a pristine tidal zone. Currently, paddlers can utilize the park's group camp area (a fee is required) by walking a quarter mile north of the kayak launch dock. For camping reservations, call the City of Atlantic Beach Recreation Department: (904) 247-5828. A primitive campsite for paddlers is being established on a small peninsula east of the kayak launch.

2. Dutton Island to Sister's Creek Marina, 5 miles
Be wary of currents and large boats as you enter the St. Johns River. You must cross the river in a diagonal direction to reach Sister's Creek. If you want to visit the Fort Caroline National Memorial in the Timucuan Preserve, paddle a short distance up the St. John's along the south shore to the low floating docks just before the reconstructed French fort. Jean Ribault landed near here in 1562, exchanged gifts with area Timucuan Indians, erected a stone monument and claimed the area for France. "It is a thing unspeakable," wrote Ribault in his journal, "to consider the things that be seen there, and shall be found more and more in this incomparable land."

The French established a colony at the site in 1564, building Fort Caroline, but only a year later, Ribault and several hundred French soldiers sailed south to raid Spanish St. Augustine. He was shipwrecked by a powerful tropical storm. Spanish Admiral Pedro Menendez saw an opportunity and raided Fort Caroline, brutally killing most of the adult males. He then hunted down Ribault and other shipwrecked sailors and killed them at a place called Matanzas ("slaughter"), part of segment 24. The fighting marked the first of many battles over European control of the "New World." Regarding the

Timucuan Indians, their numbers dwindled from tens of thousands to only a few hundred by 1700, primarily due to disease. The tribe is considered extinct today.

The [Sister's Creek Marina](#) is located on the west side of Sister's Creek just off Heckscher Drive (State Road 105), a short distance from the St. John's River. Please note that the marina is closed to the public during the Greater Jacksonville Kingfish Tournament in July and one week before. Restrooms, water and a picnic area are available.

Kayak launch at Dutton Island Park.

Segment 26
Timucuan Trails/Ft. Clinch

Emergency Contact Numbers:
911

Duval County Sheriff's Office: 904-630-0500

Nassau County Sheriff's Office: 904-225-5174

Florida Fish and Wildlife Conservation Commission 24-hour wildlife emergency/boating under the influence hotline: 1-888-404-3922

Begin: Sister's Creek Marina

End: Fort Clinch State Park

Estimated Distance: 29-30 miles

Duration: 2-4 days

Special Considerations: Paddlers need to be watchful of tides and currents, especially near river mouths. The Intracoastal Waterway can be busy with recreational boaters on weekends and holidays. This guide will focus on interior routes as the Atlantic side is considered dangerous and recommended for expert paddlers only.

Introduction
History and natural beauty combine in this exceptional segment just north of Jacksonville. In this segment of the paddling trail, five rivers either merge together or flow into the Atlantic Ocean: the St. Johns, Nassau, Amelia, St. Mary's and Fort George. The St. Johns River Blueway is a 300-mile designated paddling trail and an American Heritage River, one of only 14 in the country. Winding creeks

through unspoiled marshlands help to evoke a feeling of original Florida. Kayakers also have easy access to historic sites such as Kingsley Plantation, the Ribault Club, old Fernandina, and Fort Clinch. Paddlers have a choice of taking interior creeks and the Intercoastal Waterway (ICW), or the Atlantic shore. Those familiar with the area agree that only **expert** paddlers should attempt the Atlantic shore due to strong currents and wave action, and the fact that jetties along the mouth of the St. John's River extend almost two miles into the Atlantic. The interior route suggested here is considered safer, with more opportunities for camping and visiting points of interest.

A unique partnership of city/county, state, federal, and non-profit land managers is responsible for the waterways, lands and facilities that are included in this segment of the paddling trail. Known as the Timucuan Trail State and National Parks, the partnership includes the National Park Service, the State of Florida, the City of Jacksonville, and the Nature Conservancy. This coalition has come together to develop the Florida Sea Islands Paddling Trail, a network of 10 saltwater trails and 2 freshwater-brackish creek trails through public lands.

This segment covers the Nassau River-St. Johns River Marshes and Fort Clinch State Park Aquatic Preserves, which altogether encompass approximately 66,000 acres of open waters, marshlands, tidal creeks and rivers, and tree islands. The preserves overlap the boundaries of the Timucuan Preserve and some of the state parks. They act as buffers to help filter pollutants and protect upland areas from storm surge, and they are home for numerous aquatic species and resident and migratory birds.

The segment also traverses part of the Timucuan Ecological and Historic Preserve. Managed by the National Park Service, it is named for a Native American tribe that once inhabited the area. The 46,000-acre preserve covers encompasses wetlands, upland forests, and historic sites. Paddling trails for day trips are available in the preserve.

Five state parks are also part of the route: Fort George Island, Little Talbot Island, Big Talbot Island, Amelia Island and Fort Clinch. Besides paddling, numerous opportunities for hiking, swimming, biking, fishing and other activities are available. For primitive campsites, users are required to keep these sites clean and follow all regulations in order for them to remain open for paddlers. Most of these sites will be "pack-it-in, pack-it-out" only, with campers following Leave No Trace principles.

1. **Sister's Creek Marina to Little Talbot Island State Park; 7-8 miles**

The marina is located on the west side of Sister's Creek just off Heckscher Drive (State Road 105), a short distance from the St. John's River. Please note that the marina is closed to the public during the Greater Jacksonville Kingfish Tournament in July and one week before. Restrooms and a picnic area are available.

From the marina, paddle north up Sister's Creek, which is also the Intracoastal Waterway, so be wary of motorized craft. An incoming tide will be helpful. After about four miles, take an eastward turn at the Ft. George River. Less than a mile on your right you will spot the white wood buildings of the Kingsley Plantation, open seven days a week from 9 AM to 5 PM. You can land at a small beach about a hundred yards past the dock and visit this historic site free of charge. The plantation is located on Fort George Island and much of this 1,000-acre island was used to grow crops, especially cotton, during the plantation period (1763-1865). During your visit, you can view the planter's residence, kitchen and barn, and the half moon arc of slave quarters.

The Kingsley family was unique in that Zephaniah Kingsley took an African wife and they had several children together. Mrs. Kingsley owned her own plantation and slaves. In the 1830s, when harsh restrictions were enacted regarding free and enslaved people in Florida, most of the Kingsley family and fifty newly-freed slaves moved to Haiti, a free black colony.

The next historic stopover is less than a mile on your right down the Fort George River. Paddlers can land at a convenient boat ramp at the Fort George Island Cultural State Park and tour the Ribault Club, a 1920s style structure with grand rooms and unique architecture. The park itself is open daily, and the Club is open Wednesday through Sunday from 9:00 am to 5:00 pm. This multi-agency visitor center is cooperatively managed by the Florida State Park Service and the National Park Service.

To camp at Little Talbot Island State Park, paddle northeast from the Ribault House across the Fort George River and travel north up Simpson Creek a little over a mile. Then paddle up Myrtle Creek about a mile to the Little Talbot Island State Park campground. Sites 34, 35, 36 and 37 are near the boat ramp on your right. Time your approach to the campground with high tide. Advance reservations for these coveted spots may be made up to 11 months in advance through Reserve America or call (800) 326-3521 (8:00 a.m. to 8:00 p.m.) or TDD (888) 433-0287. When you arrive, please check in at the Talbot Islands State Parks ranger station on the West side of A1A before setting up camp. The ranger station may be reached at (904) 251-2320.

Another camping option is to proceed down the Fort George River a little more than two miles to the Huguenot Memorial Park, inside the Ft. George Inlet. Operated by the City of Jacksonville, tent camping is inexpensive and you can paddle up to the campground. Across the St. John's River mouth to the south, you can view the large naval ships of the Mayport Naval Station. It is important to walk the half mile or so to the office and check in before setting up tents. You can make reservations by calling (904) 251-3335.

2. Little Talbot Island State Park to Fort Clinch State Park, 21.5 miles via Simpson Creek and Amelia River

Paddlers have two options to get to Nassau Sound from Little Talbot campground. One option is to proceed north on Myrtle Creek, (only passable a half hour on either side of high tide) and shave off about a mile and a half. A second option is to take a highly scenic route by backtracking a half mile south on Myrtle Creek to Simpson Creek and proceeding north on Simpson Creek. This creek is passable at high or low tides. If you camped on Huguenot Park campground, proceed north on the Fort George River to Simpson Creek.

On Simpson Creek, just before the AIA Bridge on the right is an outfitter, Kayak Amelia, where restrooms, snacks and rental equipment are available along with up to date information about paddling conditions.

About a mile north of the AIA Bridge, paddlers will be greeted with an unmarred view of Half Moon Bluff, where the creek is creating a sheer cliff. Look for wading birds, wood storks and a variety of other avian creatures along this scenic creek. The cliff, combined with expansive views of unspoiled salt marsh, creates an unforgettable scene.

At the mouth of the creek, proceed along the shore of Nassau Sound. To your right is Bird Island, a bird rookery off limits to humans. Please observe birds with binoculars from a distance of at least 300 feet. If you spot birds standing up and paying attention to you, they are not performing essential functions such as resting, grooming, incubating and sheltering eggs or feeding young.

Along the shore of Big Talbot Island, you'll soon spot scenic bluffs where ocean waters are cutting into the uplands. On the map you'll see a GPS point that marks the beach end of a short trail beneath a scenic live oak canopy atop the bluff. At the end of the quarter-mile trail, you'll find a picnic area and port-o-let.

Be wary of strong currents as you cross the Nassau Sound and enter the South Amelia River, which is the Intracoastal Waterway. There is a launch site, with a small store and restrooms, at the northern end of the AIA Bridge on Amelia Island. This is part of Amelia Island State Park. Contact the Little Talbot Island Ranger office if you plan to leave a vehicle overnight at this launch site; (904) 251-2320. There is no camping allowed on Amelia Island State Park.

Paddle north up the South Amelia River. Look for flocks of white pelicans in the cool months. Numerous spoil banks provide opportunities to stretch and have a picnic. At the State Road 200 (A1A) Bridge, the current is very strong. Just past the highway bridge, you'll see one of the few remaining swinging railroad bridges. A restaurant is located at the bridge site and there are several places to disembark.

North of the bridge, you'll pass the sprawling Rayonier paper mill on the eastern shore. Within a half mile you will then see the docks and marina of Fernandina Beach, where you can find numerous restaurants and bed and breakfast establishments. An impressive fifty blocks of this historic town are listed in the National Register of Historic Places. Stroll along the streets and check out the charming Victorian architecture.

In the spring, Fernandina hosts the Isle of Eight Flags Shrimp Festival, which celebrates the town's shrimp industry and the fact that eight flags have flown over Amelia Island—more than any other spot in the United States. Since the 1500s, the flags have been French, Spanish, English, Patriots, Green Cross of Florida, Mexican, Confederate and U.S.

You have the option of camping under live oaks at a primitive site on Little Tiger Island, which is managed by Fort Clinch State Park, or you can camp at the park itself. The safest way to reach Little Tiger Island is to cross the Amelia River at the county boat ramp and hug the sandy western shore until reaching Tiger Creek. Proceed west about a quarter mile up Tiger Creek and the Little Tiger Island campsite will be on your right (see map for GPS point). No reservations are necessary for camping at Little Tiger Island at this time. Campers should adhere to Leave No Trace principles. Fort Clinch is directly east of Tiger Island, but do not attempt to cross this wide expanse of water unless conditions are calm.

You can camp at one of two campgrounds at Fort Clinch State Park. However, water access is highly restricted in the park. The park will allow for kayaks to land at the River Campground about a half mile before the fort, but you may have to carry your kayaks to your campsite. Sites 29, 30, 39, 40, 41 and 43 are near the water. Reservations are recommended. If you are registered at the campground without a vehicle and seeking to launch the next day, the park will ask you to wade and pull your boat along the shore about 1,000 feet south to the county-operated North End Boat Ramp and Nature Center. This is due to strong currents and liability concerns.

The historic red-brick fort is worth checking out. Reenactors provide an 1860s feel to the place on the first weekend of each month. Look for shark's teeth along the beaches, or hike interior trails that traverse scenic maritime hammocks.

If you are beginning or ending your journey on the circumnavigational trail, it is best to utilize the county-operated North End Boat Ramp along the state park's southern boundary. This is accessible by following North 14th Street to its terminus from Atlantic Avenue. The state park has no official kayak launch. From the ramp, you can paddle north less than half a mile to view the historic Fort Clinch and see the state of Georgia across the channel, ensuring you are at the trail's terminus. Hug the shore to avoid swift currents.

If you want to keep paddling north, you can now follow the [Georgia Saltwater Paddle Trail](#) all the way up the eastern seaboard to Chesapeake Bay. It is part of a National Park Service/multi-state effort that created a [Southeast Coast Saltwater Paddling Trail](#).

Access points:
Directions to Sister's Creek Marina (City of Jacksonville):
From Interstate 95 (south of I-295), take the Heckscher Drive/State Road 105 exit (#358A) and drive east (signs may indicate that you are northbound, but it is east) for approximately 12 miles. Sister's Creek Marina will be on the north side of the road just before you cross the Intracoastal Waterway/Sister's Creek drawbridge.

Directions to Little Talbot Island State Park:
From Sister's Creek Marina, continue east/north on Heckscher Drive/State Road 105 for an additional 6 miles. The state park entrance station is on the east side of the road. (Note: At the point where the automobile ferry crosses the St. Johns River, the highway designation changes to State Road A1A). Continue north on S.R. A1A over the Fort George River Bridge. After crossing the bridge, drive another 2 miles north on S.R. A1A to the Little Talbot Island

State Park entrance on the east side of the road (right). Proceed to the Ranger Station for camping information and instructions on how to access the launch site. A fee of $4 to use the launch is charged to non-campers.

From I-95, take the Heckscher Drive/State Road 105 exit (Exit 358A - Old Exit 124A) and then travel east for 18 miles. Heckscher Drive becomes State Road A1A once you pass the St Johns River Ferry Terminal. Continue North on S.R. A1A over the Fort George River Bridge. After crossing the bridge, drive another 2 miles North on S.R. A1A to the Little Talbot Island State Park entrance on the east side of the road (right).

Directions to access site at Ft. Clinch State Park: Fort Clinch State Park is north of the City of Fernandina Beach on State Road A1A (Atlantic Avenue). Take I–95 to the Fernandina Beach/Callahan exit (Milepost Exit 373 - Old Exit 129), and stay to the right. You will then be traveling east on A1A. (This road becomes 8th Street within the town limits of Fernandina.) Stay on this road, (A1A), for 16 miles until you come to the intersection of 8th Street and Atlantic Avenue. Turn right on Atlantic Avenue and go about two miles; Fort Clinch State Park will be on the left. A fee is charged for entrance to the park.

Alternate Inland Route Segments 2-4
Destin to Apalachicola

Emergency contact information:

911

Okaloosa County Sheriff's Office: 850-833-9200

Walton County Sheriff's Office: 850-892-8186

Bay County Sheriff's Office: 850-747-4700

Gulf County Sheriff's Office: 850-227-1115

Franklin County Sheriff's Office: 850-670-8500

Florida Fish and Wildlife Conservation Commission 24-hour wildlife emergency/boating under the influence hotline: 1-888-404-3922

Begin: Destin
End: Apalachicola
Distance: 145 miles
Duration: 9 days

It is possible to choose an alternate 'inland' route to avoid the coastal option on the CT if weather conditions are not favorable for the outside passage along the Gulf coastline in Segments 2-4 which begins at the East Pass in Destin. Also take into consideration that the outside passage between St. Andrews State Park and Mexico Beach traverses a long stretch of the coastal boundary of Tyndall Air Force Base that does not allow camping. This entails a 25-mile paddle to reach motels at Mexico Beach, the next available overnight stop after leaving St. Andrews State Park.

The inland route begins after leaving the spoil island in the Santa Rosa Sound and proceeding east under the US 98 Bridge. It skirts the north shore of the Choctawhatchee Bay and traverses through St Andrews Bay and Lake Wimico, using the Intracoastal Waterway (ICW) to Apalachicola, a distance of about 145 miles. It is also possible to return to the coastal route at several points if weather conditions are favorable. The alternate route does have its own potential challenges with long stretches of open water in the various bays and big barges that may be encountered in the narrow ICW. Plan to paddle early to avoid the bay winds that build up through the day.

The story of the ICW began in 1905 when the Gulf Intracoastal Canal Association was formed to promote the development of a single, major waterway that would connect all major ports along the Gulf Coast.
This waterway also would require the establishment of federally-protected status for it and the other inland waterways of the Gulf Coast through legislative efforts. It took more than four decades for the Association's idea to materialize, but the Gulf Intracoastal Waterway was completed in 1949 and has remained one of the most heavily-traveled and economically-significant marine routes in the nation.

The Choctawhatchee River and Bay watershed covers approximately 3,422,154 acres. About 42 percent of this is within Florida, with the remainder is in Alabama. The Choctawhatchee Bay is around 30 miles in length and 4-6 miles wide in places and bordered on the western and northern shores by Eglin Air Force Base.

1. Santa Rosa Spoil Island Site to Fred Gannon/Rocky

Bayou State Park (FGRB), 16-17 miles

A passage around the north side Choctawhatchee Bay has been created since the southern side of the Bay is almost all private residential land with very limited rest stops or overnight options. Leaving the Segment 2 spoil island campsite and passing through a narrow stretch of the Santa Rosa Sound known as the Narrows, you'll enter the wide Choctawhatchee Bay. A short distance beyond the US 98 bridge on the south side of the bay is Ross Marler Park with bathrooms, picnic pavilions, outdoor shower, and potable water. There are several restaurants within walking distance of the park. From the Ross Marler Park paddle northeast along the shoreline bordering Eglin Air Force Base. Around 6 miles beyond the US 98 Bridge the houses thin out and uninhabited stretches of beach appear. Much of the undeveloped shoreline on the north side of the bay is Eglin AFB property and short rest b r e a k s are permissible, below the mean high water mark, east of White Point and the Mid-Bay Bridge. However, Eglin AFB Main Base beach (between Black and Postal Points) is a controlled area and all non-Department of Defense affiliated paddlers should only land vessels for emergency purposes. Buoys approximately one quarter mile offshore will alert paddlers of this controlled area. Passage through this area is permitted, except during heightened security periods. Continue following the shoreline to the northeast and look for condos with red roofs on the east side of the channel leading to Rocky Bayou. Just to the north of these condos is the Bluewater Bay Marina and restaurant with a small sandy beach. From the marina keep the shoreline to your right and go under US 20 Bridge. About a half mile east of the bridge look for kayak rentals along the southern shoreline. About 200 yards further east is a small sandy beach, ideal for landing and camping at #36, 37 or 38 in the Fred Gannon/Rocky Bayou State Park. Make camping reservations well in advance by visiting Reserve America or call (800) 326-3521, TDD (888) 433-0287.

U.S. Air Force Colonel Fred Gannon was instrumental in preserving this site with beautiful old-growth longleaf pine trees, several more than 300 years old. Rocky Bayou, the main feature of the park, is the trailing arm of Choctawhatchee Bay and is popular for boating and fishing. Other opportunities for recreation include hiking, geocaching, and wildlife viewing. A well-shaded campground is available for full-facility camping. From the entrance of the state park on SR 20, it is about a one mile walk either east or west to groceries, restaurants, banks, pharmacy, etc. This is your last chance to purchase groceries until you reach St. Andrews State Park in Panama City (there will be a couple of options for restaurants along the way).

2. Fred Gannon/Rocky Bayou State Park to Basin Bayou, 16-17 miles

From the state park return to the Bay and head south, keeping the shoreline to your left. If you have military I.D. it is possible to stay in cabins or camp at the Max Gunter Recreation Area as you round White point and proceed east. Continue along the shoreline for about 9 miles to Nick's Seafood Restaurant, an excellent place for local seafood (closed on Mondays). Nick's is the landmark for the channel to Basin Bayou where a primitive campsite with tables and fire ring is located on the east side of this Eglin AFB property. It is necessary to obtain an Eglin Recreation pass and pay a fee in advance through the mail (an on-line permit system will be available in the future). To do so, send a photocopy of your current ID, along with a check for $12, your current address, and your cell phone # to: Jackson Guard, 107 Hwy 85 N, Niceville FL 32578. Call (850) 882-4164 for any other questions on Eglin permits.

3. Basin Bayou to Pt. Washington, 11-12 miles

Leaving Basin Bayou paddle towards the US 331 Bridge. On the southwest end of the bridge there are plans to create a new county park accessible from the water with restrooms, picnic pavilions, etc. On the southeast side of the bridge is a seafood restaurant with a good beach for landing kayaks. Another overnight option is to paddle to Live Oak Landing Rv Resort, a private resort on the northeast side of the Bay with RV sites and cabin rentals on Black Creek, accessible from the water about 2.5 miles east of the SR 83 Bridge. 877-436-5063.

After passing under the bridge head to Pt. Washington where there is a small public boat ramp on the southeast corner of the Bay (30.372724°/-86.114750°) and the nearby entrance to the ICW. A worthwhile stop is at the picturesque Eden Gardens State Park just to the west of the public ramp. Just in front of the park's retaining wall is an area of constructed oyster reef breakwaters, providing shelter for replanted salt marsh grasses, an effort by the non-profit Choctawhatchee Bay Alliance (CBA) to establish a Living Shoreline. In Choctawhatchee Bay and all along the state's coastline, many property owners use hardened structures such as sea walls, riprap, groins and bulkheads (as opposed to Living Shorelines) to stabilize and protect waterfront property from erosion caused by wind and wave action. While these "hard" solutions may prevent some localized shoreline erosion, they often act to increase erosion by reflecting wave energy and altering natural sediment movement. Volunteers coordinated by CBA help create living shorelines associated with natural, gradually sloping beaches, seagrass meadows and salt marshes. These efforts help restore nursery, feeding and refuge habitats for vital estuarine species while also providing protection from shoreline erosion.

There are two day-use areas at the Eden Gardens historic state park with restrooms, nature trail, and potable water. To visit the historic home, land to the east of boat dock on a small sandy spot under large magnolias. Pay an entrance fee at the park office located just south of the historic home. The house is closed on Tuesdays and Wednesdays. The focal point of this small park is the beautifully renovated, two-story Wesley house with its elegant white columns and wrap-around porch. The view from the mansion of the moss-draped, 600 year-old "Wedding Tree" and ornamental gardens inspire visions of hoop skirts and landed gentry at this popular wedding destination. Named after a wealthy Florida timber family, the park is part of the family's estate. In 1963, Lois Maxon bought and renovated the home, creating a showplace for her family heirlooms and antiques. The house holds the second largest known collection of Louis XVI furniture in the United States. Visitors can also take a stroll along the grounds and enjoy the picnic area. The old pilings visible in the water to the east side of the public boat ramp once moored large 'rafts' of logs that were floated down the Choctawhatchee River to await processing in nearby lumber mills.

For primitive camping visit the Choctawhatchee Rowing and Paddling Club next to the public boat ramp where paddlers are allowed to camp behind the building overnight. Please keep your presence discreet to not disturb adjacent neighbors. There is also a potable water tap. Visitors are asked to call 850-259-8600 for permission to stay here.

4. Pt. Washington to SR 79 Bridge, 18 miles

Point Washington has remnants of a charming bayou community with ancient oak trees and an array of historic sites. According to historian Dale Cox, Brigadier General William Miller, second-in-command of Confederate forces at the Battle of Natural Bridge, once called Point Washington home, as did a number of other Civil War veterans, both Union and Confederate. A small sign points out the location of Miller's home and a walk through the community's historic cemetery reveals the graves of a number of Civil War soldiers.

Leaving Pt. Washington, navigate to the ICW and head east. The ICW has tall sandy spoil piles lining the long channel in places and barge boats with significant wake may be encountered. Just before the SR 79 Bridge, there is a small restaurant on the south side of the ICW called BFE (Best Food Ever). Permission has been given for paddlers to camp overnight near the dock - check with the owners for location. There is also the Boondocks Restaurant on the north side of the bridge and a convenient store about a half mile walk over the SR 79 Bridge.

5. SR 79 Bridge to St. Andrews State Park, 18 miles
The ICW enters West Bay just beyond the SR 79 Bridge. It is about a 4-mile crossing to reach the mainland which you continue to keep on your right side heading eastward. Continue under the US 98 (Hathaway) Bridge and into St Andrew Bay. There is an option to sample excellent local food at a variety of restaurants and bars while taking a walking tour to visit a slice of 'Old Florida' in the vibrant Historic St Andrews District. To choose this option stay on the north side of the bay after passing under the bridge and head to the St Andrews Marina about 2.6 miles further east. Look for a small sandy cove just south of the boat dock at Uncle Ernie's Bayfront Grill. The schooner Governor Stone, a Historic National Landmark, is sometimes moored here.

If you elect to head straight for St Andrews State Park then follow the southern side of the shoreline for about 4 miles east of the bridge as it makes a sharp right and proceed to the opening of the Grand Lagoon. Make another sharp right into Grand Lagoon and paddle east past the state park boat ramp. Check Reserve America well in advance for one of the numerous campsites on the water where you can land your kayak (even numbers from 16-38, 96-114, and 101,

132, 134 and 143). There may be rip-rap (large rocks) and marsh grass in front of others. The park offers fresh water, showers and bathrooms. This is your last chance for potable water until you reach White City.

To access a large grocery store and restaurants paddle west from the state park and proceed under the bridge that crosses the Grand Lagoon. This is a very narrow and busy channel under the bridge so watch for boat traffic. Immediately turn right after the bridge and head for small boat rental business that offers a small beach area for landing a kayak. Walk north along Thomas Drive about 0.7 miles to a grocery store or visit one of many restaurants along the road. This will be your last chance for a good-sized grocery store until you reach Apalachicola.

6. St. Andrews State Park to Piney Point, 15-16 miles

Human history at St. Andrews State Park began with early Native Americans, who feasted on fish and abundant shellfish and left behind numerous middens (trash heaps of discarded shells, bones and other refuse). In the early 1900s, bathers frequently used the area, generally arriving by boat. The first known full-time resident during this period was a Norwegian-born sailor who wrecked his boat on the south bank of Grand Lagoon during a 1929 hurricane. "Teddy the Hermit" decided to homestead and remained until his death in 1954 at age 74. His makeshift shack once stood between campsites 101 and 102. The purchase of land for a state park began in 1947 when 302 acres were acquired from the federal government for the bargain price of $2.50 an acre. Today, after the addition of several adjacent parcels, at a considerably higher cost, the popular park consists of more than 1,200 acres. The inlets and bays around the park are part of the St. Andrews Aquatic Preserve. Considered one of the most diverse bays in North America, with over 2,100 recorded marine dependent species, St. Andrews Bay has the largest expanse of ecologically valuable seagrass beds in the Florida panhandle. These beds, along with expansive salt marshes, provide spawning and nursery habitats for a wide variety of fish and shellfish. The beaches and uplands along the preserve provide habitat and nesting areas for several protected species such as loggerhead and green sea turtles, the Choctawhatchee beach mouse, and snowy and piping plovers.

When leaving St. Andrews cross the pass between Shell Island and the Grand Lagoon with caution as boat traffic can be heavy and conditions challenging in the pass. The land north of Shell Island is Tyndall Air Force property and visitors are not allowed to land on the shoreline where posted. If a restaurant meal is desired before entering the remote ICW again, head to the channel just to the east of the Panama City Marina and proceed under the drawbridge into Massalina Bayou. There is a dock-side restaurant, Bayou Joe's, in the boat basin and others within walking distance.

Continue paddling east passing shipyards and industrial sites along the waterway. Your destination is Piney Point, a failed subdivision, about 5 miles east of the US 98 (Tyndall) Bridge. If you are retired or active duty military you may stay at the Tyndall Air Force Base Fam Camp located on the southwest side of the US 98 Bridge, about 10 miles east of St Andrews State Park. The Piney Point site is primitive with a great view of sunrise and directly opposite the air strip at Tyndall Air Force Base, several miles across the bay. Jet pilots known as the 'Blue Angels' may be seen practicing hair-raising maneuvers for aerial shows held around the country, an entertaining contrast against the backdrop of rugged shoreline.

7. Piney Point to Overstreet Spoil Bank Area, 17-18 miles
From Piney Point it is about 10.5 miles to the beginning of the

next stretch of the ICW. Paddle through East Bay and along the shoreline of Tyndall Air Force Base where nothing but miles of planted pines, upland woodlands and small slivers of white sand beaches are visible in this remote area. About 3.6 miles after entering the ICW the small village of Overstreet will appear below an enormous, tall bridge. On the east side of the bridge is a restroom, picnic pavilion and boat ramp, with water labeled "non-potable". There are no amenities or businesses here. About two miles east of Overstreet there are a multitude of spoil sites that are easy to access for primitive camping. Just avoid stopping anywhere posted as private land.

8. Overstreet Spoil Bank Area to Lake Wimico Campsite, 18-20 miles

It is about 12.5 miles from Overstreet to an industrial canal that heads south to the town of Port St. Joe, a distance of 6 miles. From Port St Joe it is possible to rejoin the CT coastal option of Segment 4 by crossing St Joseph Bay to the T.H. Stone/St Joseph Peninsula State Park. This is really a stunning portion of the coastline with gorgeous barrier islands worth visiting if weather conditions are favorable for a return to the Gulf.

To continue the inland route to Apalachicola it is about 1.6 miles past the industrial canal to the small town of White City. There are restrooms and potable water at the city park with a half-mile walk north on the main road to a small convenience store. This is the last option for any limited amenities before arriving in Apalachicola. There are camping options on spoil sites along the eastern bank several miles after leaving White City. It is about 6 miles from White City to Lake Wimico and 2.4 miles further to small point of land jutting into the lake on the northern shoreline that provides a shady respite for camping on a small ridge. (GPS cords on map)

Lake Wimico to Apalachicola, 13 miles
From Lake Wimico it is an easy paddle to historic Apalachicola where paddlers may be tempted to spend several days soaking up the charms of this picturesque fishing village. Stop by the Visitor's Center at 122 Commerce Street and learn about the enduring culture and maritime heritage of this still vibrant port town of Apalachicola. Grab a map and enjoy a walking tour taking in historic homes, the colorful harbor, and the John Gorrie State Museum.

John Gorrie was a young physician who moved to Apalachicola in the early 1800s when it was a prominent port of trade, commerce, and shipping in Florida. Gorrie served as postmaster, city treasurer, town councilman, and bank director. Concern for his yellow fever patients motivated Gorrie to invent a method for cooling their rooms. He became a pioneer in the field of air conditioning and refrigeration by inventing a machine that made ice, and received the first U.S. Patent for mechanical refrigeration in 1851. A replica of his ice-making machine is on display at the museum, as well as exhibits chronicling the colorful history of Apalachicola, which played an important role in Florida's economic development.

To rejoin Segment 4 from Apalachicola, paddle across the bay six or seven miles to a number of campsites on either Cape St. George or St. George Island. If you remain on the north side of the bay, the primitive campsite near Carrabelle is about 20 miles from Apalachicola (see Segment 5)

Keys Alternate Mainland Route
Segments 15-16
Flamingo to Miami

Emergency Contact Information:

911

Everglades National Park 24-hour search and rescue: 305-247-7272

Collier County Sheriff's Office: 239-774-4434

Monroe County Sheriff's Office: 305-289-2430

Dade County Sheriff's Office: ADD phone #Florida Fish and Wildlife Conservation Commission 24-hour wildlife emergency/boating under the influence hotline: 1-888-404-3922

Begin: Flamingo, Everglades National Park

End: Teachers' Island, Miami

Estimated Mileage: 75-85 miles depending on route options

Special Considerations: The alternate Florida Keys route stays close to the mainland, creating a more sheltered passage when weather conditions are challenging. The original route that borders the Atlantic side of the Keys is more exposed and has long stretches of open water between stops. Most through paddlers time their long trek around the state to be in the Keys and Everglades during the winter months when bugs are fewer. However, winter in the Keys may bring high winds and many days come with small craft advisories. Be aware that temperatures can also get surprisingly cold in the evenings, even into the 40's on rare occasions. Make sure to check the weather forecast frequently and pay attention to tides which make some areas challenging at low water; follow the depths outlined on your navigational charts. Even though the alternate route is more sheltered, you'll still be entering some long stretches of open water and you must be vigilant. Avoid getting too close to fishing boats poling in the shallows as anglers are often sight-fishing for bonefish, permit and tarpon on these flats.

You will have a choice of several routes from North Nest Key to Miami depending on wind and weather conditions, a need for resupply, etc. It is also possible to join the original Circumnavigational Trail (CT) route on the Atlantic side of the Keys at several points if conditions are favorable.

Fees and Permits in Everglades National Park:
Reservations are not accepted for any backcountry site in the Everglades National Park. A backcountry permit is required for camping on Shark Point Chickee and North Nest Key. During the winter season (mid- November through mid- April) backcountry permits must be obtained in person at the Flamingo Visitor Center or the Gulf Coast Visitor Center between the hours of 8 am - 4:30 pm. The soonest you may obtain a permit is 24 hours before your departure and a fee of $10 per permit and $2 per/person per day will be charged. During the summer season permits are free but are still required (mid- April through mid- November), not a favorable time to paddle in the Everglades due to intense heat, insects, and frequent storms. Permits are available 24/7 by following self-registration instructions at either visitor center. Permits are not issued over the telephone except for visitors coming in from the Keys to camp at North Nest Key, Little Rabbit Key, Shark Point Chickee, Johnson Key Chickee and Cape Sable. Please call 239-695-2945.

1. **Flamingo to Shark Key, 9 miles**

The U.S. National Park Service, Everglades National Park manages a campground at Flamingo and a small store, your last chance to buy supplies for several days depending on which route you select to get to Miami. The campground is about a mile before the marina and accessible by water at high tide. At low tide, you might have to wade through mud. During the busy winter season Flamingo Campground reservations can either be made online or call 1-877-444-6777 after November 20th. Reservations are not required in the summer.

The Shark Point Chickee is a favorite roosting spot for birds and is usually coated in thick droppings. Bring a tarp or plastic sheet to keep your tent and gear clean. There is a portable restroom on the platform.

2. Shark Key to North Nest Key, 20 miles

From Shark Key paddle eastward through the 'Croc Drag' opening and north of Pass Key to approach Nest Key on the north side, the only place where camping is permitted. The waters are shallow and it may be challenging to find a passage through the confusing landscape. Follow navigation charts closely. There is a portable restroom on the west end of Nest Key at the end of a dock which is experiencing rapid erosion and no longer connected to the island. There are no amenities on the island and it is a popular destination for powerboats, especially on weekends and holidays.

3. North Nest Key to Card Point, there are three options to continue your journey to Miami. Refer to map:

    A. Red Route: Nest Key via Pelican Cay to Card Point is about 18 miles. This will be the most sheltered option with presence of north/northwest winds. From Nest Key head N/NE about 4.3 miles to a small opening at Shell Creek (N 25.210047 W -80.486618) and paddle a short distance through mangroves to enter Long Sound, then head east towards distant buildings on the west end of the U.S. 1 Bridge. Look for an opening in the mangroves (N 25.235978 W -80.436184) and head under the bridge just past a couple of private marinas to Pelican Cay RV Park, (305-451-5223) for more information. It offers a limited amount of amenities with a rustic private campground, Wi-Fi and friendly retirees. Either get two gallons of potable water here or at Alabama Jacks, about seven miles further up the coast. Paddling eastward toward Card Sound Bridge, be sure to stop for conch fritters and classic Keys fare at iconic Alabama Jacks, an open-air bar floating on barges at the edge of Card Sound Road. Enter through a mangrove opening at N 25.290192 W -80.379509 or follow the canal on the west side of the bridge north about 0.4 miles. Card Sound was once a fishing community, full of characters and pioneers. Today it is a favorite destination for bikers, tourists, and colorful locals.

B. Green Route: Nest Key to Gilbert's Resort is eight miles and about another 10 miles on to Card Point. This route is more exposed, crossing both the Blackwater Sound and Barnes Sound before joining the 'Red Route' along the mainland to Card Point. This option includes a favorite watering hole of the Keys, Gilbert's Resort. This old-style resort has rooms on the water, a tiki bar, restaurant, and full service marina. Get two gallons of water here. From Nest Key paddle about 3.6 miles east to the entrance of a pleasant mangrove tunnel leading to Blackwater Sound known as the 'Bogies' (N 25.174200 W -80.451642). Exiting the 'Bogies', paddle about four miles east looking for channel markers of the Intracoastal Waterway (ICW) that passes by Gilbert's on Jewfish Creek leading to Barnes Sound. (Select the 'Orange Route' if you wish to bypass Gilbert's and part of the ICW).

C. Yellow Route: Paddling from Nest Key to Key Largo and John Pennekamp Coral Reef State Park offers two route options, southeast and east, and both choices are about 10 miles in distance. This is also where you can resupply and join the original Keys route (Segment 16). Southeast option: From Nest Key paddle southeast towards the ICW channel and follow it through Grouper and Dusenbury Creeks into Blackwater Sound. After leaving Dusenbury Creek proceed east one mile to Adams Cut, then paddle about 1.5 miles through the Cut and south to Pennekamp State Park. Boat traffic and wake, and water currents can be intense in the Cut, so exercise caution. East option, about 10 miles: From Nest Key paddle about 3.6 miles east to the entrance of a pleasant mangrove tunnel known as the 'Bogies' (N 25.174200 W -80.451642), leading to Blackwater Sound. Exiting the Bogies, head 3.6 miles southeast to Adams Cut and paddle a further 1.5 miles south to Pennekamp State Park.

Arriving at your destination one of the routes described above, you will find that Card Point is a remote and beautiful spot sheltered by Australian pines and mangroves. During a 2015 visit, a picnic table, yard furniture and a fire ring were where present. If you visit this site on weekends or holidays don't be surprised if power boaters are present during daylight hours.

4. Card Point to Homestead Bayfront Park, 11 miles:

Follow the coastline northeast, keeping a good distance from the Turkey Point Nuclear Facility. Approaching the shoreline here between the cooling canals and the facility may attract a visit by security. About 1.5 miles north of the cooling towers is Homestead Bayfront Park. Look for a narrow mangrove-covered channel at the south end of this well-developed park to access a primitive camping area screened by a concrete wall. Be sure to get permission for camping here ahead of time by calling 305-230-3033 (9 am- 5 pm) or see night security if after hours. Camping is for one night only and group size is limit to a maximum of four tents with eight kayaks. There is a restaurant (closed on Mondays), restrooms, and an outdoor shower next to a swimming lagoon, picnic pavilions and potable water. Make time to see the visitor center at Biscayne National Park, adjacent to Homestead Bayfront Park. Biscayne Bay is the largest marine park in the National Park System, with more than 180,000 acres of islands, mangrove shorelines and undersea life. The park has a number of interesting conservation programs including a sea turtle nest monitoring project, which aims to survey and monitor sea turtle nesting beaches within the park to protect nests from natural predation and unintentional damage by park visitors.

5. Homestead Bayfront Park to Teacher's Island, 27 miles:

Proceeding along the shoreline there are a couple of good rest stops—the Black Point Marina about five miles north of Homestead Bayfront Park, and Deering Point County Park five miles further north. Manatees may be seen in the Black Point area. Keep your distance to avoid disturbing them and also evade their powerful tail action if one dives to get away from you. Deering Point offers picnic pavilions, restrooms, potable water, and a few restaurants within walking distance. Heading north along the shore, you will pass a distinct Florida landscape feature, Mount Trashmore, a 225-foot high landfill site located between Coconut Creek and Deerfield Beach in northern Broward County. This is where Dade County's solid waste is disposed.

Matheson Hammock Park offers a good rest stop. If you have time, walk about a mile through the park to the fantastic Fairchild Tropical Botanic Gardens to enjoy the lush landscape and Butterfly Conservatory.

Leaving Matheson Hammock Park, head north along the opulent City of Coral Gables coastline. Exploring historic homes, enjoying exotic cuisine, and culture of Miami is an adventure but access from the water is a challenge. There are a few public access points if you want to secure your boat and create your own walking tour. It's well worth the effort to visit Vizcaya Museum and Gardens and The Barnacle Historic State Park, for a glimpse into the fascinating history of Miami's early founders. The coastline becomes increasingly developed and paddling past the mansions and high rises of Miami with fast boat traffic may seem like an assault on the senses after several days winding through the pristine Everglades and Keys.

If the Bay's waters are calm it may be worth your while to paddle east to historic Stiltsville and stay at nearby Bill Baggs Cape Florida State Park, at the primitive youth camp. It is possible to stay if the camp is not in use and if you make prior arrangements by calling 305-361-8779, M-F 8:00 am -4:30 pm. The campsite is primitive with no restrooms, shelters or power and is accessed from the No Name Harbor on the west side of the park. You must climb ladders over the seawall, secure kayaks to the bike rack near the harbor's restaurant and then carry gear a quarter mile east to the youth camp. When the park is closed (between sunset and 8:00 am), campers must remain in the youth camp. No after-hours access to the state park will be granted during sea turtle nesting season—May 1st though October 31st.

While at the state park walk about a mile to visit the Cape Florida lighthouse that was first built in 1825, destroyed by Seminole Indians in 1836, and rebuilt in 1846. The 95-foot lighthouse is the oldest standing structure in Miami-Dade County. Ponce de Leon was believed to have landed in this area in 1513 during the first Spanish expedition in Florida.

Leaving Matheson Hammock Park, paddle northeast past the horizon of high rise buildings to Teacher's Island, just past the Venetian Causeway near the mainland. This is the first of several spoil islands that Dade County is restoring into a tropical paradises with native vegetation. Most of the islands are nearly surrounded by riprap (large rocks) to stem erosion, but small beaches or docks on each island offer handy landing spots. With the exception of Bird Key, which is a bird rookery and off-limits, each island has a picnic area, and some have nature trails and shelters. No long-term camping is permitted, but the islands make great stopovers for circumnavigation paddlers as long as Leave No Trace Principles are utilized. Nearby parks on the mainland, such as Morningside Park, offer public restrooms. Bear in mind that on most weekends, the islands are very popular with boaters.

At Teacher's Island, rejoin Segment 16 and continue paddling 10.5 miles north to the next overnight stay at Oleta River State Park.

Ft. Clinch State Park

Circumnavigational Trail Data Book Summary Sheet

(Amenities listed in trail mile numbers for main route only; to be used in conjunction with data book, trail guides and maps. The complete data book is in the following section. Summary does not include Panhandle or Keys Alternate Routes.)

Medium/Large Supermarkets

Navarre, mile 35, north of Best Western Navarre, across highway

Ft. Walton Beach, mile 48.8, 1.7 miles east on Hwy. 98

Henderson Beach State Park, mile 62, across highway

Grand Cayman Motel, mile 95, 1 mile west on Alt. 98

Panama City Beach, Dan Russell Pier, mile 100.5, 1 mile west on Alt. 98

Carrabelle, mile 217.4, 4 blocks west on U.S. 98

Steinhatchee, mile 359.4; east on Riverside Drive, 5 blocks on 1st Ave to 815 1st Ave. SE (.8 mile total). Medium-sized store.

Cedar Key city park, 2.2 m off route, near 413.3; 4 blocks west on 2nd Street, corner of D Street on right. Medium-sized store.

Crystal River U.S. 19 ramp near mile 464.3; 14 blocks south on U.S. 19

Hudson ramp, mile 516; walk .8 miles to U.S. 19, take left and walk .2 mile

Bellair Causeway, 557.7, 3 blocks east on West Bay Dr.

St. Petersburg Beach, mile 28.5 of alternate segment 8 route; across road

Holmes Beach, mile 598.6, 1 mile north on main road (Gulf Dr./East Bay Dr.); or mile 595.9, 2 miles south on main road.

Matlacha, near mile 689.8, 2 miles east of Bridgewater Inn on C.R. 78

Vanderbilt Beach, mile 727.6, 1.3 miles east on Vanderbilt Beach Rd.

Marco Island after mile 747, 1 mile west on Collier Blvd.

Marathon, mile 900.7, (Sombrero Beach), 2.1 miles into Marathon on 53rd St.

Stock Island, mile 946.4 (Boyd's Campground), 2.3 miles west on U.S. 1.

Key West after mile 953. 5, On north side of island near marina; take channel under bridge across from Wisteria Island, turn right into marina area. Can land at public docks near marina area. Walk left ½ mile and then left on U.S. 1 two blocks.

Stock Island, mile 962 return trip (Boyd's Campground), 2.3 miles west on U.S. 1.

Marathon, mile 1006.3 (Sombrero Beach), Keys return trip, 2.1 miles into Marathon from on 53rd St.

Tavernier, mile 1050.4, supermarket .6 mile north on U.S. 1

Key Largo, mile 1063.5, 1 mile west of Pennekamp SP gate on U.S. 1

Oleta River State Park, mile 1135.9, across street from park

Ft. Lauderdale, mile 1152.6 (Doubletree Motel), 15 blocks west on S.R. 838

Pompano Beach, miles 1159.6 & 1159.8 (motels), 4 blocks west on E. Atlantic Ave. (S.R. 814)

Lantana, mile 1184.7 (Sportsman's Park), 1 mile north on U.S. 1

Jupiter, mile 1210.9 (Burt Reynolds Park), .5 mile south on U.S. 1

Jupiter, mile 1214.8 (Jupiter Inn), 6 blocks north on U.S. 1

Stuart, mile 1234.2 (East Island Park), .8 mile east on NE Ocean Blvd.

Oslo, mile 1264.4 (South Oslo Park), west .8 mile to U.S. 1

Micco, mile 1288, along west shore of Intracoastal on U.S. 1

Eau Gallie, mile 1306.9, .5 mile east on S.R. 518

Cocoa, near mile 1324, .7 mile east on S.R. 520

Port St. John, mile 1333, .5 mile north on U.S. 1

Edgewater, mile 1372.2 (Veteran's Park), .2 mile west on E. Indian River Blvd., .1 south on U.S. 1

Port Orange, mile 1387.1, .8 mile west of ramp at U.S. 1 junction

Ormond Beach, near mile 1398.1, 2 blocks east on S.R. 40 (E Granada)

Flagler Beach, Mile 1412.6, .6 mile west on Moody Blvd.

Jacksonville near Palm Cove Marina after 1476.9; .4 west on Beach Blvd. (U.S. 90)

Small stores (convenience/campground stores): 36.4, 48.8, 95, 138, 168, 198.5, 257.8, 318, 340, 381.4, (Chassahowitzka after 482.9), 498.8, 509.8, (Boca Grande near 662.3), (Beachcroft Motel area before 650.5), 698.8, 727.6, (Everglades City near 779), 852.2, 946.4, 953.5, 962, 1053.9, 1063.5, 1152.6, (Tomoka State Park after 1403.7), 1433.8, 1445.8, 1450.7

Primitive Campsites: 0, 6, 23, 47, 144, Alt. 145, Alt. 148.5, 147.5, 148, 156.7, 181.5, 185, 190, 194, 199.7, 204, 207, 220.5, 225.6, 232.7, 234.2, 241, 244, 250.1, 261.5, 283.6, 292.1,

300.6, (1 mile north of 318), 328, 330.5, 343, 351, 369.4, 383.4, 418, 426.3, 433.3, near 437.8, 453.6, 469.8, 499.2, 520.6, 532.4, 548.7, 565.4, 569.4, 581.7, (17.4 alt. route after 614), 632.8, 659.1, 662.3, 700.5, 717.7, 747, 758.7, 766, 772, 788, 799.5, 811.5, 820.5, 831.5, 841, 865.2, 880, 907.9, 999.1, 1027, 1067.9, 1125.3, 1226.2, 1231, 1261, 1271.6, 1283, 1295.4, 1321.5, 1345, 1361.8, (Shipyard Island after 1366), 1380.8, 1386.1, 1403.7, 1414.6, 1424.5, 1429.2, 1436, 1462.4, (Dutton Island just after 1480.9), (Little Tiger Island after 1513.2)

Campgrounds: 36.4, 62, 67.7, 73, 81, 168, 249, 257.8, 273.6, 318, 396, 408.3, (Yankeetown near 451.8), (Chassahowitzka upriver from 482.9), 498.8, 584, 621.9, 627.4, 669.3, 851, 893, 916.3, 917.3, 926.5, 946.4, 962, 980.5, 989.7, 990.7, 1004, 1014, 1063.5, 1092.5, 1097.9, 1198.2, (Jonathan Dickinson S.P. after 1212.5), 1226.2, (Sebastian S.P. after 1283), (Donald MacDonald Park after 1283), (Long Point County Park after 1283), 1335.3, (Princess Place after 1424.2), (Anastasia S.P. after 1436), 1450.7, (inland from 1480.9), (off route after 1490.8), 1493.2, 1515.2

Lodging: 17, 18, 35, 48.8, 95, 96, 137.5, 138, 217.4, 340, 359.4, 382, 396, (Cedar Key near 413.3), 498.8, (Hernando Beach before 509.8), 516, 579.3, 595.9, 598.6, (Beachcroft Motel before 650.5), 650.5, 680.3, (Matlacha near 689.8), 727.5, (Lighthouse Inn near 727.6), (Everglades City near 779), (Coconut Palm Motel and Island Bay Motel NE of 1050.4), 1135 (park cabins), 1152.6, 1159.6, 1159.8, 1173.4, 1186.8, 1187.2, 1214.8, 1234.2, 1282.2, 1392.2, 1394.3, 1445.8

Post Offices: Hours can vary, but most small town post offices are open Monday through Friday with an hour lunch break and on Saturday mornings. If you want to use a post office for a mail drop, address letters or packages to: **(your name), c/o general delivery, U.S. Post Office, (town name), FL (zip code).** All post offices use a central switchboard: 1-800-ASK-USPS. To look up more post offices, log onto http://usps.whitepages.com/post_office.

Here is a chronological list of post offices from west to east:

Mexico Beach near mile 138; 625C 15th St., 32456-2189

Carrabelle near mile 217.4; 93 Tallahassee St., 32322-9998

Steinhatchee near mile 359.4; 104 15th St. SE, 32359-3100 (closes at 3:45)

Suwannee near mile 396; 23252 SE 349 Hwy., 32692-9990 (closes at 4)

Cedar Key near mile 413.3; 518 2nd St., 32625-9998 (closes at 4)

Homosassa near mile 476.2; 10780 W. Yulee Dr., 34487-9998

Pass-a-Grille near mile 579.3; 103 8th Ave., St. Pete Beach, 33706-4334

Anna Maria near 593.7; 101B S Bay Blvd., 34216-9800

Boca Grande near mile 662.3; 434 4th St., 33921-9800 (closes at 4; closed Sat)

Matlacha near mile 689.8; 4547 Pine Island Rd, NW Unit A, 33993-9767 (closed Sat)

Everglades City near mile 779; 601 Collier Ave., 34139-9800 (opens at 10am, closes at 3pm; closed Sat)

Key West near mile 953.5; 400 Whitehead St., 33040-9998

Melbourne near mile 1303.1; 640 E. New Haven Ave., 32901-9998

Daytona Beach near mile 1392.4; 220 N Beach St., 32114-3302

St. Augustine near mile 1445.8; 99 King St., 32084-9998 (open until 6pm; 2pm on Sat)

Trail Gaps Between legal overnight camping/lodging (excess of 20 miles):

- 112.8 to 137.5 (24.7 miles), segment 3
- Chassahowitzka Campground to 498.8 (20.2 miles), segment 7 (unofficial campsite at 492 shaves off 6.8 miles)
- 598.6 to 621.9 (23.3 miles)—Turtle Crawl Inn along Gulf route will shorten distance, segment 9
- 1067.9 to 1092.5 (24.6 miles), segment 16
- 1097.9 to Teacher's Island via Bill Baggs Cape Florida State Park (21 miles), segment 16. (Bill Baggs cuts distance by 10 miles)
- 1231 to 1261 (30 miles), segments 20/21—motel 3 blocks off route at 1253.6 cuts off 7.4 miles
- 1295.4 to 1321.5 (26.1 miles), segments 21/22
- 1450.7 to 1480.9 (30.2 miles) segments 24/25—unofficial campsite at 1462.4 cuts mileage by 11.7 miles,
- 1493.2 to 1515.2 (22 miles), segment 26

Sponge Point campsite, Big Bend Coast

Florida Circumnavigational Saltwater Paddling Trail Data Book

To be used in conjunction with written guides and maps on Florida Office of Greenways and Trails (OGT) website (www.FloridaGreenwaysandTrails.com), and Google Earth maps and detailed campsite information on Florida Paddling Trails Association (FPTA) website (www.floridapaddling-trails.com). Relevant pages of the Florida Atlas will come in handy for town stops. Note: Mileage will likely be longer in certain sections due to the need to paddle farther offshore at low tide. Estimated total mileage for the trail, including paddling to Key West and back, is around 1,515 miles. This total can be more or less depending on how many points of interest are visited or if a paddler skips campsites.

Through paddlers and FPTA volunteers contributed to this document. Feedback is welcome and paddler's comments help update this guide and maps. Please contact Liz Sparks of OGT at liz.sparks@dep.state.fl.us .

PC = Primitive campsite
POI = Point of Interest
LA = Laundromat
L = Lodging
PO = Post Office
S = Shower
g = convenience/camp stores
G = medium/lg supermarkets

C = Campground
O = Outfitters
W = Water
I = Internet computer
R = Restaurant
B = Bathroom
PI = Put-In

Mile #	Type of amenity	GPS # on trail (decimal-degrees)	OGT Segment and Map#	Directions
0	PC/log-book (Big Lagoon State Park, Pensacola)	N30.3100 W87.4029	1/1-A	On trail
6	PC (Gulf Shores National Seashore)	N30.3181 W87.3321	1/1-A	On trail
8	POI (Ft. Pickens)	N30.3298 W87.3018	1/1-A	On trail
14.4	W, R (Gulf Islands National Seashore Park)	N30.3270 W87.1809	1/1-B	On trail
17	L, R, I (Comfort Inn)	N30.3329 W87.1438	1/1-B	Just before southern end of bridge
18	L, R (Paradise Inn)	N30.3357 W87.1338	1/1-B	Just past southern end of bridge
(1 mile north of	R, W (Gulf Shores Visitor's Center)	N30.3637 W87.1296	1/1-B	2 miles past bridge on north side

route)				
23	PC (Big Sabine Point)	N30.3533 W87.0524	1/2A	On Santa Rosa Island; water, restrooms and showers .5 mile south
(1 mile north of route)	PI (no facilities)	N30.3740 W87.0924	1/2A	North side of sound
27.8	PI (no facilities)	N30.3874 W86.9967	1/2A	North side of sound
35	G, L, I (Best Western),	N30.4007 W86.8592	1/2B	North side of sound just past bridge. Large grocery store
36.4	C, LA, I, g (Navarre Beach Campground)	N30.4042 W86.8377	1/2B	North side of sound; small grocery store, campsites and cabin rentals
	Segment 2			
47	PC (spoil	N30.4054	2/1B	In the

224

	islands)	W86.6625		Narrows
48.8	L, R, g, G (Bayside Inn)	N30.4048 W86.6333	2/1B	North side of Narrows; small stores in area; supermarket 1.7 miles east on Hwy 98.
52	W, B (Gulf Islands National Seashore Okaloosa Unit)	N30.3978 W86.5826	2/1B	South side of bay
56.3	PI, Bridge over East Pass	N30.3914 W86.5222	2/1B	West side of pass
56.5	W, B Clement R. Taylor Park	N30.4002 W86.5131	2/2A	East side of pass along bay
62	C, W, S, G, LA (Henderson Beach State Park	N30.3827 W86.4369	2/2A	Along Gulf, Supermarket across road
63.5	W, B (James Lee Park)	N30.3806 W86.4098	2/2A	Along Gulf
67.7	C, S, W, LA (Camping on the Gulf RV Park)	N30.3714 W86.3421	2/2A	Along Gulf
71.5	B, (Topsail Hill State Park access)	N30.3635 W86.3005	2/2B	Along Gulf
73	C, S, W (Topsail	N30.3593	2/2B	One mile

	Hill State Park access to tent campground)	W86.2798		walk or take shuttle
76	B, W (Ed Walline Park)	N30.3462 W86.2302	2/2B	Along Gulf
76.7	B, W, S (Gulfview Heights Beach) Access)	N30.3437 W86.2210	2/2B	Along Gulf
78	W, S (Blue Mtn. Beach Access)	N30.3379 W86.2009	2/2B	Along Gulf
80.3	Inlet access	N30.3262 W86.1640	2/2B	Along Gulf, inlet may be closed with sand
81	C, S, B, W (Grayton Beach State Park)	N30.3282 W86.1542	2/2B	Access via inlet
	Segment 3			
87	W, B (Deer Lake State Park)	N30.2999 W86.0781	3/1A	Along Gulf
93	B, W, POI (Camp Helen State Park)	N30.2734 W85.9896	3/1B	Along Gulf, accessible via Philips Inlet
94	G (Supermarket)	N30.2633 W85.9743	3/1B	Junction of Beach Road (Alt. 98) and Hwy 98
95	L, G, g (Grand	N30.2539	3/1B	Along Gulf;

	Cayman Motel)	W85.9591		small store across street; supermarket 1 mile west on Alt. 98
96	L (Sugar Sands Motel)	N30.2466 W85.9422	3/1B	Along Gulf
99.5	G (Supermarket)	N30.2245 W85.8916	3/2A	Junction of 98A and S.R.79 short distance from beach
100.5	B, W, S (Dan Russell Pier)	N30.2151 W85.8778	3/2A	Along Gulf
103.8	B, W, S (MB Miller Pier)	N30.1891 W85.8319	3/2A	Along Gulf
107.5	B, W (Richard Seltzer Park)	N30.1587 W85.7790	3/2A	Along Gulf
111.3	St. Andrews Jetties	N30.1223 W85.7328	3/2B	Inlet to St. Andrews Bay
112.8	C, S, W, PI (St. Andrews State Park)	N30.1335 W85.7317	3/2B	Along St. Andrews Bay
137.5	L, I (El Governor Motel, Mexico Beach)	N29.9423 W85.4106	3/3B	Along Gulf
138	L, R, I, g (La Buena Vista Inn)	N29.9384 W85.4042	3/3B	Along Gulf; small store

				across street
	PO	N29.9411 W85.3924		1 mile inland on 15th St.
144	PC #7 (St. Joseph Peninsula State Park)	N29.8612 W85.3990	3/3B	Along bay shoreline
	Segment 4			
144	PC #7 (St. Joseph Peninsula State Park)	N29.8612 W85.3990	4/1A	Along bay shoreline
Alt. 148.5 (6 miles from end of cape along Gulf)	PC #3 (St. Joseph Peninsula State Park)	N29.8067 W85.4125	4/1A	.13 mile in from Gulf
147.5	PC #2 (St. Joseph Peninsula State Park)	N29.8062 W85.4104	4/1A	Along bay shoreline
149.5	PI, W, B (park picnic area)	N29.7758 W85.4021	4/1A	Along bay shoreline
150.4	PI, W, B (park ramp)	N29.7642 W85.4029	4/1A	Along bay shoreline

156.7	PC (Deal Tower site); just before major portage to Gulf	N29.6869 W85.3625	4/1B	Along bay shoreline
162.7	W, B (Salinas Park)	N29.6832 W85.3122	4/1B	Along Gulf
168	C, S, W, LA, g (Indian Pass Campground)	N29.6833 W85.2222	4/2A	West side of Indian Pass; also cabin rentals and small store.
181.5	PC (West Pass)	N29.6272 W85.0935	4/2B	East side of West Pass
185	PC (Government Dock)	N29.6008 W85.0442	4/3A	South side of Apalachicola Bay
190	PC (Sikes Cut)	N29.6153 W84.9649	4/3A	West side of Sike's Cut
194	PC (Nick's Hole/Boy Scout)	N29.6409 W84.9176	4/3A	Dock on southwest side of cove; look for hobie sailboats
198.5	PI, g (east side St. George Island Bridge)	N29.6668 W84.8644	4/3B	Small store and restaurants on west side of main road; medium

				sized store on east side of road.
199.7	PC (Unit 4)	N29.6735 W84.8431	4/3B	About 1.5 miles past bridge along bay.
202.9	Beach near ranger station for check-in	N29.6866 W84.7945		South side of Apalachicola Bay
204	PC (Gap Point—prime campsite)	N29.7029 W84.7781	4/3B	Along East Cove
207	PC, W, S, B (Sugar Hill)	N29.7267 W84.7388	4/3B	W, S & B 200 yards SE on beachside along trail
	Alternate route to Carrabelle from Indian Pass			Island route for distance – 47.3 miles. Alternate route for distance – 36.1 miles
(15.5)	PI, L, R (Battery Park, motels nearby)	N29.7237 W84.9818	4/2B	North side of Apalachicola Bay
(21.5)	W (Millender Park)	N29.7311 W84.8843	4/3B	Just past Cat Point near

					Eastpoint.
(22)	PI (Eastpoint, restaurants nearby)	N29.7355 W84.8804	4/3B		North side of Apalachicola Bay
(34.5)	POI (Crooked River Lighthouse)	N29.8255 W84.6992			Must land on beach and walk across Hwy 98 to reach.
(35)	W, B (Carrabelle Beach Park)	N29.8293 W84.6923	5/1A		North side of Apalachicola Bay
	Segment 5				
216	Mouth of Carrabelle River	N29.8359 W84.6624			
217	PI (Timber Island ramp)	N29.8460 W84.6661	5/1A		
217.4	PI, G, L, LA, I, PO, O, R (Carrabelle town ramp; Moorings Marina has rooms and kayak friendly—866-821-2248)	N29.8523 W84.6681	5/1A		Various amenities all within a mile of ramp in either direction on Hwy. 98; supermarket 4 blocks west.
(1.5 miles up	PC (Warren Bluff)	N29.8735 W84.6965	5/1B		Along New River (left

New River)				fork)
220.5	PC (Oxbow)	N29.8705 W84.6827	5/1B	Along Crooked River
225.6	PC (Sunday Rollaway)	N29.9029 W84.6517	5/1B	Along Crooked River
232.7	PC (#1)	N29.9087 W84.6017	5/1B	Along Crooked River
234.2	PC (#2)	N29.9114 W84.5865	5/1B	Along Crooked River
241	PC (Rock Landing)	N29.9793 W84.5683	5/2A	Along Crooked River
244	PC (Loop Road)	N29.9899 W84.5355	5/2A	Along Crooked River
(left on Ochlockonee River 2.8 miles)	C, W, S, B (Womack Creek)	N30.0023 W84.5403	5/2A	Left side of Ochlockonee River going upstream
245	PI (McIntyre ramp)	N29.9818 W84.5260	5/2A	On right at junction of Crooked and Ochlockone

232

				e rivers
249	PI, C, W, S, B (Ochlockonee River State Park)	N29.9993 W84.4806	5/2A	Left side going downstream
250.1	PC, W, B (Ochlockonee River State Park Youth Camp)	N30.0084 W84.4745	5/2B	Left side of Ochlockonee River going downstream, paddle up Dead River
257.8	C, W, S, R, g (Holiday Campground)	N29.9779 W84.3847	5/2B	Left side of Ochlockonee just before bridge; restaurants & small store nearby.
261.5	PC (Bald Point State Park, Chaires Creek)	N29.9410 W84.3544	5/2B	Enter creek on right side of Ochlockonee, campsite on left
264.6	PI, W, B (Mashes Sands Park)	N29.9734 W84.3416	5/2B	Along northern point of Ochlockonee River mouth
(2.4 miles	POI, PI, W, B, R, g (Wakulla	N30.0346 W84.3889	5/3A	Located in Panacea up

233

off route)	County Visitor's Center)			tidal creek; low tide may be problematic; supermarket 4 blocks west.
273.6	C, W, B, PI, R (Spring Creek RV Park)	N30.0790 W84.3296	5/3A	Up Spring Creek on right
276.6	W, B (Shell Point Park)	N30.0575 W84.2901	5/3B	Easy access, picnic pavillions
283.6	PC (St. Marks River spoil island, aka Fog Island)	N30.1003 W84.1944	5/3B	Tall mound of rocks and trees makes it stand out
285.7	POI, PI (St. Marks Lighthouse access)	N30.0742 W84.1803	5/3B	An obvious landmark easily seen from miles away in clear weather
289.8	Palmetto Island rest stop (privately owned)	N30.0847 W84.1140		Accessible at most tide levels, no facilities
291	Deep Creek mouth	N30.0939 W84.0983	5/4A	The creek mouth can be shallow, but the

				creek itself is usually fine in low tide
292.1	PC (Ring Dike)	N30.1051 W84.1087	5/4A	Live oaks mark the campsite
298.6	Pinhook River mouth	N30.0996 W84.0157	5/4A	
300.6	PC (Pinhook River)	N30.1283 W84.0217	5/4A	50 yards west of bridge
307.6	PI, B (Lower Aucilla River)	N30.1165 W83.9795	5/4A	Upriver on right
	Segment 6			
318	PI, C, W, S, g (Econfina River Resort)	N30.0586 W83.9066	6/1A	Store and resort .2 mile north of ramp. Closed on Mondays.
(1 mile north of ramp)	PC (Econfina River)	N30.0714 W83.8967	6/1A	West side of river; low tide may inhibit passage.
328	PC (Rock Island)	N29.9720 W83.8302	6/2A	Land on north side
329.5	Spring Warrior Creek mouth	N29.9220 W83.6867	6/2B	
330.5	PC (Spring	N29.9188	6/2B	Campsite on

	Warrior)	W83.6642		right bank
340	W, S, R, L, g (Keaton Beach Park)	N29.8195 W83.5933	6/3A	Small convenience stores in town. Lodging at local marina.
343	PC (Sponge Point)	N29.7793 W83.5870	6/3B	Campsite beneath live oaks
351	PC (Dallus Creek)	N29.7138 W83.4983	6/4A	Hike trail through marsh to reach campsite
356.9	Steinhatchee River mouth	N29.6627 W83.4337	6/4A	
359.4	L, R, G, PO Boat ramps on both sides of river. Good Times Marina, which rents rooms, considered kayak friendly)	N29.6730 W83.3944	6/4A	Numerous motels to choose from. Small supermarket is about a mile inland on First Avenue.
369	Mouth of Sink Creek	N29.5565 W83.4007	6/4B	
369.4	PC (Sink Creek)	N29.5563 W83.3950	6/4B	
381.4	W, S, R, g	N29.4400	6/5A	Near

	(Horseshoe Beach Park)	W83.2933		restaurant, convenience store and small marina
382	L (El Sea's Fish Camp in Horseshoe Beach)	N29.4395 W83.2885	6/5A	.25 north along main canal thru town on right (floating dock)
383.4	PC (Butler Island)	N29.4312 W83.2697	6/5A	
388.4	C, W (Shired Island)	N29.3933 W83.2020	6/5B	County park with non-potable water, showers, restroom
393.5	Cat Island rest stop (privately owned, no facilities)	N29.3283 W83.1769	6/5B	
395	East side canal entrance	N29.3255 W83.1528	6/5B	Follow canal along east side of town to campground.
396	C, W, S, R, L, PO (Anderson Landing)	N29.3304 W83.1433	6/5B	In town of Suwannee; restaurants

				nearby. Small motel adjacent.
399.8	Mouth of Suwannee River	N29.2868 W83.1670	6/6A	
408.3	C, W, S (Shell Mound Campground)	N29.2101 W83.0632	6/6A	
413.3	PI (#4 Bridge ramp)	N29.1644 W83.0268	6/6B	
(2.2 miles off route)	L, G, R, PO, W (Cedar Key)	N29.1369 W83.0295	6/6B	Medium-sized grocery store; post office at 518 2nd St.
416.7	Mouth of Hall Creek	N29.1728 W82.9760	6/7A	
418	PC (Hall Creek)	N29.1863 W82.9694	6/7A	
425.1	Mouth of Kelly Creek	N29.1633 W82.8843	6/7A	
426.3	PC (Kelly Creek)	N29.1759 W82.8836	6/7A	
433.3	PC (Waccasassa River)	N29.1754 W82.7999	6/7B	
437.8	Turtle Creek Bay Entrance	N29.1160 W82.8009	6/7B	
(1 mile off	Turtle Creek Entrance	N29.1136 W82.7863	6/7B	

route)				
(2 miles off route)	Turtle Creek left fork to campsite	N29.1117 W82.7722	6/7B	
(2.2 miles off route)	PC (Turtle Creek)	N29.1127 W82.7703	6/7B	Small landing area on right along large tree island
451.8	PI, B (Withlacoochee River entrance to Yankeetown)	N29.0017 W82.7605	6/8A	
(3.5 miles upriver)	C, W, B, R (Yankeetown)	N29.0335 W82.6983	6/8A	Camping at B's Fish Camp and Marina
453.6	PC (Cross Florida Greenway spoil island)	N28.9764 W82.7808	6/8B	
	Segment 7			Note: The Salt River and Chassahowitzka areas can be difficult to navigate. Closely follow gps coordinates

				and maps.
455	Jetty Crossover	N28.9435 W82.7762	6/8B	Closest spot to get around Crystal River nuclear plant
460.5	Shell Island/Crystal River entrance	N28.9250 W82.6924	7/1A	Island to right of channel. Private; often used for camping by boaters
464.3	PI (Crystal River Preserve State Park)	N28.9092 W82.6371	7/1B	Left side of river going upstream
(.3 upriver)	PI, W, B (Ft. Island Park)	N28.9035 W82.6348	7/1B	Right side of river going upstream
(3.2 miles upriver)	PI, W, B (Hunter Springs Park)	N28.8951 W82.5927	7/1B	
(3.2 miles upriver in King's Bay)	PI, L, G, g, R, LA (Crystal River, Hwy 19)	N28.8992 W82.5964	7/1B	Supermarket 14 blocks south on U.S. 19

465.4	Salt River entrance	N28.9010 W82.6513	7/1B	
467	Dixie Bay entrance	N28.8837 W82.6373	7/1B	
468.1	Narrows Entrance	N28.8693 W82.6415	7/1B	
468.7	Salt Creek North entrance	N28.8593 W82.6405	7/1B	
469.8	PC (Uncle Tom's Island)	N28.8577 W82.6300	7/1B	Island about a mile up Salt Creek on left. Can be difficult at low tide.
470.5	Salt Creek south entrance	N28.8512 W82.6397	7/1B	Can exit island out south fork of creek
472.5	PI (John Brown Park)	N28.8316 W82.6559	7/1B	On right slightly off main channel
472.9	St. Martin's River entrance	N28.8262 W82.6524	7/2A	
474.1	Game Creek Bay entrance	N28.8093 W82.6466	7/2A	
476.2	Battle Creek entrance	N28.7831 W82.6342	7/2A	Half mile up Homosassa River on right
(1 mile	O, R, PO, L, POI	N28.7850	7/2A	Resort is up Homosassa

upriver)	(Homosassa)	W82.6185		River on right; post office at 10780 W. Yulee Dr.
(.5 up creek)	PI (Mason Creek)	N28.7612 W82.6337	7/2A	Ramp on left
478.3	Mason Creek entrance	N28.7573 W82.6466	7/2A	
480.1	Seven Cabbage Creek entrance	N28.7389 W82.6608	7/2B	
480.8	Reference point on Seven Cabbage Creek	N28.7306 W82.6561	7/2B	
482.9	Seven Cabbage Creek south entrance	N28.7070 W82.6530	7/2B	
(2.5 miles up Chassahowitzka River)	B (Dog Island Rest Area)	N28.7026 W82.6248	7/2B	upriver on left
(6 miles upriver)	C, PI, W, S, B, R, g (Chassahowitzka River Campground)	N28.7150 W82.5771	7/2B	Upriver on right. Small store and snack bar at ramp. Must walk to campground .3 miles.

1 mile up Ryle Creek	PC Ryle Creek emergency campsite	N28.6903 W82.6132	7/2B	Remote and unimproved. Emergency use only.
484.6	Reference point, south side of Chassahowitzka River	N28.6951 W82.6370	7/2B	Follow winding trail into South Blind Creek
487.8	Mouth of South Blind Creek	N28.6583 W82.6633	7/3A	
492	PC (10 Palms unofficial campsite)	N28.5999 W82.6599		Maneuver through rocks to land; room for 3 tents
494.3	W, B, S, R (Pine Island Park)	N28.5682 W82.6573	7/3B	On point on left
497	PI, W, B (Bayport Park, entrance to Mud River)	N28.5361 W82.6499	7/3B	On left as you enter river
498.8	C, L, B, S, W, g (Mary's Fish Camp)	N28.5428 W82.6274	7/3B	Left side of Mud River
499.2	L, PC (Riverpoint Landing Motel)	N28.5467 W82.6238	7/3B	Near end of Mud River along canal. Nearest supermarket 4 miles east on Cortez Blvd at

				Hwy 19.
(1.2 miles east)	L (Hernando Beach Motel)	N28.4939 W82.6503	7/4A	At end of canal in Hernando Beach
509.8	W, B, PI, g (Norfleet Fish Camp)	N28.4347 W82.6676	7/4B	Small general store; kayak friendly
516	L, W, B, R, PI, S, G (Hudson Beach Park)	N28.3611 W82.7102	7/4B	Land only at ramp around point along canal, not beach. Supermarket 1 mile away—walk to US 19, take left .2 mile.
520.6	PC (Werner-Boyce Salt Sprs State Park)	N28.3132 W82.7257	7/5A	Paddle .6 up Hope Bayou
523.2	W, B (Brasher Park)	N28.2852 W82.7321	7/5A	
526.1	W, B, S (Robert K. Rees Park)	N28.2537 W82.7575	7/5B	
532.4	PC (Anclote Key State Park, north end)	N28.2132 W82.8467	7/5B	6 mile open water crossing from Rees Park

	Segment 8			
535.8	POI (Anclote Key Lighthouse, southern end)	N28.1658 W82.8474	8/1A	
538.5	W, S, B (Fred Howard Park)	N28.1536 W82.8060	8/1A	
(3 miles east of direct route)	PI, W, B (Wall Springs Park)	N28.1086 W82.7758	8/1B	
545.1	W, B (West Point Honeymoon Island access)	N28.0651 W82.8334	8/1B	
546.7	W, S, B, R (Honeymoon Island State Park)	N28.0588 W82.8264	8/1B	
548.7	PC (Spoil Island #13	N28.0423 W82.7997	8/1B	
(1 miles west of route)	W, B, R (Caladesi Island State Park)	N28.0322 W82.8192	8/1B	Paddle up Seven Mouth Creek
(.7 east of route)	PI, L, R (Dunedin Marina)	N28.0109 W82.7927	8/1B	Access to lodging and restaurants
557.7	PI, W, B, G (Bellair	N27.9176 W82.8262	8/2A	Supermarkets 3 blocks east on

245

	Causeway ramp)			West Bay Dr.
565.4	PC (Island #BC 21)	N27.8279 W82.8133	8/2B	
(.3 east of route)	W, B, S, PI (Boca Ciena Park)	N27.8322 W82.8117	8/2B	Along eastern mainland shore
569.1	PI, W, B (War Veteran's Park)	N27.8004 W82.7702	8/2B	Along eastern mainland shore
569.4	PC (Island #CB 9)	N27.7975 W82.7661	8/2B	
579.3	PO, W, B, L, R, POI (Pass-A-Grill)	N27.6893 W82.7383	8/3A	Paddle through North Channel and head north .5 miles along Gulf. Post Office on 8th Ave. Museum across street.
581.7	PC (Shell Key)	N27.6569 W82.7452	8/3B	
584	C, W, S (Ft. De Soto Park)	N27.6354 W82.7192	8/3B	
	Alternate Gulf route from			Intracoastal

	Spoil Island #13 to Pass-A-Grill			and. Gulf route distances are same – 30.6 miles
(6.1)	Clearwater Pass to Gulf (CR 183 Bridge)	N27.9624 W82.8225	8/2A	
(7.4)	W, B, S (Sand Key Park)	N27.9612 W82.8314	8/2A	
(11.9)	W, B, S (Indian Rocks Beach)	N27.9003 W82.8493	8/2A	
(15.4)	W, B, S (Tiki Gardens Indian Shores Beach)	N27.8539 W82.8465	8/2B	
(16.3)	PI, B, W (Park Blvd. launch)	N27.8425 W82.8392	8/2B	
(18)	W, B, S (Redington Shores)	N27.8319 W82.8346	8/2B	
(21)	W, B, S (Archibald Memorial Beach)	N27.8017 W82.8031	8/2B	
(21.6)	W, B ((Madeira Beach)	N27.7971 W82.7973	8/2B	
(23)	Johns Pass	N27.7831 W82.7824	8/2B	1.4 miles to PC at Island CB#9 if desired. Strong

247

				currents!
(24.2)	W, B, R (municipal beach)	N27.7711 W82.7732	8/3A	
(26.5)	W, B, S (Treasure Island Beach)	N27.7434 W82.7591	8/3A	
(27.3)	W, B, R (Upham Beach)	N27.7356 W82.7512	8/3A	
(28.5)	W, B, G, L (St. Petersburg Park)	N27.7209 W82.7415	8/3A	Supermarket across road. Motels nearby.
(30.6)	PO, L, W, B, R, POI (Pass-A-Grill)	N27.6893 W82.7383	8/3A	Museum across street. Post Office on 8th Ave.
	Segment 9			
589.2	POI (Egmont Key Lighthouse)	N27.5976 W82.7621	9/1A	
593.7	PO, R, Northern point, Anna Maria Island	N27.5385 W82.7452	9/1B	Reference point; post office on 101B S Bay; restaurants nearby
595.9	L, G (Holmes Beach Motels)	N27.5147 W82.7253	9/1B	Gulf side of Anna Maria Island; supermarket

				2 miles south on main road in Holmes Beach.
598.6	L, G (Bradenton Beach Econolodge)	N27.4812 W82.7049	9/1B	Gulf side of Bradenton Beach; supermarket 1 mile north on main road in Holmes Beach.
600.6	B, W, S (Coquina Beach)	N27.4551 W82.6947	9/2A	Access is inside bay just north of pass
604.6	B, W (Joan Durante Park)	N27.4159 W82.6552	9/2A	Along bay on Longboat Key
(Along Gulf, 5.8 miles from Coquina Beach)	L (Turtle Crawl Inn)	N27.3903 W82.6439	9/2A	Along Gulf (6.9 miles to Lido Beach).
614	R, B, S, W (Lido Beach)	N27.3114 W82.5766	9/2B	Gulfside of Lido Key

(1.1 mile north of Big Pass)	PI, B, W (South Lido Park)	N27.3094 W82.5687	9/2B	Bay side of Lido Key
	Alternate bay route from Ft. DeSoto Park to South Lido Beach			Main route – 31.1 miles Bay route – 39.2 miles
(3.4)	W, B (North Skyway Bridge rest area)	N27.6491 W82.6771	9/1A	West side of Skyway Bridge
(10.5)	W, B (South Skyway Bridge rest area)	N27.5847 W82.6132	9/1A	East side of Skyway Bridge
(16.2)	POI (Native American temple mound)	N27.5302 W82.6269	9/1B	South shore of Emerson Point Park
(17.3)	POI, W, B (DeSoto Memorial)	N27.5242 W82.6439	9/1B	North side of Riverview Point Park
(17.4)	PC unofficial spoil island campsite	N27.5143 N82.6870		
(19.2)	W, B, PC, PI (Robinson Preserve)	N27.5147 W82.6621	9/1B	Group camping only; detailed map of preserve

				helpful.
(25.5)	B, W, S (Coquina Beach)	N27.4551 W82.6947	9/2A	Access is inside bay just north of pass
(29.5)	W, B (Joan Durante Park)	N27.4159 W82.6552	9/2A	Bay side of Longboat Key
(39.2)	PI, B, W (South Lido Park)	N27.3094 W82.5687	9/2B	Bay side of Lido Key
	Segment 10			
618	R, B, W, S (Siesta Beach Park)	N27.2661 W82.5526	10/1A	Gulf side of Siesta Key
621.9	C, S, B, W (Turtle Beach Campground)	N27.2201 W82.5178	10/1B	Gulf side of Siesta Key; marked by 3 tiki huts
622.8	Midnight Pass portage	N27.2081 W82.5113	10/1B	100-foot stretch of sand to portage
625.2	PI (Blackburn Point)	N27.1809 W82.4955	10/1B	Along mainland at Bridge
627.1	Oscar Scherer State Park ranger station access	N27.1699 W82.4753	10/1B	Along South Creek on left
627.4 (1.1 miles	C, S, W, B, PI (Oscar Scherer State Park	N27.1711 W82.4697	10/1B	Farther along South Creek on

251

from bay)	launch and campground access)			left. Either walk to campground or inquire about sites accessible from water.
631.5	PI (Casey Key)	N27.1283 W82.4704	10/2 A	On Casey Key along Intracoastal Waterway
632.7	W, B, R (North Jetty Park)	N27.1136 W82.4672	10/2 A	North side of Venice Inlet
632.8	PC (Snake Island)	N27.1128 W82.4633	10/2 A	Just inside the Venice Inlet. Crow's Nest Marina and Restaurant on south bank.
638.4	PI (Red Lake)	N27.0577 W82.4406	10/2 A	Just north of Intracoastal Waterway.
642.3	PI (Manasota Bridge)	N27.0103 W82.4104	10/2B	SW side of bridge
647	W, B, PI, POI (Indian Mound Park)	N26.9575 W82.3632	10/2B	Along mainland
650.5	L (Weston's Resort)	N26.9123 W82.3527	10/3 A	Bay side of Englewood Beach area

	Alternate Gulf route from Snake Island to Weston's Resort			
(.2)	W, B, R (Humphris Park)	N27.1114 W82.4667	10/2 A	South side of Venice Inlet on point.
(1)	W, B, R, S (Venice Beach)	N27.1002 W82.4604	10/2 A	
(2.5)	W, R, S (Service Club Park)	N27.0786 W82.4522	10/2 A	
(4.3)	W, B (Caspersen Beach)	N27.0564 W82.4429		
(8)	W, B, S (Manasota Beach)	N27.0104 W82.4126	10/2B	On Gulf side. Can walk to park from bridge launch.
(11.7)	W, B, S (Blind Pass Park)	N26.9631 W82.3851	10/2B	
(14.7)	L, R, g (Beach Croft Motel— kayak friendly!)	N26.9266 W82.3621	10/3 A	Access along Gulf; restaurants and small store nearby
(18.7)	L (Wanna B Inn)	N26.9123 W82.3527	10/3 A	Bay side of Englewood Beach area
	Segment 11			

655.7	W, B (Don Pedro Island S.P. land base)	N26.8559 W82.3029	11/1A	along mainland
(.5 miles to west of route)	W, B (Don Pedro Island State Park)	N26.8468 W82.3020	11/1A	Bayside access point
(5.7 miles from Weston's; 6 miles to Hoagen Key)	W, B (Don Pedro Island State Park)	N26.8464 W82.3036	11/1A	Gulfside access point
659.1	PC (Dog Island)	N26.8201 W82.2668	11/1B	
662.3	PC (Hoagen Key)	N26.7741 W82.2536	11/1B	Free!
(1 miles west of route)	PI, PO, G, R (Gasparilla Island)	N26.7637 W82.2629	11/1B	On bayside of island; post office at 434 4th St (12 blocks south); restaurants & small store nearby
(1	L (The Innlet	N26.7579	11/1B	On bayside

miles west of route)	Motel)	W82.2626		of Gasparilla Island
(along Gulf)	W, B, S (Gasparilla Island beach)	N26.7424 W82.2637	11/1B	Along Gulf
666.5	W, B, POI (Gasparilla Island S.P.)	N26.7186 W82.2587	11/2 A	Bayside access point near Boca Grande Pass
669.3	C, W, B, S (Cayo Costa S.P.)	N26.6857 W82.2455	11/2 A	Bayside access point. Take shuttle or walk to campground.
(Gulfside access point)	C, W, B, S (Cayo Costa S.P.)	N26.6866 W82.2589	11/2 A	Along Gulf
	Segment 12			
675.3	POI, B, W (Pineland/Randell Research Center)	N26.6593 W82.1529	12/1 A	West side of Pine Island
680.3	L (Jug Creek Cottages)	N26.7042 W82.1593	12/1 A	North side of Pine Island
(.4 south	PI (Bokeelia)	N26.6942 W82.1459	12/1 A	North side of Pine

255

of route)				Island down canal
689.8	W, B, PI, PO, g (Matlacha Park)	N26.6273 W82.0698	12/1B	Small store in town; post office at 4547 Pine Island Rd.
(.9 east of Matlacha Park)	L, G (Sun and Moon Inn)	N26.6386 W82.0607	12/1B	NE side of CR78 Bridge; supermarket 1.5 miles east on C.R. 78
695.8	PI (Tropical Point Park)	N26.5469 W82.0805	12/1B	
700.5	PC (Picnic Island)	N26.4897 W82.0493	12/2A	
	Alternate route from Cayo Costa to Picnic Island			Runs on inside of Sanibel-Captiva islands. Main route – 31.2 Alternate route – 26.7
(2.6)	W, B, L, R (Cabbage Key)	N26.6566 W82.2224	12/1A	Site of "Cheeseburger in Paradise"
(15)	PI (Blind Pass)	N26.4827	12/2	North side of Blind

		W82.1834	A	Pass
(15.7)	L, PI, G (Castaways Launch & Cottages)	N26.4815 W82.1803	12/2 A	South side of Blind Pass; adjacent to small store
(26.7)	PC (Picnic Island)	N26.4897 W82.0493	12/2 A	
	Main route continued			
703	PI (Punta Rassa Launch)	N26.4846 W82.0105	12/2B	NE end of Sanibel Causeway
(2 miles south of route)	POI (Sanibel Lighthouse)	N26.4531 W82.0144	12/2B	NE tip of Sanibel Island
705.8	B (Bunche Beach)	N26.4750 W81.9674	12/2B	Along mainland
(.5 miles south of route)	W, B, S, R (Bowditch Point)	N26.4631 W81.9662	12/2B	NW tip of Estero Island
708.9	POI (Matanzas Preserve access)	N26.4513 W81.9365	12/2B	Bay side of Estero Island
709.5	POI, PI, W, B (Mound House Park)	N26.4468 W81.9276	12/2B	Bay side of Estero Island
(4	C, W, S, PI	N26.4368	12/3	South shore

miles up Estero River)	(Koreshan State Park)	W81.8196	A	of Estero River
713.9	POI (Mound Key)	N26.421 W81.861	12/3 A	
715.8	W, B (Lover's Key picnic area)	N26.4009 W81.8704	12/3 A	
(Gulfside access)	W, B, S (Lover's Key Beach)	N26.3899 W81.8796	12/3 A	Along Gulf
717.7	PC (Bowtie Island)	N26.3766 W81.8536	12/3 A	Access on SE corner of the island just west of the boat channel
	Segment 13			
721.6	W, B, S (Bonita Beach)	N26.3313 W81.8458	13/1 A	Along mainland
723.8	W, B, S (Barefoot Beach)	N26.3044 W81.8357	13/1 A	Along mainland
725	W, B, S (Delnor-Wiggins State Park)	N26.2877 W81.8316	13/1B	
(2.7 miles south at end of canal)	L, R (Lighthouse Inn)	N26.2551 W81.8222	13/1B	South end of canal; high dock. 900-foot portage to Vanderbilt

				Beach can shave off 5.3 miles (need wheels)
727.5	L, R (Vanderbilt Beach Resort)	N26.2560 W81.8239	13/1B	Along Gulf
727.6	W, B, S, g, G (Vanderbilt Beach)	N26.2538 W81.8230	13/1B	Along Gulf. Convenience store nearby; supermarkets 1.3 miles east
734.1	W, B (Lowdermilk Park)	N26.1627 W81.8106	13/2A	Along Gulf
736.4	W, B, S (Naples Pier)	N26.1317 W81.8060	13/2A	Along Gulf
747	PC (Keewaydin/ Sea Oat Island)	N25.9864 W81.7478	13/2B	Inland passage route more protected but up to 2 miles longer
750.4	W, B (Tigertail Beach)	N25.9477 W81.7442	13/3A	West side of Marco Island
(1.1 miles east of route)	PI	N25.9126 W81.7170	13/3A	Southern end of Marco Island

758.7	PC (Cape Romano)	N25.8435 W81.6814	13/3B	Southern point of Cape Romano
	Alternate inside route from Cannon Island to Cape Romano			Main route - 11.7 miles Alternate route – 15.8
(2)	L (Boathouse Motel)	N25.9733 W81.7319	13/3A	North side of Marco Island
(3.8)	PI, G (Hwy. 951 Bridge)	N25.9612 W81.7104	13/3A	Launch is along SW side of bridge; supermarket less than mile west on Collier Blvd.
(8.4)	PI (CR 92 Bridge)	N25.9325 W81.6559	13/3A	SW side of bridge
(.5 west of route)	PI, G (Calusa Island Marina)	N25.9209 W81.6517	13/3A	small store in town of Goodland
(15.8)	PC (Cape Romano)	N25.8435 W81.6814	13/3B	Southern point of Cape Romano
	Main route continued			

766	PC (White Horse Key)	N25.8666 W81.5723	13/3B	Outer island; no permit needed
(1 mile north of route)	PC (Tiger Key, ENP)	N25.8322 W81.4907	13/4 A	Outer island, need permit
772	PC (Picnic Key, ENP)	N25.8231 W81.4851	13/4 A	Outer island, need permit
779	W, B, S, PI, L, g (Everglades N. P. Visitor's Center. Ivy House B&B in town kayak friendly and free shuttle!)	N25.8456 W81.3873	13/4 A	Along mainland through Indian Key Pass; obtain camping permits. Small store in town with limited groceries.
	Segment 14			
782	POI (Smallwood's Store Museum)	N25.8099 W81.3625	14/1 A	South side of Chokoloskee
788	PC (Rabbit Key, ENP)	N25.7517 W81.3740	14/1 A	Outer island
799.5	PC (Turkey Key, ENP)	N25.6438 W81.2725	14/1B	Outer island

811.5	PC (Highland Beach ENP)	N25.5014 W81.2064	14/2B	Along mainland
820.5	PC (Graveyard Creek, ENP)	N25.3824 W81.1429	14/3A	Just past Shark Point along Graveyard Creek
831.5	PC (Northwest Cape Sable, ENP)	N25.2197 W81.1702	14/3B	Along mainland
841	PC (East Cape Sable, ENP)	N25.1180 W81.0850	14/4A	Along mainland
851	C, W, B, S (Flamingo Campground)	N25.1368 W80.9380	14/4B	Along mainland
852.2	PI, W, g (Flamingo)	N25.1423 W80.9232	14/4B	Along mainland; small store/limited groceries
858.7	PC (Johnson Key chickees, ENP)	N25.0517 W80.9072	14/5A	Add half mile to distance to Little Rabbit Key
865.2	PC (Little Rabbit Key, ENP)	N24.9819 W80.8253	14/5A	Island in Florida Bay
868.7	Upper Arsnicker Keys rest stop	N24.9329 W80.8266	14/5A	Small island in Florida Bay
880	C Long Key State Park	N24.8126 W80.8224	14/6A	South side of Long

				Key in Florida Keys
	Segment 15			Note: Keys maps are in mile markers
887.7	Tom's Harbor Keys rest stop	N24.7653 W80.9276	15/M M 71-59	Along Atlantic
893	C, W, B, S (Curry Hammock State Park)	N24.7416 W80.9601	15/M M 60-48	Along Atlantic
900.7	B, W, S, PI, R, G (Sombrero Beach Park)	N24.6912 W81.0866	15/M M 60-48	Along Atlantic; (R, G, 2.1 miles into Marathon on 53rd St.)
905.3	POI, W, B (Pigeon Key)	N24.7048 W81.1560	15/M M 50-27	Along Seven Mile Bridge
907.9	PC (Molasses Key)	N24.6836 W81.1909	15/M M 50-27	South of Seven Mile Bridge
910.4	W, B, S (Little Duck Key Veteran's Park)	N24.6814 W81.2302	15/M M 50-27	Along Seven Mile Bridge
(.9 off route along Florid	C, W, B, S (Bahia Honda S.P., campsite	N24.6626 W81.2729	15/M M 39-27	Can paddle bay side around Bahia

a Bay)	#80 for paddlers)			Honda if using campsite. Arrive by 3pm or call 305-872-2353
916.3	C, W, B, S Camp Sawyer	N24.6477 N81.3133	15/MM 39-27	Must have advanced confirmed reservation
917.3	C, W, B, S, G (Big Pine Key Fishing Lodge)	N24.6461 W81.3285	15/MM 39-27	Just south of Hwy 1
920	Pass to Ramrod Key/Howell Key	N24.6303 W81.3653	15/MM 39-27	Can use to paddle inside of outer islands in Atlantic
922	Picnic Island rest stop	N24.6362 W81.3946	15/MM 39-27	
(2.5 miles NW of route)	U.S. 1 Bridge reference point	N24.6617 W81.4018	15/MM 39-27	
926.5	C, W, B, S, R (Sugarloaf Key KOA)	N24.6602 W81.5180	15/MM 27-17	
933.5	Sugarloaf Creek rest stop	N24.6034 W81.5702	15/MM 17-7	Along Atlantic

945	Reference point for inlet to campground	N24.5607 W81.723	15/M M 8-0	
946.4	C, W, B, S, PI, G, g (Boyd's Key West Campground)	N24.5741 W81.7330	15/M M 8-0	Tricky to find; at end of canal. Convenience store nearby. Supermarket 2.3 miles west on U.S. 1.
953.5	PI, W, B (Ft. Taylor State Park)	N24.5453 W81.8097	15/M M 8-0	SW end of Key West; land on east end of beach.
953.5 (2 miles off route)	PO (R, g)	N24.5504 W81.8004		PO 10 blocks NE of park at 400 Whitehead St. (U.S. 1); restaurants and small stores nearby
(3.9 miles north and east)	PI (public docks)	N24.5615 W81.7880		On north side of island near marina; take channel

265

				under bridge across from Wisteria Island, turn right into marina area.
	G (Key West Supermarket on U.S. 1. Restaurants and motels in area)	N24.5649 W81.7719		Can land at public docks near marina area. Walk left ½ mile and then left on U.S. 1 two blocks.
	Return trip along Keys			
960.6	Reference point for inlet to campground	N24.5607 W81.723	15/M M 8-0	
962	C, W, B, S, PI, G, g (Boyd's Key West Campground)	N24.5741 W81.7330	15/M M 8-0	At end of canal; Convenience store nearby. Supermarket 2.3 miles west on U.S. 1.
973.5	Sugarloaf Creek rest stop	N24.6034 W81.5702	15/M M 17-7	Along Atlantic
980.5	C, W, B, S, R	N24.6602	15/M	

	(Sugarloaf Key KOA)	W81.5180	M 27-17	
985	Picnic Island rest stop	N24.6362 W81.3946	15/MM 39-27	
989.7	C, W, B, S, G (Big Pine Key Fishing Lodge)	N24.6461 W81.3285	15/MM 39-27	Just south of Hwy 1
990.7	C, W, B, S (Camp Sawyer)	N24.6477 W81.3133	15/MM39-27	Must have advanced confirmed reservation
(.9 off route along Florida Bay)	C, W, B, S (Bahia Honda S.P., campsite #80 for paddlers)	N24.6626 W81.2729	15/MM 39-27	Can paddle bay side around Bahia Honda if using campsite.
996.6	W, B, S (Little Duck Key Veteran's Park)	N24.6814 W81.2302	15/MM 50-27	Along Seven Mile Bridge
999.1	PC (Molasses Key)	N24.6836 W81.1909	15/MM 50-27	Along Seven Mile Bridge
1001.7	POI, W, B (Pigeon Key)	N24.7048 W81.1560	15/MM 50-27	Along Seven Mile Bridge
1006.3	B, W, S, PI, R, G (Sombrero Beach Park)	N24.6912 W81.0866	15/MM 60-48	Along Atlantic; (R, G, 2.1 miles into Marathon

				on 53rd St.)
1014	C, W, B, S (Curry Hammock State Park)	N24.7416 W80.9601	15/M M 60-48	Along Atlantic
1019.3	Tom's Harbor Keys rest stop	N24.7653 W80.9276	15/M M 71-59	Along Atlantic
1027	C Long Key State Park	N24.8126 W80.8224	15/M M 71-59	Along Atlantic
1037.4	POI, W (Indian Key)	N24.8797 W80.6777	15/M M 82-70	In Atlantic south of U.S. 1
(just north of U.S. 1)	POI, W, B, R (Robbie's Marina—tarpon feeding)	N24.8830 W80.6906	15/M M 82-70	Restaurants nearby on U.S. 1
(10.5 m from Indian Key)	L (Lookout Lodge)	N24.9711 W80.5588	15/M M 91-81	Along Florida Bay
(1.8 miles NE of Tavernier Creek)	L (Coconut Palm Motel)	N25.0124 W80.5179	15/M M 98-89	Along Florida Bay
(2.1	L (Island Bay	N25.0165	15/M	Along

268

miles NE of Tavernier Creek)	Motel)	W80.5133	M 98-89	Florida Bay
1053.9	W, B, S, R, g (Harry Harris Park)	N25.0242 W80.4943	15/M M 98-89	Along Atlantic; 1 mile walk to restaurant and small store
1063.5	C, W, B, S, R, LA, g, G (John Pennekamp S.P.)	N25.1252 W80.4054	15/M M 104-96	Along Atlantic; small stores just left of park gate; supermarket 1 mile west of park gate on U.S. 1.
	Segment 16			
1067.9	PC (Garden Cove)	N25.173 W80.3654	16/1B	Along Atlantic
1082.1	POI (Palo Alto Key rest stop)	N25.3405 W80.2632	16/2A	Along tidal creek; need map
1087.6	POI (Jones Homesite)	N25.3405 W80.2632	16/2A	North side of Porgy Key
1087.9	W, B (Adam's Key)	N25.3970 W80.2337	16/2A	North side of pass to Biscayne

				Bay
1092.5	C, W, B, S (Elliott Key)	N25.4534 W80.1963	16/2B	Along Biscayne Bay
1097.9	C, B (Boca Chita Key)	N25.5253 W80.1753	16/2B	Along Biscayne Bay
1119.6 (mainland route)	POI, W, B (Virginia Key Beach Park)	N25.7432 W80.1442	16/4A	
1125.3	PC (Teacher's Island)	N25.7983 W80.1768	16/4A	
1135	L, G, R (Oleta River State Park).	N25.9063 W80.1322	16/4B	Access park past beach up tidal creek on left. Supermarket & restaurants across street from park
	More direct route from Boca Chita to Teacher's Island			4-6 miles shorter; about the same open water mileage. Check wind direction.
(10.8	W, B, PC, S, PI	N25.6762	16/4	From No

270

miles)	(Bill Baggs Cape Florida State Park)	W80.1603	A	Name Harbor, Climb sea wall and portage 0.2 miles east to youth camp
(15.7 miles)	POI, W, B (Virginia Key Beach Park)	N25.7432 W80.1442	16/4 A	
(21 miles)	PC (Teacher's Island)	N25.7983 W80.1768	16/4 A	
	Segment 17			
1142.9	W, B (Hollywood Marina)	N26.0143 W80.1215	17/2 A	South side of North Lake
1142.2	W, B, PI (Holland Park)	N26.0185 W80.1182	17/2 A	West side of Intracoastal
1143.7	POI, W, B (Kolb Nature Center)	N26.0386 W80.1193	17/2 A	West side of Intracoastal
1146.9	W, B, PI (Mizell/Johnson State Park Launch)	N26.0814 W80.1125	17/2 A	East side of Intracoastal
1148.1	W, B, S (Mizell/Johnson State Park)	N26.0910 W80.1087	17/2B	South side of Port Everglades entrance
1152.6	L, R, g, G (Doubletree	N26.1371 W80.1087	17/2B	S.R. 838 Bridge.

	Gallery one Motel)			High dock at low tide. Supermarket 15 blks west.
1153.2	Hugh Taylor Birch State Park dock on ICW	N26.1427 W80.1067	17/2B	East side of ICW
(1.1 miles west of route)	W, B (George English Park)	N26.1384 W80.1157	17/2B	West of Intracoastal
	Alternate Atlantic Route from Oleta to Ft. Lauderdale			
(3)	W, B (Haulover Park)	N25.9013 W80.1223	17/1A	Access to Atlantic Ocean
(8.7)	W, B (Hallandale Beach)	N25.9832 W80.1181	17/1A	Along Atlantic
(10.2)	W, B, S (Harry Berry Beach)	N26.0042 W80.1159	17/2A	Along Atlantic
(11.7)	W, B (Hollywood Beach)	N26.0280 W80.1145	17/2A	Along Atlantic
(16.1)	W, B, S (Mizell/Johnson State Park)	N26.0910 W80.1087	17/2B	South side of Port Everglades entrance

(17.8)	W, B, PI, R (Ft. Lauderdale South Beach Park)	N26.1142 W80.1043	17/2B	Along Atlantic. Restaurant across street.
(19.3)	POI, W, B (Bonnet House)	N26.1344 W80.1029	17/2B	Along Atlantic
(19.9)	W, B (Birch S.P. Tunnel Entrance)	N26.1406 W80.1024	17/2B	Along Atlantic
(20.8)	L (Backpacker's Beach Hostel Access)	N26.1550 W80.0999	17/2B	Along Atlantic
	Segment 18			
1159.6	L, R, LA, G (Sands Harbor Resort and Marina)	N26.2335 W80.0927	18/1A	East side of Intracoastal; supermarket 4 blocks west on E. Atlantic Blvd. (SR 814)
1159.8	L, R, G (Stratford Motel)	N26.2388 W80.0919	18/1A	East side of Intracoastal; supermarket 4 blocks west on E. Atlantic Blvd. (SR 814)
1160.9	W, B, PI (William Alsdorf Park)	N26.2518 W80.0919	18/1B	Along Intracoastal

1161.9	W, B (Hillsborough Inlet Park)	N26.2606 W80.0836	18/1B	Access to Atlantic
1165.6	W, B, R (Cove Marina)	N26.3135 W80.0814	18/1B	Along Intracoastal
(1.5 miles west of Intracoastal)	W, B, PI (Pioneer Park)	N26.3220 W80.0969	18/1B	
(.6 east of route)	W, B (Boca Raton Inlet Park)	N26.3354 W80.0722	18/1B	Access to Atlantic
1168.2	W, B, PI (Silver Palm Park)	N26.3499 W80.0761	18/2A	West side of Intracoastal
1169.5	POI, W, B (Gumbo Limbo Nature Center)	N26.3676 W80.0710	18/2A	East side of Intracoastal
1170.3	W, B, S, PI (Spanish River Park)	N26.3799 W80.0703	18/2A	East side of Intracoastal
1173.4	L, R, I (Holiday Inn)	N26.4235 W80.0644	18/2A	Intracoastal access
1175	W, B, PI (Knowles Park)	N26.4468 W80.0659	18/2A	West side of Intracoastal
1182	W, B, PI (Boat Club Park)	N26.5463 W80,0534	18/2B	West side of Intracoastal
1184.7	W, B, PI, R, G (Sportsman	N26.5839 W80.0475	18/3A	Along CR 812 Bridge;

	Park)			supermarket 1 mile north on U.S. 1
1186.6	W, B, PI, R (Bryant Park)	N26.6144 W80.0477	18/3 A	West side of Intracoastal
1186.8	PI (Snook Islands)	N26.6160 W80.0461	18/3 A	Just north of 802 Bridge, west side of Intracoastal
1186.8	L, R (Sabal Palm House B&B)	N26.6168 W80.0487	18/3 A	2 blocks north of Bryant Park
1187.2	L, R, I (Fairfield Inn)	N26.6157 W80.0400	18/3 A	East side of Intracoastal
	Alternate Atlantic Route to Boynton Inlet (continued from segment 17)			
(26.3)	W, B, S (Pompano Beach Park)	N26.2329 W80.0886	18/1 A	Along Atlantic
(28.3)	W, B (Hillsborough Inlet Park)	N26.2606 W80.0836	18/1B	Access to Intracoastal
(32.3)	W, B (Deerfield Beach Park)	N26.3090 W80.0758	18/1B	Along Atlantic
(34.1)	W, B (Boca Raton Inlet Park)	N26.3354 W80.0722	18/1B	Access to Intracoastal
(35.3)	W, B, S (South	N26.3508	18/2	Along

	Beach Park)	W80.0696	A	Atlantic
(36.1)	W, B, S (Red Reef Park)	N26.3625 W80.0687	18/2 A	Along Atlantic
(40.4)	L (Holiday Inn)	N26.4239 W80.0629	18/2 A	Beach access
(42.7)	W, B, S (Delray Beach Park)	N26.4562 W80.0586	18/2 A	Along Atlantic
(46.2)	W, B, S (Gulfstream Park)	N26.5049 W80.0515	18/2B	Along Atlantic
(48.1)	W, B, S (Ocean Front Park)	N26.5313 W80.0469	18/2B	Along Atlantic
(49.1)	W, B, R (Ocean Inlet Park)	N26.5440 W80.0450	18/2B	Along Atlantic
	Segment 19			
1195.6	W, B, PI (Currie Park)	N26.7357 W80.0498	18/1B	West side of Intracoastal
1198.2	C, W, B, S (Peanut Island Campground) Call to check status and make reservations: 866-383-5730	N26.7732 W80.0492	18/1B	East side of Peanut Island; primitive camping on west side. Lake Worth Inlet directly east.
(.8 west of Peanu	W, B, PI (Riviera Marina)	N26.7748 W80.0521	18/1B	West side of Intracoastal

t Island Campground)				
1199.2	W, B, PI (Phil Foster Park)	N26.7853 W80.0429	18/1B	East side of Intracoastal
(.6 miles west of route)	W, S, PI (Adventure Kayaks Outfitters)	N26.8084 W80.0616	18/1B	Along Earman River
1201.3	POI (Munyon Island)	N26.8153 W80.0473	18/1B	Along Intracoastal
(1.5 miles west of route)	PI (MacArthur State Park)	N26.8268 W80.0430	18/1B	Along lagoon off Intracoastal
1204.4	W, B, PI (Juno Park)	N26.8529 W80.0664	18/2A	East side of Intracoastal
1205.9	W, B, PI (Bert Winters Park)	N26.8739 W80.0662	19/2A	East side of Intracoastal
1210.9	W, B, PI, G (Burt Reynolds Park)	N26.9404 W80.0850	19/2A	East side of Intracoastal; supermarket .5 south on U.S. 1
1211.7	POI, W, B (Jupiter Lighthouse)	N26.9477 W80.0841	19/2B	North side of Jupiter Inlet
1212.5	POI, W, B	N26.9437	19/2B	South side

277

	(Dubois Park)	W80.0747		of Jupiter Inlet
(5 miles west of route)	C, W, B, S (Jonathan Dickinson S.P.)	N26.9880 W80.1429	19/2B	5 miles up Loxahatchee River; walk 200 yards to campground
1214	W, B, S (Coral Cove Park)	N26.9629 W80.0795	19/2B	East side of Intracoastal
1214.8	L, R, G (Jupiter Waterfront Inn)	N26.9739 W80.0874	19/2B	West side of Intracoastal; supermarket 6 blocks north on U.S. 1
	Segment 20			
1219.8	W, B (Hobe Sound Refuge center)	N27.0374 W80.1110	20/1 A	West side of Intracoastal
1224.6	W, B, PI (Jimmy Graham Park)	N27.1015 W80.1417	10/2 A	West side of Intracoastal
1225.2	W, B (Peck Lake Park)	N27.1082 W80.1422	10/2 A	West side of Intracoastal
1226.3	PC, Informal	N27.1201 W80.1490	10/2 A	West side of ICW
1228.5	W, B (St. Lucie Preserve S.P.)	N27.1513 W80.1636	10/2B	West side of Intracoastal
(.4 across inlet)	PI, W, B (Cove Road Launch)	N27.1493 W80.1684	10/2B	East side of Intracoastal

1231	PC (Spoil Island MC3)	N27.1812 W80.1810	10/2B	Along Intracoastal
1232.7	POI, W, B (House of Refuge Museum)	N27.1999 W80.1659	10/2B	East side of Intracoastal
1234.2	W, B, PI, L, I, G (East Island Park)	N27.2082 W80.1884	20/2B	Marriott Motel at east end of bridge (772-225-3700); supermarket .8 east
1236.1	W, B, PI (Indian Riverside Park)	N27.2251 W80.2118	20/2B	
1238.1	PI, B (S.R. 732 Bridge)	N27.2527 W80.2219	20/3A	
(.5 east of route)	PI (Blind Creek Park)	N27.3781 W80.2556	20/3B	East side of Intracoastal
1249.6	POI (Vitolo Family Park viewing tower)	N27.4098 W80.2775	20/3B	East side of Intracoastal
(.6 east of route)	PI (Bear Point Sanctuary Launch)	N27.4294 W80.2815	20/3B	East side of Intracoastal
1253.6	W, B, PI, L (Veteran's Park)	N27.4520 W80.3228	20/3B	West side of Intracoastal
(1.5 miles east of	W, B, PI (Jaycee Park)	N27.4520 W80.2894	20/3B	East side of Intracoastal

route)				
1254.4	W, B, PI (Causeway Island Launch)	N27.4611 W80.3139	20/3B	
	Segment 21			
(1.4 miles east of route)	W, B, S, PI (Ft. Pierce Inlet S.P.)	N27.4722 W80.2954	21/1 A	North side of Ft. Pierce Inlet)
(1.9 miles east of route)	W, B (Pepper Park Launch)	N27.4952 W80.3031	21/1 A	East side of Intracoastal
1255.5	PI (Barry Sanders Bridge)	N27.4736 W80.3224	21/1 A	
1258.3	PI, W, B (Village Marina launch)	N27.5088 W80.3448	21/1 A	West side of Intracoastal
1259.8	PI (DJ Wilcos)	N27.5282 W80.3481	21/1 A	West side of Intracoastal
1261	PC (Run-a-Muck Island or SL2)	N27.5441 W80.3414	21/1 A	
(1.3 miles east of route)	PI (Round Island); B, W, S across street, beachside	N27.5619 W80.3292	21/1 A	East side of Intracoastal
1264.4	PI, G, R (South Oslo)	N27.5866 W80.3653	21/1B	West side of Intracoastal; follow road .8 mile west to supermarket

				on U.S. 1
1268.7	PI, B, R, O (Riverside Park)	N27.6479 W80.3671	21/1B	East side of Intracoastal; free bus service to restaurants, outfitters (Kayaks Etc.)
1269.5	W, B, R (Royal Palm Point Park)	N27.6502 W80.3747	21/1B	West side of Intracoastal
1271.6	PC (Gifford Point)	N27.6765 W80.3816	21/2A	
1277.7	PI, W, B, S (Wabasso Causeway)	N27.7568 W80.4222	21/2A	
1282.2	PI, W, B, S, R, L (Sebastian Park)	N27.8096 W80.4642	21/2B	West side of Intracoastal
1283	PC (IR5 Spoil Island)	N27.8196 W80.4590	21/2B	
(.3 west of route)	PI (Sebastian ramp)	N27.8173 W80.4683	21/2B	West side of Intracoastal
(1.2 miles east of route)	C, W, B, S, PI (Sebastian S.P)	N27.8501 W80.4549	21/2B	East side of Intracoastal
(3 miles up	C, W, B, S, PI (Donald MacDonald	N27.8198 W80.5079	21/2B	West side of Intracoastal

281

Sebastian River)	Park)			
(1.8 miles east of route)	W, B, R (Sebastian S.P.)	N27.8608 W80.4492	21/2B	
(1 miles east of route)	C, W, B, S, PI (Long Point County Park)	N27.8733 W80.4713	21/2B	East side of Intracoastal
1288	G (supermarket)	N27.8818 W80.5022	21/2B	West side of Intracoastal; just across highway
1291.2	W, B, PI (Fisherman's Landing Park)	N27.9240 W80.5217	21/3A	West side of Intracoastal
(1.2 miles east of route)	POI, PI (Honest John's Fish Camp)	N27.9339 W80.5041	21/3A	East side of Intracoastal
1295.4	PC (Island BC 38)	N27.9821 W80.5423	21/3A	
(.8 off route up Turkey Creek)	W, B, R, PI (Goode Park)	N28.0296 W80.5827	21/3B	West side of Intracoastal; south side of creek

1300	W, B, PI (Castaway Point Park)	N28.0403 W80.5801	21/3B	West side of Intracoastal
(1.5 miles east of route)	W, B (Melbourne Beach Park)	N28.0684 W80.5661	21/3B	East side of Intracoastal
1302.5	PI (Riverside Park)	N28.0719 W80.5986	21/3B	West side of Intracoastal
1303.1	PI, W, B, PO, R (Front Street Park)	N28.0798 W80.5999	21/3B	West side of Intracoastal; post office at 640 E. New Haven 6 blocks west; restaurants nearby
	Segment 22			
1306.9	PI, B, G, R (S.R. 518 Bridge Ramp)	N28.1359 W80.6064	22/1B	Near eastern end of bridge; supermarket and restaurants .5 mile east on S.R. 518
(1 mile west of route)	I, R, W, B (Eau Gallie Library)	N28.1319 W80.6253	22/1B	Just past 518 Bridge along western shore adjacent to

				restaurant
1313	PI, B, W (Pineda Landing)	N28.2065 W80.6617	22/1B	West side of Intracoastal
1321.5	PC (Island #35)	N28.3247 W80.6994	22/2A	
1324	PI, W, B, R (Lee Wenner Park)	N28.3556 W80.7226	22/2B	West side of S.R. 520 Bridge; restaurants nearby
(.7 east of route)	PI, W, B, G (southeast side of S.R. 520 Bridge)	N28.3561 W80.7155	22/2B	Supermarket .7 mile east on S.R. 520
Veer right at S.R. 518 Bridge	**Alternate route through Banana Lagoon and Canaveral Barge Canal**			two campsites; 6.8 extra miles
(2.9)	PC, B (Samson's Island Park)	N28.1797 W80.6117	22/1B	East side of Banana Lagoon
(12.5)	PI, W, B (Jones Creek/1000 Islands)	N28.3094 W80.6147	22/2A	East side of Banana Lagoon
(21.3)	PC (Ski Island)	N28.4111 W80.6419	22/2B	From island, head due west through Canaveral

				Barge Canal
(27.3)	Rendevous point with main route	N28.4041 W80.7399	22/2B	Just north of Bennett Causeway
	Continue main route			
1333	PI, G, R (Port St. John Ramp)	N28.4750 W80.7667	22/3 A	Supermarket .5 north on U.S. 1; restaurants across street.
1335.3	C, W, B, S (Manatee Hammock Campground)	N28.5054 W80.7798	22/3 A	West side of Intracoastal; fills up quickly around shuttle launch
1339.1	PI, W, B (Kennedy Point Park)	N28.5536 W80.7954	22/3B	West side of Intracoastal
1343.9	PI, W, B (Hwy 406 Bridge Ramp)	N28.6236 W80.7954	22/3B	
1345	PC (Titusville Spoil Island)	N28.6384 W80.8021	22/4 A	Other islands closer to 406 bridge.
(1.2 miles west of	PI (Jones Ramp)	N28.6778 W80.8266	22/4 A	West side of Intracoastal

route)				
1352.9	PI (Blairs Cove Ramp)	N28.7330 W80.7568	22/4 A	
1355.2	PI (Mosquito Ramp)	N28.7562 W80.7663	22/4B	West side of Mosquito Lagoon
1361.8	PC County Line Island (see maps for more nearby options)	N28.8408 W80.8157	22/4B	West side of Mosquito Lagoon
1363.8	PI, W, B (Lefils Fish Camp)	N28.8657 W80.8331	22/4B	West side of Mosquito Lagoon
1364.1	POI (Seminole Rest Timucuan Mound)	N28.8693 W80.8370	22/4B	West side of Mosquito Lagoon
1366.4	W, PI, B, S (River Breeze Park)	N28.8983 W80.8513	22/5 A	West side of Mosquito Lagoon
(4.2 miles west of route)	W, B, PI (Canaveral Seashore Visitor's Center)	N28.9267 W80.8248	22/5 A	East side of Mosquito Lagoon; Obtain camping permits and detailed map of campsite locations.
(another .3	POI (Turtle Mound)	N28.9305 W80.8275	22/5 A	East side of Mosquito

miles north)				Lagoon
(additional .3 miles north)	PI	N28.9343 W80.8293	22/5A	East side of Mosquito Lagoon; follow map back to main route.
(additional 1 mile north-west)	PC (Shipyard Island)	N28.9409 W80.8448	22/5A	Northwest side of island
1372.2	W, B, G (Veterans Park)	N28.9731 W80.8921	22/5B	West side of Mosquito Lagoon; supermarket .2 west and just south on U.S. 1.
1373.6	PI	N28.9888 W80.9012	22/5B	West side of Mosquito Lagoon
1379.6	W, B (Smyrna Dunes Park)	N29.0658 W80.9173	22/5B	East side of Mosquito Lagoon
	Segment 23			
1380.8	PC (spoil island)	N29.0771 W80.9338	23/1A	Across from lighthouse
1381.1	PI, POI (Ponce de Leon Inlet	N29.0792	23/1	West side of

		Lighthouse)	W80.9285	A	Intracoastal
(2 miles west of route)		PI, W, B (Spruce Creek Park)	N29.0931 W80.9741	23/1A	.5 miles up Spruce Creek on north shore.
1386.1		PC (spoil island)	N29.1357 W80.9697	23/1A	
1387.1		PI, W, B, G (Port Orange Causeway)	N29.1475 W80.9767	23/1A	Supermarket .8 mile west of ramp at U.S. 1 junction
1389.6		W, B (Riverfront Veteran's Park)	N29.1760 W81.0010	23/1B	West side of Intracoastal
1391.3		W, B, PI (Bethune Point Park)	N29.2001 W81.0081	23/1B	West side of Intracoastal
1392.2		PI, L	N29.2094 W81.0144	23/1B	West side of Intracoastal; Bayview Motel 1 block west on Orange Ave (386-253-6844)
1392.4		W, B, PI, PO, R (Daytona Beach town park)	N29.2119 W81.0158	23/1B	West side of Intracoastal; post office short distance at 220 N. Beach St.;

				restaurants nearby
1394.3	W, B, PI, L (Ross Point Park)	N29.2382 W81.0315	23/1B	West side of Intracoastal; River Lily Inn B&B across street.
1395.1	W, B, PI, R (Sunrise Park)	N29.2474 W81.0364	23/1B	West side of Intracoastal
1398.1	W, B, R, PI (Granada Pier, Ormond Beach)	N29.2856 W81.0544	23/2A	West side of Intracoastal; restaurants begin 1 block west on S.R. 40
(.2 mile east of route)	PI, R, G	N29.2891 W81.0490	23/2A	Northeast side of S.R. 40 Bridge; supermarket / restaurant 2 blocks east on S.R. 40 (E. Granada Blvd.)
1403.7	PC (spoil island)	N29.3627 W81.0822	23/2A	
(1.3 miles west of route)	POI, W, B, PI, g (Tomoka State Park)	N29.3487 W81.0888	23/2A	Southern side of Tomoka Basin; small camp store

				near ramp
1405	PI (Seabridge Park)	N29.3815 W81.0870	23/2B	East side of Intracoastal
1407	PI (Highbridge Park)	N29.4083 W81.1002	23/2B	East side of Intracoastal along C.R. 2001 Bridge
1407.1	W, B, PI (North Peninsula State Park)	N29.4103 W81.0998	23/2B	East side of Intracoastal
1409.2	W, B, PI (Gamble Rogers State Park)	N29.4368 W81.1091	23/2B	East side of Intracoastal
1412.6	PI, G (Moody Ramp)	N29.4774 W81.1357	23/2B	Along S.R. 100 Bridge; supermarket .6 mile west on Moody Blvd.
(.4 miles east of route)	PI (Silver Lake Park)	N29.4971 W81.1372	23/3A	East side of Intracoastal
1414.6	PC (Silver Lake spoil island)	N29.5050 W81.1448	23/3A	
1423.2	PI, W, B (Bing's Landing)	N29.6155 W81.2041	23/3B	East side of Intracoastal
1424.2	POI (Washington Oaks Gardens	N29.6276 W81.2090	23/3B	East side of Intracoastal

	S.P. access)			
(1.3 miles up Pellicer Creek)	PI, W, B, C (Princess Place Preserve)	N29.6563 W81.2357	23/3B	Along southern shore
(2.8 miles up Pellicer Creek)	W, B, PI (Faver-Dykes State Park)	N29.6671 W81.2571	23/3B	North shore of creek
(.3 miles east of route)	PI (River to Sea Preserve Launch)	N29.6719 W81.2147	23/3B	East side of Intracoastal
1427.5	PC (Jordan Island)	N29.6730 W81.2211	23/3B	
1429.2	PC (Mellon Island)	N29.6958 W81.2304	23/3B	
	Segment 24			
1430.6	POI, W, B (Ft. Matanzas access)	N29.7147 W81.2349	24/1A	East side of Intracoastal
1433.8	PI, W, B, g (Devil's Elbow)	N29.7532 W81.2496	24/1A	East side of Intracoastal; small store
1434.8	PI (Hwy 206 Bridge)	N29.7643 W81.2615	24/1A	West side of Intracoastal

(.3 miles east of route)	PI (Coastal Outfitters)	N29.7675 W81.2564	24/1 A	East side of Intracoastal
1435.3	Moses Creek mouth	N29.7729 W81.2694	24/1 A	West side of Intracoastal. Navigate oyster beds and marsh at low tide.
1436	PC, W (Moses Creek)	N29.7693 W81.2776	24/1 A	West side of Intracoastal on north shore of Moses Creek.
(.5 miles east of route)	PI (Frank Butler)	N29.7908 W81.2686	24/1 A	East side of Intracoastal
(1.5 miles up Salt Run)	PI, POI (St. Augustine Lighthouse)	N29.8857 W81.2859	24/1B	
(2.8 miles up Salt Run)	C, B, W, S, PI (Anastasia State Park)	N29.8718 W81.2755	24/1B	
1445.8	W, B, S, L, R, PO, g (St. Augustine	N29.8920 W81.3098	24/1B	West side of Intracoastal; restaurants

	Marina)			and lodging nearby; post office at 99 King St. 6 blocks SW; only small stores in area
1446.4	POI (Castillo de San Marcos fort)	N29.8988 W81.3113	24/1B	West side of Intracoastal
1447.6	PI, B, W	N29.9119 W81.3085	24/1B	West side of Intracoastal
1450.2	PI	N29.9428 W81.3086	24/2A	East side of Intracoastal
1450.7	C, W, B, S, LA, g (North Beach Campground)	N29.9490 W81.3100	24/2A	East side of Intracoastal
1451.2	R (Caps on the Water)	N29.9550 W81.3129	24/2A	East side of Intracoastal
1456.2	POI (GTMNERR Shell Bluff access)	N30.0153 W81.3457	24/2A	East side of Intracoastal
1462.4	PC (unofficial spoil island campsite)	N30.0956 W81.3665	21/2B	West side of Intracoastal near Smith Creek outlet
1465.3	PI, R (Palm Valley Road Bridge)	N30.1327 W81.3851	24/2B	East side of Intracoastal
	Segment 25			

1471.1	R	N30.2105 W81.4099	25/1A	East side of Intracoastal
(.7 miles up tidal creek)	PI (Cradle Creek Preserve)	N30.2747 W81.4095	25/1B	East side of Intracoastal; low tide problematic
1476.9	PI (U.S. 90 Bridge)	N30.2900 W81.4199	25/1B	East side of Intracoastal
(.6 miles west of route)	G, R, W, B (Palm Cove Marina)	N30.2905 W81.4314	25/1B	West side of Intracoastal; supermarket .4 west on Beach Blvd. (U.S. 90)
(.5 miles west of route)	PI, W, B (Castaway Park)	N30.2961 W81.4315	25/1B	West side of Intracoastal; low tide problematic
(.9 miles east of route)	PI (Tideviews Preserve)	N30.3259 W81.4255	25/1B	East side of Intracoastal; low tide problematic
1480.9	PI (Dutton Island)	N30.3361 W81.4339	25/1B	East side of Intracoastal
(.1 miles east)	PC (Dutton Island)	N30.3355 W81.4324	25/1B	East side of Intracoastal along Dutton Creek
(.5 miles	W, B, S (Dutton	N30.3386	25/1B	

inland on island)	Island facilities)	W81.4332		
(1.3 miles east of route)	PI (St. Johns River, south shore)	N30.3821 W81.4387	25/2 A	
1485.7	PI, W, B (Sister's Creek Marina)	N30.3951 W81.4604	25/2 A	West side of Sister's Creek
	Segment 26			
1490.8	POI, W, B (Kingsley Plantation)	N30.4392 W81.4332	26/1 A	South side of Sister's Creek
(3.2 miles south of route)	C, W, B, S (Huguenot Memorial Park)	N30.4058 W81.4026	26/1 A	
1493.2	C, W, B, S (Little Talbot State Park)	N30.4596 W81.4218	26/1 A	East side of Myrtle Creek
1495	W, B, I, O (Kayak Amelia Outfitters 9-5 daily; 904-251-0016). Info source for tides and access.	N30.4623 W81.4281	26/1 A	Along Simpson's Creek near Hwy 105 Bridge; water available after hours as well.

1499.8	POI (Big Talbot Beach trailhead)	N30.5058 W81.4522	26/2A	Along mainland
1513.2	PI, W, B, R (Fernandina Harbor Marina ramp)	N30.6703 W81.4653	26/2B	(access to Old Fernandina; east side of Amelia River)
(1.6 miles west of route)	PC (Little Tiger Island)	N30.7055 W81.4879	26/2B	West side of Amelia River
1515	PI, W, B (North End Ramp on border of state park)	N30.6958 W81.4600	26/2B	East side of Amelia River; land here if not camping at state park.
1515.2	C, W, B, S (Ft. Clinch S.P. River Campground)	N30.6986 W81.4611	26/2B	East side of Amelia River; check on access rules.
1515.9	POI (Historic Fort Clinch in Ft. Clinch State Park)	N30.7052 W81.4565	26/2B	Eastern terminus of trail! Note: no official launch area in park.

Panhandle Alternate Route
Segments 2-4, Destin to Apalachicola
Circumnavigational Trail Data Book

PC = Primitive campsite
POI = Point of Interest
LA = Laundromat
L = Lodging
PO = Post Office
S = Shower
g = convenience/camp stores
G = medium/lg supermarkets

C = Campground
O = Outfitters
W = Water
I = Internet computer
R = Restaurant
B = Bathroom
PI = Put-In

Mile #	Type of amenity	GPS # on trail (decimal-degrees)	CT Segment and Map #	Directions
0	R,B,S,W,PI (Ross Marler Park, just past 98 Bridge)	N 30.40030 W-86.59260	Alt 1A	On trail
16 (5 miles north of	C, B, S, W, LA, G, PI (Rocky	N 30.50163 W-86.43725	Alt 1A	East of US 20 bridge. Shopping

297

route)	Bayou State Park)				center one mile east of park entrance
12-13 (alt. for Rocky Bayou SP)	C, S, L, LA, W (Maxwell-Gunter Recreation Area Military Only)	N 30.45740 W-86.41163	Alt 1A		On trail Requires military ID
19	B, PI, W Choctaw Beach	N30.476676 W-86.330760	Alt 1B		On trail
23	R, B, W, PI Nick's Seafood Restaurant	N 30.486592 W-86.250917	Alt 1B		On trail
(1 mile north of route)	PC Basin Bayou Primitive Campsite	N 30.496910 W-86.240160	Alt 1B		North of Nick's. Go under bridge and head to northeast side of Basin Bayou
2.5 miles east of SR 83 Bridge	C, L, LA, I, B, W, PI (Live Oak Landing RV Resort)	N 30.430074° W - 86.114335°	Alt 2A		On trail
	R, W, PI Seafood	N 30.387342° W -	Alt 2A		SE corner of SR 83 Bridge Small beach

298

	Restaurant	86.174294°		in front of restaurant for access
34.5	POI, B, W Eden Gardens State Park (no camping)	N 30.373613° W- 86.117191°	Alt 2A	On trail
35	PC, PI, W (Choctawhatchee Rowing and Paddling Club)	N 30.372820 W- 86.114970	Alt 2A	On trail, camp behind club building
53	R,B,W,PC,PI BFE Restaurant, SR 79 Bridge	N 30.293973° W - 85.860306°	Alt 3A	On trail, next to bridge. There is also another restaurant on east side of the bridge.
0.5 mile north	G, W, B Small grocery store	N 30.299013° W - 85.852304°	Alt 3A	Walk north over bridge on SR 79.
67	POI, R, B, W, L, I Historic St Andrews	N 30.169433° W - 85.702729°	Alt 3B	Land on small beach next to Uncle Ernies Bayfront Grill.
70.5	C,R,S,B,G,W,PI	N 30.133946°	Alt 4A	On trail

	St Andrews State Park	W - 85.732256°		
79	C,L,W,B,S, Tyndall AFB Fam Camp (Military only)	N 30.099278° W 30.099278°	Alt 4A	On trail Restricted to military with ID
84.5	PC, no facilities Piney Point	N 30.094056° W - 85.522627°	Alt 4B	On trail
92	B,P, PI Overstreet	N 29.997630° W - 85.370707°	Alt 5A	On trail Water must be treated
104	POI Gulf County Canal	N 29.887165° W - 85.249186°	Alt 5B	On trail, six-mail long canal that leads to coastal CT route near town of Port St Joe.
105.5	G,B,W,PI White City	N 29.879865° W - 85.220956°	Alt 5B	Small convenience store 0.5 miles north of bridge on CR 71.
114	PC, no facilities Lake Wimico	N 29.800620° W -	Alt 6A	On trail, east side of Lake Wimico,

			85.137452°		small point mid-way of lake
121		POI ICW joins Apalachicola River	N 29.778106° W - 85.050790°	Alt 6A	On trail
121.5		PC, no facilities Large sand bar, east side of river	N 29.772759° W - 85.043145°	Alt 6A	On trail, 0.5 miles downstream confluence of Apalachicola River and ICW
122		PI,P Abercrombie Boat Ramp	N 29.768459° W - 85.043253°	Alt 6A	On trail
127		L,R,B,G,POI,PI Apalachicola	N 29.723839° W - 84.980832°	Alt 6B	On trail, join Segment 4 here

Keys Alternate Route
Segments 15-16, Flamingo to Miami
Circumnavigational Trail Data Book

PC = Primitive campsite
POI = Point of Interest
LA = Laundromat
L = Lodging
PO = Post Office
S = Shower
g = convenience/camp stores
G = medium/lg supermarkets

C = Campground
O = Outfitters
W = Water
I = Internet computer
R = Restaurant
B = Bathroom
PI = Put-In

Mile #	Type of amenity	GPS # on trail (decimal-degrees)	CT Segment and Map #	Directions
0	C,L,R,S,PI,W PO,G Flamingo, (Everglades NP	N25.1368 W-80.9380	Map 1A	On trail
9	PC, B Shark Point Chickee	N25.1407 W-80.8024	Map 1A	On trail Permit required
29	PC, B Nest Key,	N25.1510	Map 2A	On Trail

	(Everglades NP)	W-80.5136		Permit required
	Three Route options from Nest Key to Miami: Red Route, Green Route, Yellow Route			
RED ROUTE:	**Most sheltered route**			
33.5	Opening to Shell Creek between Nest Key and Pelican Cay	N25.20780 W80.48710	Map 2A	On red route
38	C, W, B, S, LA Pelican Cay Harbor	N25.2361 W80.43141	Map 2A&B	On red route
45	R,W Alabama Jacks	N25.29012 W80.379509	Map 3A	On red & green route
48	PC Card Point	N25.3233 W80.3426	Map 3A	On red & green route
	Red & Green Routes join at Card Point and proceed to Miami			
GREEN ROUTE	Nest Key to Card Point via 'the Bogies' &			

303

	Gilberts			
33	The Bogies	N25.175688 W80.453860		On green route, mangrove tunnel entrance
37	L,I,PI,R,W Gilberts	N25.18286 W80.38947	Map 2A & B	On green route
	R,W Alabama Jacks	N25.29012 W80.379509	Map 3A	On red & green route
47	PC Card Point	N25.3233 W80.3426	Map 3A	On red & green route
YELLOW ROUTE	Nest Key to Segment 16 Atlantic Coast Route			
39	Grouper Creek	N25.121640 W80.446235	Map 2B	Opening to channel
41.5	Dusenbury Creek	N25.131184 W80.442245	Map 2B	Opening to channel
43.5	Adams Cut	N25.13791 W80.40295	Map 2B	Opening to channel
45	C,S,R,I,POI, John Pennekamp State Park	N25.12429 W80.40687	Map 2B	Resume Segment 16 information
Red & Green routes merge at Card Point to proceed north to Miami				

58	PC, R, S, W, R, PI Homestead Bayfront Park	N25.459269 W80.337512	Map 4A	On trail
58.5	POI, B, W, PI Biscayne Park Visitor Center	N25.463366 W80.334027	Map 4A	On trail
63.5	PI, W, R, g, B, Black Point Marina	N25.538482 W80.327508	Map 4B	On trail
68	B, W, R Deering Point County Park	N25.610956 W80.306895	Map 4B	On trail, short walk north on Old Cutler Rd. to several restaurants
75	W, R, B Matheson Hammock Park	N25.677105 W80.259238	Map 5A	On trail
86	PC Teacher's Island	N25.7432 W80.1442	Map 5A	On trail, route rejoins Segment 16

Along Cape St. George on bay side, segment 4.

Trip Planning

Thinking of a long distance journey on the Florida Circumnavigational Saltwater Paddling Trail? Several factors and considerations should be part of your preparation and planning.

Pre-Planning. Besides this guide book, the trail map book should be obtained or downloaded from the Office of Greenways and Trails website.

In addition, the Florida Paddling Trails Association offers valuable information about the trail, including links to blogs from past and sometimes current thru paddlers. Some of the information is only available to members. The website is: http://www.floridapaddlingtrails.com/. The purchase of navigational charts, available at most marine supply stores, is also recommended.

Reservations and Permits. Maintaining the circumnavigational trail is a low-budget operation that largely depends upon volunteers, so there is no central permitting/reservation body for the trail. Where required, permits and reservations must be obtained from the many parks and private businesses along the trail. These may be found by perusing the segment trail guides. Many motels and state park and private campgrounds, especially in central and south Florida and in the Keys during peak seasons (holidays and early spring), require advance reservations in order to be assured a spot. Bring a cell phone and call ahead as soon as you have a good idea of your schedule. Regarding the Big Bend portion of the trail managed by the Florida Fish and Wildlife Conservation Commission (Aucilla River to the town of Suwannee, part of segment 6), free permits are required and can be reserved online at

http://www.myfwc.com/RECREATION/WMASites_BigBend_paddling_trail.htm.

Be sure to leave a detailed float plan with a reliable friend or relative before you begin your journey.

Experience. Long distance paddlers should be competent in all types of environments and conditions, capable of dealing with strong winds and currents, and skilled at crossing open water stretches and boat channels. You should be able to navigate at night and in poor visibility, capable of using navigational maps and charts and a GPS system, and trained in advanced rescue techniques, wilderness first aid and primitive camping skills. The trail is marked by GPS points on a map, not by signs. Cell phone coverage can be spotty in some sections. A SPOT tracking device is recommended.

It is especially important to field test your equipment beforehand under various conditions, especially all electronic equipment and items such as dry bags, tents and rain gear. Some paddlers have learned the hard way that the "waterproof" label is not always accurate. Online and magazine reviews of equipment can also be helpful, along with consultation with outfitters and other paddlers.

Distances. In several stretches, one must paddle more than 20 miles to reach a legal campsite or motel. For this reason, proper conditioning and equipment, and awareness of weather forecasts and wind conditions, are all imperative. Stiff fines and possible arrest can result from illegally camping on private or public lands, especially military lands and national wildlife refuges. Only emergency conditions such as injury or dangerous weather should dictate a decision to stop short of an authorized overnight stop.

Weather. As with any long distance paddling journey, weather may not always be ideal. Storms and high winds can prohibit travel for a day or more. Lightning can be especially dangerous. Occasional storm days should be factored into your planning. A weather radio is an important addition to your equipment list along with the ability to read changing weather conditions while in the field.

Timing. Generally, it is best to avoid the summer hurricane season for a long distance journey. Recommended paddling months are late October through April. Bugs and hot steamy weather, along with lightning storms, will be less prevalent as well. The entire trail is about 1,515 miles, but side trips and extreme low tides can add more miles. Allowing for some days off, plan to take about four months if planning to traverse the entire trail. Or, paddle the trail in segments over a longer period of time. Make your trip a journey of discovery, not a race.

Budget. Be realistic about costs. While every effort has been made to provide low cost or free campsites for paddlers, motel stays will occasionally be necessary. Waterfront motels, and some established campgrounds, can be expensive, depending on the season and locale.

Supplies. Plan on having 4 to 7 days worth of supplies at any given time, depending on the segment. The longest stretch without an opportunity to re-supply will be from Everglades City to the Keys in segments 14 and 15. While we list or describe a few supermarkets within easy walking distance of the trail, there are several more that may require a longer walking distance. Inquire locally for directions. Some small towns or fish camps may only have a convenience store for re-supply. In some places, care packages can be sent ahead to post offices in care of general delivery, but your arrival time needs to coincide with post office hours. Also, for those with special dietary restrictions and/or the need for certain prescription medications, post office drops may be essential in some areas. See data book summary for list of recommended post offices.

Regarding water, you'll be able to replenish water supplies almost daily in developed sections of the trail due to the many parks along the route. However, in the Big Bend and Ten Thousand Islands/Everglades in particular, fresh water re-supply opportunities can be spaced several days apart. See segment guides for specifics. The general rule is to figure on one gallon of water per person per day. Be mindful that animals such as raccoons on remote coastal islands may seek your fresh water as much as your food. Hang food and water or store in secure hatches.

Trail Direction and Camping. Note that the trail is designed to go north to south along the Gulf Coast, and south to north along the East Coast. This will help to prevent trail groups from overlapping at campsites. For many fragile coastal camping sites, the size limit is 8 persons and 4 small tents. Campsites are often on a first-come, first-serve basis and are not always limited to paddlers. Camping rules may differ according to the managing entity. Follow Leave No Trace guidelines when primitive camping, http://www.lnt.org.

Trail changes. Hurricanes, business closings and other factors can alter trail conditions and overnight stays. Check the Circumnavigational Trail website for trail updates. Maps and segment guides on the website will occasionally be revised, so download or peruse the latest versions before beginning serious planning. Contact the trail manager if you encounter situations that differ from what is currently on the website.

Launching kayaks at Crystal River.

Trip Tips and Safety

- Do not paddle alone

- If inexperienced, join with experienced paddlers and/or outfitters and try short trips first. Peruse books and articles about sea kayaking in Florida and talk with experts.

- File a float plan that contains departure location, time and date, and expected arrival date, time and location

- Five short blasts on a whistle is the international signal for an emergency

- Waving a brightly colored shirt or towel can attract the attention of a passing boater

- Take careful note of weather conditions and forecasts. If in doubt, don't proceed into open water. Be especially vigilant during hurricane season, from June through November. Warm weather thunderstorms can also bring high winds and heavy rains, along with the risk of lightning strikes.

- The prime paddling period in Florida is from October through April

- Parts of the trail may require motel stays as there is no legal camping available. Budget accordingly, and bring a locking security cable for securing your craft to pilings, docks, fences, etc.

- Stay well hydrated. Paddlers should carry at least one gallon of freshwater per person per day. In remote areas such as the Big Bend and Everglades, there can be two or more days between replenishment stops.

- Carry a tide chart. Some areas can be very shallow at low tide. In certain tidal creeks, rivers and passes, changing tides can cause strong currents that might help or hinder.

- When primitive camping, employ leave no trace principles (www.lnt.org). In high use areas, you may even be required to carry out human waste in bags designed for this purpose.

- If fishing, a Florida fishing license is required for persons 16 years of age and older (free for Florida residents 65 or older). Visit http://myfwc.com/license/ or call 1-888-347-4356

- Sub-freezing winter temperatures can be experienced in almost all parts of Florida. Plan accordingly.

- Snakes, including venomous ones, can be active in coastal environments, even in salt marshes. Proceed with caution when you can't see the ground. If encountering a snake, back away and admire these beautiful animals as they go about their lives.

- Poison ivy, poisonwood trees and other plants that cause allergic reactions can be found along the trail. If in doubt, do not touch.

- Don't walk on oysters or coral barefoot. Cactus, sandspurs, glass and other items can cause problems, too. Wear appropriate footwear.

- Long-distance paddling can be rigorous. Adverse tides, currents and head winds can hinder progress and challenge physical endurance. Be physically fit before embarking.

- By setting a relaxed pace for your trip, with plenty of time set aside for side trips and land explorations, you will likely have a richer experience.

Recommended Gear and Safety Equipment for Extended Trips

- A sea kayak with rudder suitable for open water
- Lightweight paddle and spare paddle
- Spray skirt/cockpit cover
- U.S. Coast Guard approved personal flotation device (wear at all times!)
- Marine whistle, bell or horn within easy reach
- Flares, laser flare
- Marine radio
- Waterproof GPS and extra batteries
- Deck compass
- Pertinent maps, NOAA charts and tide charts
- Cell phone & solar charger (although some areas may be out of range)

- SPOT Personal satellite tracking system (can give outgoing message where cell phones do not work)
- First aid kit (ace bandage, butterfly bandages, asst. bandaids, snake bite kit, moleskin, eyedrops, tweezer, scissors, cold/hot pads)
- Medication (bi-ox, Tylenol, anti-itch cream, antifungal cream, diarrhea tablets, sinus/cold, antacid, painkiller, antibiotic, vomiting medication, nasal spray, seasick pills, thermometer)
- Towline
- Bilge pump/sponge/paddle float
- Paddle Leash
- Dry bags, deck bag and chart case (for map and GPS)
- Sunscreen, sun hat, waterproof sunscreen, and long-sleeved, light-colored shirts
- Polarized sunglasses. Ski goggles may be optimal for those with sensitive eyes
- Insect repellent, head net, and net clothing
- Rain gear
- Appropriate clothing for anticipated weather
- Water containers and easily accessible water bottle
- Lightweight camp stove, fuel container and funnel
- Matches or lighter
- Mess kit
- Tent with fine mesh screen and rain fly
- Sleeping bag
- Flashlight and/or head lamp
- Several feet of cord
- Small trowel
- Toilet paper
- Garbage bags
- Pocket multi-tool
- Repair items (duct tape, nails/screws, epoxy putty, super glue, aquaseal)

- Biodegradable soap and scrubbie
- Dish towel
- Ziplock bags
- Sewing kit
- Dental supplies
- Small can of lubricant to spray zippers and other metal parts to prevent corrosion
- Solid brass lock and stainless steel chain or cable (corrosion resistant) for securing kayak
- Small brass brush to clean off corrosion on metal objects.
- Optional items include binoculars, walkie-talkies, paddling gloves, folding stool, folding toilet seat, sleeping pad, inflatable pillow, battery operated tent fan, camera, small jungle hammock, wheels for transporting kayak, and a tarp for use as a camp rain fly or ground cover.

Packing kayaks in Everglades City, Ten Thousand Islands

Circumnavigational Paddling Trail Glossary
(Some terms found in the guide)

Bank – The slope of land adjoining a body of water or a large elevated area of the sea floor.

Bay – A body of water partly enclosed by land but with a wide outlet to the sea.

Buoys and channel markers – Floating objects of defined shape and color, which are anchored at given positions and serve as an aid to navigation. The meanings of the colors and numbers of navigation markers can be found by logging onto http://www.boat-ed.com/fl/course/p3-7_navaidsbuoys.htm.

Channel - The deeper part of a river or harbor; a deep navigable passage sometimes marked by buoys.

Cove – A small, sheltered bay in the shoreline of a sea, river, or lake.

Flag warnings on beaches – Means to alert swimmers and boaters of potential dangers in the water. Flag warnings and colors for Florida beaches are:

 Green: Low hazard, calm conditions, exercise caution.

 Yellow: Medium hazard, moderate surf and/or currents.

 Red: High hazard, high surf and/or strong currents.

 . Red over Red (two flags flying): Water closed to the public.

 Purple: Dangerous marine life such as stinging jellyfish.

Global Positioning System – (GPS) A satellite based radionavigation system providing continuous worldwide coverage. It provides navigation, position, and timing information to air, marine, and land users.

Knot – A unit of speed: one nautical mile (1.852 kilometres) per hour. Originally speed was measured by paying out a line from the stern of a moving boat. The line had a knot every 47 feet 3 inches (14.4 m), and the number of knots passed out in 30 seconds gave the speed through the water in nautical miles per hour

Lagoon – A shallow body of water, especially one separated from the sea by sandbars or coral reefs. Example: Indian River Lagoon.

Midden - a refuse pile made by early native inhabitants, consisting primarily of shells.

Nautical mile - A distance of 1,852 meters = 2000 yards = 6080 feet. A speed of one nautical mile per hour is called a *knot*. By contrast, a statute mile, normally used to measure objects on land in the United States, is 1609 meters = 1,760 yards = 5,280 feet. The circumnavigational guide uses statute miles.

Nero day (near zero) - usually a reference to a relaxing half day of paddling or backpacking.

Pass - A way through a barrier island or body of land that is generally navigable by boat.

Portage - To carry goods or boat between two navigable points.

Primitive campsite - A campsite with no amenities or with minimal amenities such as a fire ring and composting toilet.

Put-In - The starting point of a paddling trip; where the boats are launched into the water.

Reef - Rock or coral, possibly only revealed at low tide, shallow enough that the vessel will at least touch if not go aground.

Salt Flat – Barren areas with highly saline and usually alkaline soils formed by the evaporation of sea water. In Florida, they are more similar to tidal flats and not the dry salt flats of Utah.

Sandbar – An offshore shoal of sand built up by the action of waves or currents.

Shoal – Shallow water that is a hazard to navigation.

Take-Out - The ending point of a paddling trip; where the boats are finally taken from the water. See Put-In.
Tidal flat – Nearly flat coastal area alternately covered and exposed by tides, usually muddy.
Waypoint – A location defined by navigational coordinates, especially as part of a planned route.

Zero Day—A day in which a paddler or group of paddlers on a journey does not paddle; rest day.

Matt Keene, first paddler to complete entire trail
(east to west, 9/15/08 – 1/5/09)

Dan Dick and Mike Ruso, first paddlers to complete trail going west to east (11/12/08 – 3/26/09)

Jodi Eller, first woman to complete the trail, December 2013. Photo by Matt Keene. Mary Mangiapia was the first woman to complete the trail in one paddling season (2014).

Thru paddlers Carl Anderson, Ian Brown, Jim Windle, Marc DeLuca, Gus Bianchi and Daniel Alvarez at first annual CT gathering at Silver Springs, May 2014.

Scott Warren finishes CT in 2017.
Photo courtesy of Scott Warren.

Camille Richards was the 28th person to complete the trail, finishing in 2019.

Made in the USA
Columbia, SC
11 March 2020